DOM Scripting

Web Design with JavaScript and the Document Object Model

Jeremy Keith

friendsof

DESIGNER TO DESIGNER™

an Apress® company

DOM Scripting
Web Design with JavaScript and the Document Object Model

ISBN-13 (pbk): 978-1-59059-533-6
ISBN-10 (pbk): 1-59059-533-5

Printed and bound in the United States of America 9 8 7 6 5 4 3

Distributed to the book trade worldwide by Springer-Verlag New York, Inc., 233 Spring Street, 6th Floor, New York, NY, 10013. Phone 1-800-SPRINGER, fax 201-348-4505, e-mail orders-ny@springer-sbm.com, or visit www.springeronline.com.

For information on translations, please contact Apress directly at 2560 Ninth Street, Suite 219, Berkeley, CA 94710. Phone 510-549-5930, fax 510-549-5939, e-mail info@apress.com, or visit www.apress.com.

The source code for this book is freely available to readers at www.friendsofed.com in the Downloads section.

For Jessica, my wordridden wife.

CONTENTS AT A GLANCE

Foreword . . . . **xv**

About the Author . . . . **xvii**

About the Technical Reviewer . . . . **xviii**

About the Foreword Writer . . . . **xix**

Acknowledgments . . . . **xx**

Introduction . . . . **xxi**

Chapter 1: A Brief History of JavaScript **3**

Chapter 2: JavaScript Syntax **13**

Chapter 3: The Document Object Model **41**

Chapter 4: A JavaScript Image Gallery **57**

Chapter 5: Best Practices **77**

Chapter 6: Image Gallery Revisited **93**

Chapter 7: Creating Markup on the Fly **119**

Chapter 8: Enhancing Content **145**

Chapter 9: CSS-DOM **177**

Chapter 10: Animated Slideshow **207**

Chapter 11: Putting It All Together **243**

Chapter 12: The Future of DOM Scripting **293**

Reference **311**

Index **329**

CONTENTS

Foreword. xv

About the Author xvii

About the Technical Reviewer xviii

About the Foreword Writer xix

Acknowledgments. xx

Introduction. xxi

Chapter 1: A Brief History of JavaScript. 3
The origins of JavaScript 4
    What is a Document Object Model? 5
The browser wars 6
    The D word: DHTML 6
    Clash of the browsers 7
Raising the standard 7
    Thinking outside the browser 8
    The end of the browser wars 8
    A new beginning 9
What's next? 10

Chapter 2: JavaScript Syntax 13

What you'll need 14
Syntax. 16
Statements 16
    Comments 16
Variables 18
    Data types 20
        Strings 20
        Numbers. 21
        Boolean values 22
    Arrays 22
        Associative arrays 24
Operations 25
    Arithmetic operators 25
Conditional statements 27
    Comparison operators 29
    Logical operators 29
Looping statements 30
    while 31
        do...while 31
    for 32
Functions 33
        Variable scope 35
Objects 36
    Native objects 38
    Host objects 38
What's next? 39

Chapter 3: The Document Object Model. 41

D is for document 42
Objects of desire. 42
Dial M for model 43
    Nodes 45
        element nodes 45
        text nodes 46
        attribute nodes 46
        Cascading Style Sheets 47
    getElementById 49
    getElementsByTagName 50
Taking stock 52
    getAttribute 52
    setAttribute 54
What's next? 55

Chapter 4: A JavaScript Image Gallery 57

The markup 58
The JavaScript 61
   A DOM diversion 62
   Finishing the function. 62
Applying the JavaScript 63
   Event handlers. 63
Expanding the function 65
   Introducing childNodes. 66
   Introducing the nodeType property 67
   Adding a description in the markup. 68
   Changing the description with JavaScript 69
   Introducing the nodeValue property 69
   Introducing firstChild and lastChild 70
   Using nodeValue to update the description 70
What's next? 74

Chapter 5: Best Practices 77

Please don't let me be misunderstood 78
   Don't blame the messenger 78
   The Flash mob. 79
   Question everything 80
Graceful degradation 81
   The javascript: pseudo-protocol 82
   Inline event handlers 82
   Who cares? 83
The lessons of CSS. 84
   Progressive enhancement 85
Unobtrusive JavaScript 86
Backwards compatibility 88
   Browser sniffing 90
What's next? 90

Chapter 6: Image Gallery Revisited. 93

A quick recap 94
Does it degrade gracefully?. 95
Is the JavaScript unobtrusive? 96
   Adding the event handler 97
   Checkpoints 97
   What's in a name?. 99
   Looping the loop 100
   Changing behavior. 101
   Closing it up 102
   Share the load 102

CONTENTS

Assuming too much 104
   Fine-tuning 107
   Keyboard access 109
   Beware of onkeypress 110
   Sharing hooks with CSS 112
DOM Core and HTML-DOM 115
What's next? 117

Chapter 7: Creating Markup on the Fly 119

document.write 120
innerHTML 122
   Pros and cons 125
DOM methods 125
   createElement 126
   appendChild 127
   createTextNode 128
      A more complex combination 130
Revisiting the image gallery 132
   insertBefore 135
      Writing the insertAfter function 136
      Using the insertAfter function 137
   The finished image gallery 138
Summary 142
What's next? 143

Chapter 8: Enhancing Content 145

What not to do 146
Making the invisible visible 147
The content 148
   HTML or XHTML? 149
The markup 149
The CSS 151
The JavaScript 152
   Displaying abbreviations 152
      Writing the displayAbbreviations function 153
      Creating the markup 155
      A browser bomb 161
   Displaying citations 164
      Writing the displayCitations function 165
   Displaying access keys 171
      The markup 171
      The JavaScript 173
Summary 174
What's next? 175

Chapter 9: CSS-DOM 177

Three sheets to the Web 178
    Structure 178
    Presentation 178
    Behavior 179
    Separation 180
The style property 180
    Getting styles 182
        Inline only 186
    Setting styles 188
Knowing when to use DOM styling 189
    Styling elements in the node tree 189
    Repetitive styling 193
    Responding to events 198
className 200
    Abstracting a function 203
What's next? 204

Chapter 10: Animated Slideshow 207

What is animation? 208
    Position 208
    Time 211
        setTimeout 211
        Increments 212
    Abstraction 215
Practical animation 222
    The situation 222
    The solution 223
    CSS 225
    JavaScript 227
    A question of scope 231
Refining the animation 233
Final touches 236
    Generating markup 238
What's next? 241

Chapter 11: Putting It All Together 243

The brief 244
    Raw materials 244
    Site structure 244
    Page structure 246
Design 247
CSS 248
Color 250
    Layout 251
    Typography 254

Markup 255
JavaScript 256
   Page highlighting. 257
   JavaScript slideshow 262
   Internal navigation. 267
   JavaScript image gallery 272
   Table enhancements. 276
   Form enhancements. 281
      Labels. 283
      Default values 284
      Form validation 286
Summary 290
What's next? 291

Chapter 12: The Future of DOM Scripting **293**

The state of the Web 294
   Web browsers 294
      Crazy like a Firefox 295
   Web designers 296
   The three-legged stool 297
      The DOM Scripting Task Force 297
Ajax 298
   The XMLHttpRequest object 300
   An explosion of Ajax. 302
      Ajax challenges 305
   Progressive enhancement with Ajax 305
      Hijax 306
   The future of Ajax 307
Applications on the Web 308
What's next? 309

Reference **311**

Methods. 312
   Creating nodes. 312
      createElement 312
      createTextNode 313
   Duplicating nodes 314
      cloneNode 314
   Inserting nodes. 316
      appendChild 316
      insertBefore 317
   Removing nodes. 318
      removeChild 318
   Replacing nodes 318
      replaceChild 318
   Manipulating nodes 319
      setAttribute 319

Finding nodes 320
    getAttribute 320
    getElementById 321
    getElementsByTagName 321
    hasChildNodes 322
Properties 323
    Node properties 323
        nodeName 323
        nodeType 323
        nodeValue 324
    Traversing the node tree 325
        childNodes 325
        firstChild 325
        lastChild 326
        nextSibling 326
        parentNode 327
        previousSibling 327

Index **329**

FOREWORD BY DAVE SHEA

"JavaScript? No way. It's inaccessible, you know. Relying on it will make your site unusable, too. It's the root of many an evil pop-up window. I mean, it probably even kicked your dog when no one was looking."

Or so I thought...

Are you like me, a web designer or developer who has avoided JavaScript on principle? There are a lot of us out there, and no wonder. With so many examples of bad scripting living on in outdated web tutorials from the height of the dot-com era, the overwhelming resistance to using it is no large surprise.

Thankfully, there are people out there like Jeremy Keith working to point us back in the right direction. In this book, he shows us that, hey, it's not as bad as all that. When used properly, with care and attention paid to the traditional JavaScript gotchas, DOM Scripting is a powerful and even vital addition to the web development toolbox.

In fact, the state of DOM Scripting at the moment reminds me of where CSS was in 2002. Up to that point, CSS had been considered this quirky little web display language that no one used for anything more than font styling.

But then interest in CSS-based layouts exploded, and the tide started to turn. High-profile commercial redesigns by Wired and ESPN, the first of many, triggered a change in opinion. I contributed by launching the CSS Zen Garden in early 2003, a project meant to spark interest in the capability of CSS amongst designers. By the end of that year, CSS had shifted from a specialty item to an expected method of development for many organizations.

And now we see DOM Scripting sitting at the beginning of a similar curve. With high-profile applications like Google Maps and Flickr recently taking advantage of DOM Scripting, the demand is growing. More than ever, people like you and me are interested in honing our scripting skills and learning how to make the power of the DOM work for us in ways that will enhance usability, not hinder it.

Lucky for us, we now have this book to lead the way. And I couldn't think of a better person to learn from than Jeremy Keith. As a driving force behind the Web Standards Project's Scripting Task Force, he's on top of all the latest developments in powerful, unobtrusive scripting. Besides, I've been stealing his code for ages anyway, at least now that it's in convenient book form I don't have to feel so guilty about it.

And it is a great book to learn from. After stumbling through the first few code examples, I was hungry for more. After reading through the first chapter, I knew I was hooked. Jeremy Keith is blessed with the rare ability to explain advanced concepts in simple, easy-to-understand English. He takes the time to back up his claims with commonsense examples, so that you don't simply know what to do, you also know why you should be doing it.

It's time to toss out the browser sniffing in favor of object detection. No more assuming every visitor has JavaScript enabled either. Let's lose the inline event handlers, once and for all. The web is getting an upgrade, and the techniques in this book are going to help it come about in a way that benefits everybody.

ABOUT THE AUTHOR

Jeremy Keith is a web developer living and working in Brighton, England. Working with the web consultancy firm Clearleft (www.clearleft.com), Jeremy enjoys building accessible, elegant websites using the troika of web standards: XHTML, CSS, and the DOM. His online home is adactio.com. Jeremy is also a member of the Web Standards Project (webstandards.org) where he serves as joint leader of the DOM Scripting Task Force.

When he's not building websites, Jeremy plays bouzouki in the alt.country band Salter Cane (www.saltercane.com). He is also the creator and curator of one of the web's largest online communities dedicated to Irish traditional music, The Session (www.thesession.org).

ABOUT THE TECHNICAL REVIEWER

Jon Stephens got his start in the IT and technical writing fields in the mid-1990s by teaching computers how to operate radio stations (and then teaching humans how to operate the computers). He's been working with Web and Open Source technologies since 1996, and almost from the beginning of that time gravitated to using JavaScript, both client-side and server-side as well as PHP, Python, and MySQL. He is a co-author of *Professional JavaScript, Second Edition.* (Wrox Press, 2001) and has contributed his JavaScript and DOM scripting expertise to numerous other books on web technologies as an author or reviewer, including *The JavaScript Programmer's Reference* (Wrox, 2001), *Usable Web Menus* (glasshaus, 2001), *Professional PHP 4 XML Programming* (Wrox, 2002), and *Constructing Usable Shopping Carts* (glasshaus, 2002; reissued by Apress, 2004). Most recently he was the co-author (with Chad Russell) of *MySQL Database Design and Optimization* (Apress, 2004) and is currently working on *PHP 5 Recipes* for Apress. Jon is a regular contributor to *International PHP magazine*, for whom he's written a couple of articles on DOM scripting in PHP 4 and 5. He's also been active on a number of developer websites (including HiveMinds.org and Experts-Exchange.com) as well as several JavaScript/DOM mailing lists.

Jon hung up his freelancer's hat in 2004 when he accepted a full-time job as a technical writer with MySQL AB. He helps maintain the MySQL Manual and other MySQL documentation, wrestles with the vagaries of DocBook XML, and hangs out on the MySQL User Forums. Jon is known to become quite excited when occasionally he gets to do some JavaScript or PHP DOM scripting in connection with his job.

Having lived most places where one can reasonably live in the USA, Jon migrated in 2002 to Australia. He shares a house in Brisbane's South End with several cats and computers, both of whose numbers constantly fluctuate. In his spare time, he likes going to the ocean, finding new places to drink coffee, reading the odd detective thriller, and listening to his daughter sing.

ABOUT THE FOREWORD WRITER

Dave Shea is the creator and cultivator of the highly influential CSS Zen Garden website (www.csszengarden.com). As well as being a member of the Web Standards Project, Dave is the owner and director of Bright Creative, and he writes about all things Web for his daily weblog, mezzoblue.com. With more than six years of experience working on the Web, Dave is a leader of the new generation of web designers that believe in responsible web design.

ACKNOWLEDGMENTS

This book owes its existence to my friends and colleagues, Andy Budd (www.andybudd.com) and Richard Rutter (www.clagnut.com). Andy runs a (free) training event in our home town of Brighton called Skillswap (www.skillswap.org). In July 2004, Richard and I gave a joint presentation on JavaScript and the Document Object Model. Afterward, we adjourned to the cozy confines of a nearby pub, where Andy put the idea in my head of expanding the talk into a book.

I took this idea and presented it to Chris Mills at friends of ED. Chris was gracious enough to give me the green light, despite the fact that I had never written a book before. Everyone at friends of ED has been helpful and encouraging. I'd particularly like to thank my project manager, Beckie Stones, and my copy editor, Julie Smith, for their support and good humor in dealing with this rookie author.

I would never have learned to write a single line of JavaScript if it weren't for two things. The first is the view source option built in to almost every web browser. Thank you, view source. The second is the existence of JavaScript giants who have been creating amazing code and explaining important ideas over the years. Scott Andrew, Aaron Boodman, Steve Champeon, Peter-Paul Koch, Stuart Langridge, and Simon Willison are just some of the names that spring to mind. Thank you all for sharing.

Thanks to Molly Holzschlag for sharing her experience and advice with me and for giving me feedback on early drafts. Thanks to Derek Featherstone for many a pleasurable JavaScript-laden chat; I like the way your mind works.

Extra-special thanks to Aaron Gustafson who provided invaluable feedback and inspiration during the writing of this book.

While I was writing this book, I had the pleasure of speaking at two wonderful events: South by Southwest in Austin, Texas, and @media in London. Thanks to Hugh Forrest and Patrick Griffiths respectively for orchestrating these festivals of geekery that allowed me to meet and befriend the nicest, friendliest bunch of people I could ever hope to call my peers.

Finally, I'd like to thank my wife, Jessica Spengler, not only for her constant support, but also for her professional help in proofreading my first drafts. Go raibh míle maith agat, a stór mo chroí.

INTRODUCTION

This book deals with a programming language, but it isn't intended for programmers. This is a book for web designers. Specifically, this book is intended for standards-aware designers who are comfortable using CSS and XHTML. If that sounds like you, read on...

This book is made up of equal parts code and concepts. Don't be frightened by the code: I know it might look intimidating at first, but once you've grasped the concepts behind the code, you'll find yourself reading and writing in a new language. Learning a programming language might seem like a scary prospect, but it needn't be. DOM Scripting might appear to be more verbose than, say, CSS, but once you've got the hang of the syntax, you'll find yourself armed with a powerful web development tool.

In any case, the code is there simply to illustrate the concepts. I'll let you in on a secret: nobody memorizes all the syntax and keywords that are part and parcel of any programming language. That's what reference books are for.

This isn't a reference book. I'm going to cover the bare minimum of syntax required to get up and running with JavaScript. I'm really going to focus on the ideas behind DOM Scripting. A lot of these ideas might already be familiar to you: graceful degradation, progressive enhancement, and user-centered design are important concepts in any aspect of front-end web development.

These ideas inform all the code examples given in this book. You'll find scripts for creating image galleries, animating slideshows, and enhancing the look and feel of page elements. If you want, you can simply cut and paste these examples, but it's more important to understand the hows and whys that lie behind the code.

If you're already using CSS and XHTML to turn your designs into working web pages, then you already know how powerful web standards can be. Remember the thrill you experienced when you realized you'd never have to use a <font> tag again? Remember when you discovered that you could change the design throughout an entire site just by changing one CSS file? The Document Object Model offers an equal level of power.

But with great power comes great responsibility. That's why I'm not just going to show you cool DOM Scripting effects; I'm also going to show you how to use DOM Scripting to enhance your web pages in a usable, accessible way.

To get hold of all the code examples discussed in the book, pay a visit to http://www.friendsofed.com and find this book's page. At this site, you can also find out about all the other great books friends of ED have to offer, on web standards, Flash, Dreamweaver, and much more besides.

Your exploration of DOM Scripting needn't end when you close this book. I've set up a website at http://domscripting.com/, where I'm going to continue the discussion of modern, standards-based JavaScript. I hope you'll pay the site a visit. In the meantime, enjoy the book.

1 A BRIEF HISTORY OF JAVASCRIPT

What this chapter covers:

- The origins of JavaScript
- The browser wars
- The evolution of the DOM

This is an exciting time to be a web designer. In recent years, web design has evolved from its chaotic, haphazard roots into a mature design discipline. Designers are adopting a standards-based approach to building websites, and the term "web standards" has been coined to describe the technologies that enable this approach.

Whenever designers discuss the subject of web standards, e**X**tensible **H**yper**T**ext **M**arkup **L**anguage (XHTML) and **C**ascading **S**tyle **S**heets (CSS) usually take center stage. However, there's a third technology, approved by the **W**orld **W**ide **W**eb **C**onsortium (W3C) and supported by all standards-compliant web browsers, called the **D**ocument **O**bject **M**odel (DOM). The DOM allows us to add interactivity to our documents in much the same way that CSS allow us to add styles.

Before looking at the DOM, let's examine the language that you'll be using to make your web pages interactive. The language is JavaScript, and it's been around for quite some time.

The origins of JavaScript

JavaScript was developed by Netscape, in collaboration with Sun Microsystems. Before JavaScript, web browsers were fairly basic pieces of software capable of displaying hypertext documents. JavaScript was later introduced to add some extra spice to web pages and to make them more interactive. The first version, JavaScript 1.0, debuted in Netscape Navigator 2 in 1995.

At the time of JavaScript 1.0's release, Netscape Navigator dominated the browser market. Microsoft was struggling to catch up with its own browser, Internet Explorer, and was quick to follow Netscape's lead by releasing its own VBScript language, along with a version of JavaScript called JScript, with the delivery of Internet Explorer 3.

As a response to this, Netscape and Sun set about standardizing the language, together with the **E**uropean **C**omputer **M**anufacturers **A**ssociation (ECMA). The result was ECMAScript, yet another name for the same language. Though the name never really stuck, we should really be referring to JavaScript as ECMAScript.

JavaScript, ECMAScript, JScript—whatever you want to call it—was gaining ground by 1996. Version 3 browsers from Netscape and Microsoft both supported the JavaScript 1.1 language to varying degrees.

I should point out that JavaScript has nothing to do with Java, a programming language developed by Sun Microsystems. JavaScript was originally going to be called LiveScript. "JavaScript" was probably chosen to make the new language sound like it was in good company. Unfortunately, the choice of this name really only had the effect of confusing the two languages in people's minds—a confusion that was amplified by the fact that web browsers also supported a form of client-side Java. However, while Java's strength lies in the fact that it can theoretically be deployed in almost any environment, JavaScript was always intended for the confines of the web browser.

JavaScript is a scripting language. This means that unlike a program that does everything itself, the JavaScript language simply tells the web browser what to do. The web browser interprets the script and does all the work, which is why JavaScript is often compared unfavorably with compiled programming languages like Java and C++. But JavaScript's relative simplicity is also its strength. Because it has a low barrier to entry, non-programmers who wanted to cut and paste scripts into their existing web pages quickly adopted the language.

JavaScript also offered developers the chance to manipulate aspects of the web browser. For example, the language could be used to manipulate the properties of a browser window, such as its height, width, and position. Addressing the browser's own properties in this way can be thought of as a Browser Object Model (BOM). Early versions of JavaScript also provided a primitive sort of Document Object Model.

What is a Document Object Model?

In short, a Document Object Model (DOM) is a way of conceptualizing the contents of a document.

In the real world, we all share something I'll call a World Object Model. We can refer to objects in our environment using terms like "car," "house," and "tree" and be fairly certain that our terms will be understood. That's because we have mutually agreed upon which objects the words refer to specifically. If I say "The car is in the garage," it's safe to assume that you won't take that to mean "The bird is in the cupboard."

Our World Object Model isn't restricted to tangible objects though—it also applies to concepts.

For instance, I might refer to "the third house on the left," when giving you directions. For that description to make sense, the concepts of "third" and "left" must be understood. If I give that description to somebody who can't count, or who can't tell left from right, then the description is essentially meaningless, whether or not the words have been understood. In reality, because people agree on a conceptual world model, very brief descriptions can be full of meaning. I can be fairly sure that others share my concepts of "left" and "third."

It's the same situation with web pages. Early versions of JavaScript offered developers the ability to query and manipulate some of the actual contents of web documents—mostly images and forms. Because the terms "images" and "forms" had been predefined, JavaScript could be used to address "the third image in the document" or "the form named 'details,'" as shown:

```
document.images[2]
document.forms['details']
```

This first, tentative sort of Document Object Model is often referred to as DOM Level 0. In those early, carefree days, the most common usage of DOM Level 0 was for image rollovers and some client-side form validation. But when the fourth generation of browsers from Netscape and Microsoft appeared, the DOM really hit the fan.

The browser wars

Netscape Navigator 4 (NN4) was released in June 1997, and by October of that year, Internet Explorer 4 (IE4) had also been released. Both browsers promised many improvements on previous versions, along with many additions to what could be accomplished with JavaScript, using a greatly expanded DOM. Web designers were encouraged to test-drive the latest buzzword: **DHTML**.

The D word: DHTML

DHTML was short for dynamic HTML. Not a technology in and of itself, DHTML was a shorthand term for describing the marriage of HTML, CSS, and JavaScript. The thinking behind DHTML went like this:

- You could use HTML to mark up your web page into elements.
- You could use CSS to style and position those elements.
- You could use JavaScript to manipulate and change those styles on the fly.

DHTML referred to the combination of those three techniques. Using DHTML, complex animation effects suddenly became possible. Let's say you used HTML to mark up a page element like this:

```
<div id="myelement">This is my element</div>
```

You could then use CSS to apply positioning styles like this:

```
#myelement {
  position: absolute;
  left: 50px;
  top: 100px;
}
```

Then, using JavaScript, you could change the left and top styles of myelement to move it around the page. Well, that was the theory anyway.

Unfortunately for developers, both browsers used different, incompatible DOMs. Although the browser manufacturers were promoting the same ends, they each approached the DOM issue in completely different ways.

Clash of the browsers

The Netscape DOM made use of proprietary elements called layers. These layers were given unique IDs and then addressed through JavaScript like this:

```
document.layers['myelement']
```

Meanwhile, the Microsoft DOM would address the same element like this:

```
document.all['myelement']
```

The differences didn't end there. Let's say you wanted to find out the left position of myelement and assign it to the variable xpos. In Netscape Navigator 4 you would do it like this:

```
var xpos = document.layers['myelement'].left;
```

Here's how you would do the same thing in Internet Explorer 4:

```
var xpos = document.all['myelement'].leftpos;
```

This was clearly a ridiculous situation. Developers had to fork their code to accomplish any sort of DOM scripting. In effect, many scripts were written twice, once for NN4 and once for IE4. Convoluted browser sniffing was often required to serve up the correct script.

DHTML promised a world of possibilities. But anybody who actually attempted to use it discovered a world of pain instead. It wasn't long before DHTML became a dirty (buzz)word. The technology quickly garnered a reputation for being both over hyped and overly difficult to implement.

Raising the standard

While the browser manufacturers were busy engaging in their battle for supremacy, and using competing DOMs as weapons in their war, the W3C was quietly putting together a standardized Document Object Model. Fortunately, the browser vendors were able to set aside their mutual animosity. Netscape, Microsoft, and other browser manufacturers worked together with the W3C on the new standard and DOM Level 1 was completed in October 1998.

Going back to our example, let's take a look at how the new standardized DOM would tackle the same situation. Remember, we have a <div> with the ID myelement and we're trying to ascertain the value that has been applied to its left position so that we can store that value as the variable xpos. Here's the syntax we would use:

```
var xpos = document.getElementById('myelement').style.left
```

At first glance, that might not appear to be an improvement over the non-standard, pro-prietary DOMs. However, the standardized DOM is far more ambitious in its scope.

While the browser manufacturers simply wanted some way to manipulate web pages with JavaScript, the W3C proposed a model that could be used by *any* programming language to manipulate *any* document written in *any* markup language.

Thinking outside the browser

The DOM is what's known as an Application Programming Interface (API). APIs are essentially conventions that have been agreed upon by mutual consent. Real-world equivalents would be things like

- Morse code
- International time zones
- The periodic table of the elements

All of these things are standards, and they make it easier for people to communicate and cooperate. In situations where a single convention hasn't been agreed upon, the result is often disastrous. Remember, competition between metric and imperial measurements has resulted in at least one failed Mars mission.

In the world of programming, there are many different languages, but there are many similar tasks. That's why APIs are so handy. Once you know the standard, you can apply it in many different environments. The syntax may change depending on the language you're using, but the convention remains the same.

So, while I focus specifically on using the DOM with JavaScript in this book, your new knowledge of the DOM will also be very useful if you ever need to parse an XML document using a programming language like PHP or Python.

The W3C defines the DOM as

"A platform- and language-neutral interface that will allow programs and scripts to dynamically access and update the content, structure, and style of documents."

The independence of the standardized DOM, together with its powerful scope, places it head and shoulders above the proprietary DOMs created by the bickering browser manufacturers.

The end of the browser wars

Microsoft won the battle for browser market-share supremacy. Ironically, the clash of competing DOMs and proprietary markup had little effect on the final outcome. Internet Explorer was destined to win simply by virtue of the fact that it came pre-installed on all PCs running the Windows operating system.

The people who were hit hardest by the browser wars were web designers. Cross-browser development had become a nightmare. As well as the discrepancies in JavaScript implementations that I mentioned earlier, the two browsers also had very different levels of support for CSS. Creating style sheets and scripts that worked on both browsers became a kind of black art.

A backlash began against the proprietary stance of the browser manufacturers. A group was formed calling itself the **W**eb **S**tandards **P**roject, or the WaSP for short (http://webstandards.org/). The first task that the WaSP undertook was to encourage browser makers to adopt W3C recommendations—the very same recommendations that the browser manufacturers had helped draft.

Whether it was due to pressure from the WaSP or the result of internal company decisions, there was far greater support for web standards in the next generation of web browsers.

A new beginning

Internet Explorer 5 shipped with built-in support for WC3's standardized DOM, while also maintaining support for the old, proprietary Microsoft DOM.

Netscape decided to make a clean break and released a browser that had next to nothing in common with NN4. Netscape Navigator 6 even skipped a version number, and it used a completely different rendering engine with far, far greater CSS support. It also supported the standardized DOM, but without any backwards compatibility for the old Netscape DOM.

Subsequent releases from both Netscape and Microsoft improved on previous incarnations with increased support for web standards. Unfortunately, development of Internet Explorer has stagnated at version 6. This is a pity, as some problems still remain with the browser's implementation of CSS. Support for DOM Level 1, however, is rock solid.

In the meantime, other browsers have appeared on the scene. When Apple debuted its Safari web browser in 2003, there was no question that it would follow the DOM standards. Firefox, Mozilla, and Camino, all based on the same open-source rendering engine as Netscape 6 and 7, have excellent support for the DOM. Opera and Konquerer also offer great DOM support.

Over 95% of the browsers in active use today have built-in support for the DOM. The browser wars of the late nineties appear to be well and truly behind us. Although no single browser has implemented the W3C DOM perfectly, all modern browsers cover about 95% of the specifications. This means there's a huge amount that we can accomplish without having to worry about branching code.

The stagnated development of Internet Explorer notwithstanding, life has improved greatly for web designers. Instead of writing scripts with forked code served up with complicated browser sniffing, we are now in a position to write something once and publish it everywhere. As long as we follow the DOM standards, we can be sure that our scripts will work almost universally.

What's next?

One thing you should definitely take away from my brief JavaScript history lesson is that different browsers used to accomplish the same tasks in different ways. This inescapable fact dominated not just the writing of JavaScript scripts, it also dictated how books about JavaScript were written.

Any JavaScript books aimed at demonstrating how to learn the language by example often had to show the same scripts written in different ways for different browsers. Just like the code found on most websites, the examples in most JavaScript books were full of browser sniffing and code branching. Similarly, technical reference books on JavaScript couldn't simply contain lists of functions and methods. They also had to document which functions and methods were supported by which browsers.

The situation has changed now. Thanks to the standardization of the DOM, different browsers do the same things in much the same way. This means that when I'm showing you how to do something using JavaScript and the Document Object Model, we won't get sidetracked by browser inconsistencies.

I am going to try to avoid mentioning any specific browsers in this book.

I'm also not going to use the term DHTML any more. The term always worked better as a marketing buzzword than as a technical description. For one thing, it sounds confusingly like another flavor of HTML or XHTML. Also, the term comes with a lot of baggage. If you mention DHTML to anyone who tried using it in the late nineties, you'll have a hard time convincing them that it's a straightforward, standardized technology now.

DHTML was supposed to refer to the combination of (X)HTML, CSS, and JavaScript, but in actual fact, what binds these things together is the DOM. If we need any term to describe this process, let's use something more accurate. While the term DHTML could be used to refer to browser-specific coding, it doesn't seem right to try to apply the same term to standards-based coding. **DOM Scripting** is a more accurate way to describe the manipulation of documents and style sheets using the W3C Document Object Model.

Whereas DHTML referred only to web documents, DOM Scripting can be used in conjunction with any marked-up document using any language that supports the DOM API. In the case of web documents, the ubiquity of JavaScript makes it the best choice for DOM Scripting.

Before I get down to the nitty-gritty of DOM Scripting, I'm going to give you a brief refresher in JavaScript syntax, which is what you'll find in the next chapter.

2 JAVASCRIPT SYNTAX

What this chapter covers:

- Statements
- Variables and arrays
- Operators
- Conditional statements and looping statements
- Functions and objects

This chapter is a brief refresher in JavaScript syntax, taking on the most important concepts.

What you'll need

You don't need any special software to write JavaScript. All you need is a plain text editor and a web browser.

Code written in JavaScript must be executed from a document written in (X)HTML. There are two ways of doing this. You can place the JavaScript between <script> tags within the <head> of the document:

```
<!DOCTYPE html PUBLIC "-//W3C//DTD XHTML 1.1//EN"
"http://www.w3.org/TR/xhtml11/DTD/xhtml11.dtd">
<html>
<head>
<script type="text/javascript">
JavaScript goes here...
</script>
</head>
<body>
Mark-up goes here...
</body>
</html>
```

A much better technique, however, is to place your JavaScript code into a separate file. Save this file with the file extension .js. You can then use the src attribute in a <script> tag to point to this file:

```
<!DOCTYPE html PUBLIC "-//W3C//DTD XHTML 1.1//EN"
"http://www.w3.org/TR/xhtml11/DTD/xhtml11.dtd">
<html>
<head>
<script type="text/javascript" src="file.js">
</script>
</head>
<body>
Mark-up goes here...
</body>
</html>
```

If you'd like to try the examples in this chapter, go ahead and create two files in a text editor. First, create a simple bare-bones HTML or XHTML file. You can call it something like test.html. Make sure that it contains a <script> tag in the <head> that has a src attribute with a value like example.js. That's the second file you can create in your text editor.

Your test.html file should look something like this:

```
<!DOCTYPE html PUBLIC "-//W3C//DTD XHTML 1.1//EN"
"http://www.w3.org/TR/xhtml11/DTD/xhtml11.dtd">
<html xmlns="http://www.w3.org/1999/xhtml" xml:lang="en">
 <head>
  <meta http-equiv="content-type" content="text/html; charset=utf-8" />
  <title>Just a test</title>
  <script type="text/javascript" src="example.js">
  </script>
 </head>
 <body>
 </body>
</html>
```

You can copy any of the examples in this chapter and write them into example.js. None of the examples are going to be particularly exciting, but they may be illuminating.

In later chapters, I'll be showing you how to use JavaScript to alter the behavior and content of your document. For now, I'll be using simple dialog boxes to display messages.

Whenever you change the contents of example.js, you can test its effects by reloading test.html in a web browser. The web browser will interpret the JavaScript code immediately.

Programming languages are either interpreted or compiled. Languages like Java or C++ require a **compiler**. A compiler is a program that translates the source code written in a high-level language like Java into a file that can be executed directly by a computer.

Interpreted languages don't require a compiler—they just need an interpreter instead. With JavaScript, in the context of the World Wide Web, the web browser does the interpreting. The JavaScript interpreter in the browser executes the code directly from the source. Without the interpreter, the JavaScript code would never get executed.

If there are any errors in the code written in a compiled language, those errors will pop up when the code is compiled. In the case of an interpreted language, errors won't become apparent until the interpreter executes the code.

Although compiled languages tend to be faster and more portable than interpreted languages, they often have a fairly steep learning curve.

One of the nice things about JavaScript is that it's relatively easy to pick up. Don't let that fool you though: JavaScript is capable of some pretty complex programming operations. For now, let's take a look at the basics.

Syntax

English is an interpreted language. By reading and processing these words that I have written in English, you are acting as the interpreter. As long as I follow the grammatical rules of English, my writing can be interpreted correctly. These grammatical rules include structural rules known as **syntax**.

Every programming language, just like every written language, has its own syntax. JavaScript has a syntax that is very similar to that of other programming languages like Java and C++.

Statements

A script written in JavaScript, or any other programming language, consists of a series of instructions. These are called **statements**. These statements must be written with the right syntax in order for them to be interpreted correctly.

Statements in JavaScript are like sentences in English. They are the building blocks of any script.

Whereas English grammar demands that sentences begin with a capital letter and end with a period, the syntax of JavaScript is much more forgiving. You can simply separate statements by placing them on different lines:

```
first statement
second statement
```

If you place a number of statements on the same line, you must separate them with semi-colons like this:

```
first statement; second statement;
```

However, it is good programming practice to place a semicolon at the end of every statement even if they are on different lines:

```
first statement;
second statement;
```

This helps to make your code more readable. Putting each statement on its own line makes it easier to follow the sequence that your JavaScript is executed in.

Comments

Not all statements are (or need to be) executed by the JavaScript interpreter. Sometimes you'll want to write something purely for your own benefit, and you'll want these statements to be ignored by the JavaScript interpreter. These are called **comments**.

Comments can be very useful when you want to keep track of the flow of your code. They act like sticky notes, helping you to keep track of what is happening in your script.

JavaScript allows you to indicate a comment in a number of different ways. For example, if you begin a line with two forward slashes, that line will be treated as a comment:

```
//  Note to self: comments are good.
```

If you use this notation, you must put the slashes at the start of each comment line. This won't work, for instance:

```
//  Note to self:
    comments are good.
```

Instead, you'd need to write

```
//  Note to self:
//  comments are good.
```

If you want to comment out multiple lines like that, you can place a forward slash and an asterisk at the start of the comment block and an asterisk and forward slash at the end:

```
/*  Note to self:
    comments are good  */
```

This is useful when you need to insert a long comment that will be more readable when it is spread over many lines.

You can also use HTML-style comments, but only for single lines. In other words, JavaScript treats <!– the same way that it treats //:

```
<!– This is a comment in JavaScript.
```

In HTML, you would need to close the comment with –>:

```
<!– This is a comment in HTML –>
```

JavaScript would simply ignore the closing of the comment, treating it as part of the comment itself.

Whereas HTML allows you to split comments like this over multiple lines, JavaScript requires the comment identifier to be at the start of each line.

Because of the confusing differences in how this style of comment is treated by JavaScript, I don't recommend using HTML-style comments. Stick to using two forward slashes for single-line comments and the slash-asterisk notation for multi-line comments.

Variables

In our everyday lives there are some things about us that are fixed and some things that are changeable. My name and my birthday are fixed. My mood and my age, on the other hand, will change over time. The things that are subject to change are called **variables**.

My mood changes depending on how I'm feeling. Suppose I had a variable with the name mood. I could use this variable to store my current state of mind. Regardless of whether this variable has the value "happy" or "sad", the name of the variable remains the same: mood. I can change the value as often as I like.

Likewise, my age might currently be 33. In one year's time, my age will be 34. I could use a variable named age to store how old I am and then update age on my birthday. When I refer to age now, it has the value 33. In one year's time, the same term will have the value 34.

Giving a value to a variable is called **assignment**. I am assigning the value "happy" to the variable mood. I am assigning the value 33 to the variable age.

This is how you would assign these variables in JavaScript:

```
mood = "happy";
age = 33;
```

When a variable has been assigned a value, we say that the variable **contains** the value. The variable mood now contains the value "happy". The variable age now contains the value 33. You could then display the values of these two variables in annoying pop-up alert windows by using the statements

```
alert(mood);
alert(age);
```

Here is an example of the value of the variable called mood:

Here is an example of the value of the variable called age:

We'll get on to doing useful things with variables later on in the book, don't you worry!

Notice that you can jump right in and start assigning values to variables without introducing them first. In many programming languages, this isn't allowed. Other languages demand that you first introduce, or **declare**, any variables.

In JavaScript, if you assign a value to a variable that hasn't yet been declared, the variable is declared automatically. Although declaring variables beforehand isn't required in JavaScript, it's still good programming practice. Here's how you would declare mood and age:

```
var mood;
var age;
```

You don't have to declare variables separately. You can declare multiple variables at the same time:

```
var mood, age;
```

You can even kill two birds with one stone by declaring a variable and assigning it a value at the same time:

```
var mood = "happy";
var age = 33;
```

You could even do this:

```
var mood = "happy", age = 33;
```

That's the most efficient way to declare and assign variables. It has exactly the same meaning as doing this:

```
var mood, age;
mood = "happy";
age = 33;
```

The names of variables, along with just about everything else in JavaScript, are case-sensitive. The variable mood is not the same variable as Mood, MOOD or mOOd. These statements would assign values to two different variables:

```
var mood = "happy";
MOOD = "sad";
```

The syntax of JavaScript does not allow variable names to contain spaces or punctuation characters (except for the dollar symbol, $). The next line would produce a syntax error:

```
var my mood = "happy";
```

Variable names can contain letters, numbers, dollar symbols, and underscores. In order to avoid long variables looking all squashed together, and to improve readability, you can use underscores in variable names:

```
var my_mood = "happy";
```

19

The text "happy" in that line is an example of a **literal**. A literal is something that is literally written out in the JavaScript code. Whereas the word var is a keyword and my_mood is the name of a variable, the text "happy" doesn't represent anything other than itself. To paraphrase Popeye, "It is what it is!"

Data types

The value of mood is a *string literal*, whereas the value of age is a *number literal*. These are two different types of data, but JavaScript makes no distinction in how they are declared or assigned. Some other languages demand that when a variable is declared, its data type is also declared. This is called **typing**.

Programming languages that require explicit typing are called **strongly typed** languages. Because typing is not required in JavaScript, it is a **weakly typed** language. This means that you can change the data type of a variable at any stage.

The following statements would be illegal in a strongly typed language but are perfectly fine in JavaScript:

```
var age = "thirty three";
age = 33;
```

JavaScript doesn't care whether age is a *string* or a *number*.

Now let's review the most important data types that exist within JavaScript.

Strings

Strings consist of zero or more characters. Characters include letters, numbers, punctuation marks, and spaces. Strings must be enclosed in quotes. You can use either single quotes or double quotes. Both of these statements have the same result:

```
var mood = 'happy';
var mood = "happy";
```

Use whichever one you like, but it's worth thinking about what characters are going to be contained in your string. If your string contains the double-quote character, then it makes sense to use single quotes to enclose the string. If the single-quote character is part of the string, you should probably use double quotes to enclose the string:

```
var mood = "don't ask";
```

If you wanted to write that statement with single quotes, you would need to ensure that the apostrophe (or single quote) between the n and the t is treated as part of the string. In this case, the single quote needs to be treated the same as any other character, rather than as a signal for marking the end of the string. This is called **escaping**. In JavaScript, escaping is done using the backslash character:

```
var mood = 'don\'t ask';
```

Similarly, if you enclose a string with double quotes, but that string also contains a double-quote character, you can use the backslash to escape the double-quote character within the string:

```
var height = "about 5'10\" tall";
```

These backslashes don't actually form part of the string. You can test this for yourself by adding this to your example.js file and reloading test.html:

```
var height = "about 5'10\" tall";
alert(height);
```

Here's an example of an output of a variable using backslashes to escape characters:

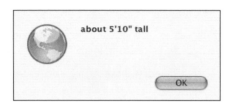

Personally, I like to use double quotes. Whether you decide to use double or single quotes, it's best to be consistent. If you switch between using double and single quotes all the time, your code could quickly become hard to read.

Numbers

If you want a variable to contain a numeric value, you don't have to limit yourself to whole numbers. JavaScript also allows you to specify numbers to as many decimal places as you want. These are called **floating-point numbers**:

```
var age = 33.25;
```

You can also use negative numbers. A minus sign at the beginning of a number indicates that it's negative:

```
var temperature = -20;
```

Negative values aren't limited to whole numbers either:

```
var temperature = -20.33333333
```

These are all examples of the *number* data type.

Boolean values

Another data type is *Boolean*.

Boolean data has just two possible values: true or false. Let's say I wanted a variable to store one value for when I'm sleeping and another value for when I'm not sleeping. I could use the string data type and assign it values like "sleeping" or "not sleeping", but it makes much more sense to use the Boolean data type:

```
var sleeping = true;
```

Boolean values lie at the heart of all computer programming. At a fundamental level, all electrical circuits use only Boolean data: either the current is flowing or it isn't. Whether you think of it in terms of "true and false", "yes and no", or "one and zero", the important thing is that there can only ever be one of two values.

Boolean values, unlike string values, are not enclosed in quotes. There is a difference between the Boolean value false and the string value "false".

This will set the variable married to the Boolean value true:

```
var married = true;
```

In this case, married is a string containing the word "true":

```
var married = "true";
```

Arrays

Strings, numbers, and Boolean values are all examples of **scalars**. If a variable is a scalar, then the variable can only ever have one value at any one time. If you want to use a variable to store a whole set of values, then you need an **array**.

An array is a grouping of multiple values under the same name. Each one of these values is an **element** of the array. For instance, you might want to have a variable called beatles that contains the names of all four members of the band at once.

In JavaScript, you declare an array by using the Array keyword. You can also specify the number of elements that you want the array to contain. This number is the **length** of the array:

```
var beatles = Array(4);
```

Sometimes you won't know in advance how many elements an array is eventually going to hold. That's OK. Specifying the number of elements is optional. You can just declare an array with an unspecified number of elements:

```
var beatles = Array();
```

Adding elements to an array is called **populating**. When you populate an array, you specify not just the value of the element, but also where the element comes in the array. This is the **index** of the element. Each element has a corresponding index. The index is contained in square brackets:

```
array[index] = element;
```

Let's start populating our array of Beatles. We'll go in the traditional order of John, Paul, George, and Ringo. Here's the first index and element:

```
beatles[0] = "John";
```

I know it might seem counterintuitive to start with an index of zero instead of one, but I'm afraid that's just the way that JavaScript works. It's easy to forget this. Many novice programmers have fallen into this common pitfall when first using arrays.

Here's how we'd declare and populate our entire beatles array:

```
var beatles = Array(4);
beatles[0] = "John";
beatles[1] = "Paul";
beatles[2] = "George";
beatles[3] = "Ringo";
```

You can now retrieve the element "George" in your script by referencing the index 2 (beatles[2]). It might take a while to get used to the fact that the length of the array is four when the last element has an index of three. That's an unfortunate result of arrays beginning with the index number zero.

That was a fairly long-winded way of populating an array. You can take a shortcut by populating your array at the same time that you declare it. When you are populating an array in a declaration, separate the values with commas:

```
var beatles = Array("John","Paul","George","Ringo");
```

An index will automatically be assigned for each element. The first index will be zero, the next will be one, etc. So referencing beatles[2] will still give us "George".

You don't even have to specify that you are creating an array. Instead, you can use square brackets to group the initial values together:

```
var beatles = ["John","Paul","George","Ringo"];
```

Still, it's good to get into the habit of using the Array keyword when you declare or populate an array. Your scripts will be more readable and it will be easy to spot arrays at a glance.

The elements of an array don't have to be strings. You can store Boolean values in an array. You can also use an array to store a series of numbers:

```
var years = Array(1940,1941,1942,1943);
```

You can even use a mixture of all three:

```
var lennon = Array("John",1940,false);
```

An element can be a variable:

```
var name = "John";
beatles[0] = name;
```

This would assign the value "John" to the first element of the beatles array.

The value of an element in one array can be an element from another array. This will assign the value "Paul" to the second element of the beatles array:

```
var names = Array("Ringo","John","George","Paul");
beatles[1] = names[3];
```

In fact, arrays can hold other arrays! Any element of an array can contain an array as its value:

```
var lennon = Array("John",1940,false);
var beatles = Array();
beatles[0] = lennon;
```

Now the value of the first element of the beatles array is itself an array. To get the values of each element of this array, we need to use some more square brackets. The value of beatles[0][0] is "John", the value of beatles[0][1] is 1940 and the value of beatles[0][2] is false.

This is quite a powerful way of storing and retrieving information, but it's going to be a frustrating experience if we have to remember the numbers for each index (especially when we have to start counting from zero). Luckily, there is a far more readable way of populating arrays.

Associative arrays

The beatles array is an example of a **numeric array**. The index for each element is a number that increments with each addition to the array. The index of the first element is zero, the index of the second element is one, and so on.

If you only specify the values of an array, then that array will be numeric. The index for each element is created and updated automatically.

It is possible to override this behavior by specifying the index of each element. When you specify the index, you don't have to limit yourself to numbers. The index can be a string instead:

```
var lennon = Array();
lennon["name"] = "John";
lennon["year"] = 1940;
lennon["living"] = false;
```

This is called an **associative array**. Actually, all arrays are associative arrays when you think about it. It just so happens that each index of a numeric array is created automatically. Each index is still associated with a specific value. So a numeric array is really just another example of an associative array.

Using associative instead of numeric arrays means you can reference elements by name instead of relying on numbers. It also makes for more readable scripts.

Let's create a new array named beatles and populate one of its elements with the array lennon that we created previously. Remember, an element in an array can itself be an array:

```
var beatles = Array();
beatles[0] = lennon;
```

Now we can get at the elements we want without using any numbers. beatles[0]["name"] is "John", beatles[0]["year"] is 1940, and beatles[0]["living"] is false.

That's an improvement, but we can go one further. What if beatles was an associative array instead of a numerical array? Then, instead of using numbers to reference each element of the array, we could use descriptive strings like "drummer" or "bassist":

```
var beatles = Array();
beatles["vocalist"] = lennon;
```

Now the value of beatles["vocalist"]["name"] is "John", beatles["vocalist"]["year"] is 1940, and beatles["vocalist"]["living"] is false.

Operations

All the statements I've shown you have been very simple. All I've done is create different types of variables. In order to do anything useful with JavaScript, we need to be able to do calculations and manipulate data. We want to perform **operations**.

Arithmetic operators

Addition is an operation. So are subtraction, division, and multiplication. Every one of these **arithmetic operations** requires an **operator**. Operators are symbols that JavaScript has reserved for performing operations. You've already seen one operator in action. We've been using the equals sign (=) to perform assignment. The operator for addition is the plus sign (+), the operator for subtraction is the minus sign (-), division uses the backslash (/), and the asterisk (*) is the symbol for multiplication operations.

Here's a simple addition operation:

```
1 + 4
```

You can also combine operations:

```
1 + 4 * 5
```

To avoid ambiguity, it's best to separate operations by enclosing them in parentheses:

```
1 + (4 * 5)
(1 + 4) * 5
```

A variable can contain an operation:

```
var total = (1 + 4) * 5;
```

Best of all, you can perform operations on variables:

```
var temp_fahrenheit = 95;
var temp_celsius = (temp_fahrenheit - 32) / 1.8;
```

JavaScript provides some useful operators that act as shortcuts in frequently used operations. If you wanted to increase the value of a numeric variable by one, you could write

```
year = year + 1;
```

You can achieve the same result by using the ++ operator:

```
year++;
```

Similarly, the -- operator will decrease the value of a numeric variable by one.

The + operator is a bit special. You can use it on strings as well as numbers. Joining strings together is a straightforward operation:

```
var message = "I am feeling " + "happy";
```

Joining strings together like this is called **concatenation**. This also works on variables:

```
var mood = "happy";
var message = "I am feeling " + mood;
```

You can even concatenate numbers with strings. This is possible because of JavaScript's weakly typed nature. The number will automatically be converted to a string:

```
var year = 2005;
var message = "The year is " + year;
```

Remember, if you concatenate a string with a number, the result will be a longer string, but if you use the same operator on two numbers, the result will be the sum of the two numbers. Compare the results of these two alert statements:

```
alert ("10" + 20);
alert (10 + 20);
```

The first alert returns the string "1020". The second returns the number 30.

Here's the result of concatenating the string "10" and the number 20:

The result of adding the number 10 and the number 20 is as follows:

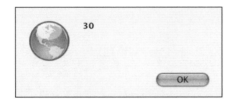

Another useful shorthand operator is += which performs addition and assignment (or concatenation and assignment) at the same time:

```
var year = 2005;
var message = "The year is ";
message += year;
```

The value of message is now "The year is 2005". You can test this yourself by using another
alert dialog box:

```
alert(message);
```

The result of concatenating a string and a number is as follows:

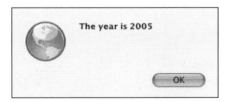

Conditional statements

All the statements you've seen so far have been relatively simple declarations or operations. The real power of a script is its ability to make decisions based on the criteria it is
given. JavaScript makes those decisions by using **conditional statements**.

When a browser is interpreting a script, statements are executed one after another. You can use a conditional statement to set up a condition that must be successfully evaluated before more statements are executed. The most common conditional statement is the if statement. It works like this:

```
if (condition) {
   statements;
}
```

The condition is contained within parentheses. The condition always resolves to a Boolean value, which is either true or false. The statement or statements contained within the curly braces will only be executed if the result of the condition is true. In this example, the annoying alert message never appears:

```
if (1 > 2) {
   alert("The world has gone mad!");
}
```

The result of the condition is false because one is not greater than two.

I've indented everything between the curly braces. This is not a syntax requirement of JavaScript—I've done it purely to make my code more readable.

In fact, the curly braces themselves aren't completely necessary. If you only want to execute a single statement based on the outcome of an if statement, you don't have to use curly braces at all. You can just put everything on one line:

```
if (1 > 2) alert("The world has gone mad!");
```

However, the curly braces help make scripts more readable so it's a good idea to use them anyway.

The if statement can be extended using else. Statements contained in the else clause will only be executed when the condition is false:

```
if (1 > 2) {
   alert("The world has gone mad!");
} else {
   alert("All is well with the world");
}
```

This is returned when 1>2 is false:

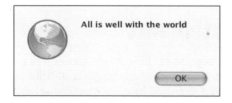

Comparison operators

JavaScript provides plenty of operators that are used almost exclusively in conditional statements. There are comparison operators like greater than (>), less than (<), greater than or equal to (>=), and less than or equal to (<=).

If you want to find out if two values are equal, you can use the equality operator. It consists of two equals signs (==). Remember, a single equals sign is used for assignment. If you use a single equals sign in a conditional statement, the operation will always be true as long as the assignment succeeds.

This is the *wrong* way to check for equality:

```
var my_mood = "happy";
var your_mood = "sad";
if (my_mood = your_mood) {
  alert("We both feel the same.");
}
```

I've just assigned the value of your_mood to my_mood. The assignment operation was carried out successfully so the result of the conditional statement is true.

This is what I should have done:

```
var my_mood = "happy";
var your_mood = "sad";
if (my_mood == your_mood) {
 alert("We both feel the same.");
}
```

This time, the result of the conditional statement is false.

There is also an operator that tests for inequality. Use an exclamation point followed by an equals sign (!=).

```
if (my_mood != your_mood) {
  alert("We're feeling different moods.");
}
```

Logical operators

It's possible to combine operations in a conditional statement. Say I want to find out if a certain variable, let's call it num, has a value between five and ten. I need to perform two operations. First, I need to find out if the variable is greater than or equal to five, and next I need to find out if the variable is less than or equal to ten. These operations are called **operands**. This is how I combine operands:

```
if ( num>=5 && num<=10 ) {
  alert("The number is in the right range.");
}
```

I've used the "and" operator, represented by two ampersands (&&). This is an example of a **logical operator**.

Logical operators work on Boolean values. Each operand returns a Boolean value of either true or false. The "and" operation will be true only if both operands are true.

The logical operator for "or" is two vertical pipe symbols (||). The "or" operation will be true if one of its operands is true. It will also be true if both of its operands are true. It will be false only if both operands are false.

```
if ( num > 10 || num < 5 ) {
  alert("The number is not in the right range.");
}
```

There is one other logical operator. It is represented by a single exclamation point (!). This is the "not" operator. The "not" operator works on just a single operand. Whatever Boolean value is returned by that operand gets reversed. If the operand is true, the "not" operator switches it to false:

```
if ( !(1 > 2) ) {
  alert("All is well with the world");
}
```

Notice that I've placed the operand in parentheses to avoid any ambiguities. I want the "not" operator to act on everything between the parentheses.

You can use the "not" operator on the result of a complete conditional statement to reverse its value. I'm going to use another set of parentheses so that the "not" operator works on both operands combined:

```
if ( !(num > 10 || num < 5) ) {
  alert("The number IS in the right range.");
}
```

Looping statements

The if statement is probably the most important and useful conditional statement. The only drawback to the if statement is that it can't be used for repetitive tasks. The block of code contained within the curly braces is executed once. If you want to execute the same code a number of times, you'll need to use a looping statement.

Looping statements allow you to keep executing the same piece of code over and over. There are a number of different types of looping statements, but they all work in much the same way. The code within a looping statement continues to be executed as long as the condition is met. When the condition is no longer true, the loop stops.

while

The while loop is very similar to the if statement. The syntax is the same:

```
while (condition) {
  statements;
}
```

The only difference is that the code contained within the curly braces will be executed over and over as long as the condition is true. Here's an example of a while loop:

```
var count = 1;
while (count < 11) {
  alert (count);
  count++;
}
```

Let's take a closer look at the code I just showed you. I began by creating a numeric variable, count, containing the value one. Then I created a while loop with the condition that the loop should repeat as long as the value of count is less than eleven. Inside the loop itself, the value of count is incremented by one using the ++ operator. The loop will execute ten times. In your web browser, you will see an annoying alert dialog box flash up ten times. After the loop has been executed, the value of count will be eleven.

> It's important that something happens within the while loop that will affect the test condition. In this case, we increase the value of count within the while loop. This results in the condition evaluating to false after ten loops. If we didn't increase the value of the count variable, the while loop would execute forever.

do...while

As with the if statement, it is possible that the statements contained within the curly braces of a while loop may never be executed. If the condition evaluates as false on the first loop, then the code won't be executed even once.

There are times when you will want the code contained within a loop to be executed at least once. In this case, it's best to use a do loop. This is the syntax for a do loop:

```
do {
  statements;
} while (condition);
```

This is very similar to the syntax for a regular while loop, but with a subtle difference. Even if the condition evaluates as false on the very first loop, the statements contained within the curly braces will still be executed once.

Let's look at our previous example, reformatted as a do...while loop:

```
var count = 1;
do {
  count++;
  alert (count);
} while (count < 11);
```

The result is exactly the same as the result from our while loop. The alert message appears ten times. After the loop is finished, the value of the variable count is eleven.

Now consider this variation:

```
var count = 1;
do {
  alert (count);
  count++;
} while (count < 1);
```

In this case, the condition never evaluates as true. The value of count is one to begin with so it is never less than one. Yet the do loop is still executed once because the condition comes after the curly braces. You will still see one alert message. After these statements are executed, the value of count is two even though the condition is false.

for

The for loop is a convenient way of executing some code a specific number of times. In that sense, it's similar to the while loop. In a way, the for loop is just a reformulation of the do loop we've already used. If we look at our do loop example, we can formulate it in full like this:

```
initialize;
while (condition) {
  statements;
  increment;
}
```

The for loop simply reformulates that as follows:

```
for (initial condition; test condition; alter condition) {
  statements;
}
```

This is generally a cleaner way of executing loops. Everything relevant to the loop is contained within the parentheses of the for statement.

If we reformulate our do loop example, this is how it looks:

```
for (var count = 1; count < 11; count++ ) {
  alert (count);
}
```

Everything related to the loop is contained within the parentheses. Now we can put code between the curly braces, secure in the knowledge that the code will be executed exactly ten times.

One of the most common uses of the for loop is to act on every element of an array. This is achieved using array.length, which provides the number of elements in array:

```
var beatles = Array("John","Paul","George","Ringo");
for (var count = 0 ; count < beatles.length; count++ ) {
  alert(beatles[count]);
}
```

If you run this code, you will see four alert messages, one for each Beatle.

Functions

If you want to re-use the same piece of code more than once, you can wrap the statements up inside a **function**. A function is a group of statements that can be invoked from anywhere in your code. Functions are, in effect, miniature scripts.

It's good practice to define your functions before you invoke them.

A simple function might look like this:

```
function shout() {
  var beatles = Array("John","Paul","George","Ringo");
  for (var count = 0 ; count < beatles.length; count++ ) {
    alert(beatles[count]);
  }
}
```

This function performs the loop that pops up the names of each Beatle. Now, whenever you want that action to occur later in your script, you can invoke the function by simply writing

```
shout();
```

That's a useful way of avoiding lots of typing whenever you want to carry out the same action more than once. The real power of functions is that you can pass data to them and then have them act on that data. When data is passed to a function, it is known as an **argument**.

Here's the syntax for defining a function:

```
function name(arguments) {
  statements;
}
```

JavaScript comes with a number of built-in functions. You've seen one of them already: the alert function takes a single argument and then pops up a dialog box with the value of the argument.

You can define a function to take as many arguments as you want by separating them with commas. Any arguments that are passed to a function can be used just like regular variables within the function.

Here's a function that takes two arguments. If you pass this function two numbers, the function will multiply them:

```
function multiply(num1,num2) {
  var total = num1 * num2;
  alert(total);
}
```

You can invoke the function from anywhere in your script, like this:

```
multiply(10,2);
```

The result of passing the values 10 and 2 to the multiply() function is as follows:

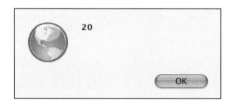

This will have the effect of immediately popping up an alert dialog with the answer (20). It would be much more useful if the function could send the answer back to the statement that invoked the function. This is quite easily done. As well as accepting data (in the form of arguments), functions can also return data.

You can create a function that returns a number, a string, an array, or a Boolean value. Use the **return** statement to do this:

```
function multiply(num1,num2) {
  var total = num1 * num2;
  return total;
}
```

Here's a function that takes one argument (a temperature in degrees Fahrenheit) and returns a number (the same temperature in degrees Celsius):

```
function convertToCelsius(temp) {
  var result = temp - 32;
  result = result / 1.8;
  return result;
}
```

The really useful thing about functions is that they can be used as a data type. You can assign the result of a function to a variable:

```
var temp_fahrenheit = 95;
var temp_celsius = convertToCelsius(temp_fahrenheit);
alert(temp_celsius);
```

The result of converting 95 degrees Fahrenheit into Celsius is as follows:

2

In this example, the variable `temp_celsius` now has a value of 35, which was returned by the `convertToCelsius` function.

You might be wondering about the way I've named my variables and functions. For my variables, I've used underscores to separate words. For my functions, I've used capital letters after the first word (this is called **camel case**). I've done this purely for my own benefit so that I can easily distinguish between variables and functions. As with variables, function names cannot contain spaces. Camel casing is simply a convenient way to work within that restriction.

Variable scope

I've mentioned already that it's good programming practice to use var when you are assigning a value to a variable for the first time. This is especially true when you are using variables in functions.

A variable can be either global or local. When we differentiate between local and global variables, we are discussing the **scope** of variables.

A **global variable** can be referenced from anywhere in the script. Once a global variable has been declared in a script, that variable can be accessed from anywhere in that script, even within functions. Its scope is global.

A **local variable** exists only within the function in which it is declared. You can't access the variable outside the function. It has a local scope.

So, you can use both global and local variables within functions. This can be useful, but it can also cause a lot of problems. If you unintentionally use the name of a global variable within a function, JavaScript will assume that you are referring to the global variable, even if you actually intended the variable to be local.

Fortunately, you can use the var keyword to explicitly set the scope of a variable within a function.

If you use var within a function, the variable will be treated as a local variable. It only exists within the context of the function. If you don't use var, the variable will be treated as a global variable. If there is already a variable with that name, the function will overwrite its value.

Take a look at this example:

```
function square(num) {
  total = num * num;
  return total;
}
var total = 50;
var number = square(20);
alert(total);
```

The value of the variable has been inadvertently changed:

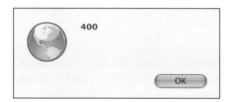

The value of the variable total is now 400. All I wanted from the square() function was for it to return the value of number squared. But because I didn't explicitly declare that the variable called total within the function should be local, the function has changed the value of the global variable called total.

This is how I should have written the function:

```
function square(num) {
  var total = num * num;
  return total;
}
```

Now I can safely have a global variable named total, secure in the knowledge that it won't be affected whenever the square() function is invoked.

Remember, functions should behave like self-contained scripts. That's why you should always declare variables within functions as being local in scope. If you always use var within functions, you can avoid any potential ambiguities.

Objects

There is one very important data type that we haven't looked at yet: **objects**. An object is a self-contained collection of data. This data comes in two forms: **properties** and **methods**:

- A property is a variable belonging to an object.
- A method is a function that the object can invoke.

These properties and methods are all combined in one single entity, which is the object.

Properties and methods are both accessed in the same way using JavaScript's dot syntax:

```
Object.property
Object.method()
```

You've already seen how variables can be used to hold values for things like mood and age. If there were an object called, say, Person, then these would be properties of the object:

```
Person.mood
Person.age
```

If there were functions associated with the Person object—say, walk() or sleep()—then these would be methods of the object:

```
Person.walk()
Person.sleep()
```

Now all these properties and methods are grouped together under one term: Person.

To use the Person object to describe a specific person, you would create an **instance** of Person. An instance is an individual example of a generic object. For instance, you and I are both people, but we are also both individuals. We probably have different properties (our ages may differ, for instance), yet we are both examples of an object called Person.

A new instance is created using the new keyword:

```
var jeremy = new Person;
```

This would create a new instance of the object Person, called jeremy. I could use the properties of the Person object to retrieve information about jeremy:

```
jeremy.age
jeremy.mood
```

I've used the imaginary example of a Person object just to demonstrate objects, properties, methods, and instances. In JavaScript, there is no Person object. It is possible for you to create your own objects in JavaScript. These are called **user-defined objects**. But that's quite an advanced subject that we don't need to deal with for now.

Fortunately, JavaScript is like one of those TV chefs who produce perfectly formed creations from the oven, declaring, "Here's one I made earlier." JavaScript comes with a range of pre-made objects that you can use in your scripts. These are called **native objects**.

Native objects

You've already seen objects in action. Array is an object. Whenever you initialize an array using the new keyword, you are creating a new instance of the Array object:

```
var beatles = new Array();
```

When you want to find out how many elements are in an array, you do so by using the length property:

```
beatles.length;
```

The Array object is an example of a native object supplied by JavaScript. Other examples include Math and Date, both of which have very useful methods for dealing with numbers and dates respectively. For instance, the Math object has a method called round which can be used to round up a decimal number:

```
var num = 7.561;
var num = Math.round(num);
alert(num);
```

The Date object can be used to store and retrieve information about a specific date and time. If you create a new instance of the Date object, it will be automatically be pre-filled with the current date and time:

```
var current_date = new Date();
```

The date object has a whole range of methods like getDay(), getHours(), and getMonth() that can be used to retrieve information about the specified date. getDay(), for instance, will return the day of the week of the specified date:

```
var today = current_date.getDay();
```

Native objects like this provide invaluable shortcuts when you're writing JavaScript.

Host objects

Native objects aren't the only kind of pre-made objects that you can use in your scripts. Another kind of object is supplied not by the JavaScript language itself, but by the environment in which it's running. In the case of the Web, that environment is the web browser. Objects that are supplied by the web browser are called **host objects**.

Host objects include Form, Image, and Element. These objects can be used to get information about forms, images, and form elements within a web page.

I'm not going to show you any examples of how to use those host objects. There is another object that can be used to get information about any element in a web page that you might be interested in: the document object. For the rest of this book, we are going to be looking at lots of properties and methods belonging to the document object.

What's next?

In this chapter, I've shown you the basics of the JavaScript language. Throughout the rest of the book, I'll be using terms that have been introduced here: statements, variables, arrays, functions, and so on. Some of these concepts will become clearer once you see them in action in a working script. You can always refer back to this chapter whenever you need a reminder of what these terms mean.

I've just introduced the concept of objects. Don't worry if it isn't completely clear to you just yet. The next chapter will take an in-depth look at one particular object, the document object. I want to start by showing you some properties and methods associated with this object. These properties and methods are provided courtesy of the Document Object Model.

In the next chapter, I want to introduce you to the idea of the DOM and show you how to use some of its very powerful methods.

3 THE DOCUMENT OBJECT MODEL

What this chapter covers:

- The concept of nodes
- Four very handy DOM methods: getElementById, getElementsByTagName, getAttribute, and setAttribute

It's time to meet the DOM. I'd like to introduce you to the Document Object Model and show you the world through its eyes.

D is for document

The Document Object Model can't work without a document. When you create a web page and load it in a web browser, the DOM stirs into life. It takes the document that you have written and turns it into an object.

In normal everyday English, the word "object" isn't very descriptive. It simply means thing. In programming languages, on the other hand, "object" has a very specific meaning.

Objects of desire

At the end of the last chapter, I showed you some examples of **objects** in JavaScript. You'll remember that objects are self-contained bundles of data. Variables associated with an object are called **properties** of the object, while functions that can be executed by an object are called **methods** of the object.

There are three kinds of objects in JavaScript:

- User-defined objects created from scratch by the programmer. We won't be dealing with these.
- Native objects like Array, Math, and Date that are built in to JavaScript.
- Host objects that are provided by the browser.

From the earliest days of JavaScript, some very important host objects have been made available for scripting. The most fundamental of these is the window object.

This object is nothing less than a representation of the browser window itself. The properties and methods of the window object are often referred to as the Browser Object Model, although perhaps Window Object Model would be more semantically correct. The Browser Object Model has methods like window.open and window.blur. These methods, incidentally, are responsible for all those annoying pop-up and pop-under windows that now plague the Web. No wonder JavaScript has a bad reputation!

Fortunately, we won't be dealing with the Browser Object Model very much. Instead, I'm going to focus on what's inside the browser window. The object that handles the contents of a web page is the document object.

For the rest of this book, we're going to be dealing almost exclusively with the properties and methods of the document object.

That explains the letter D (document) and the letter O (object) in DOM. But what about the letter M?

Dial M for model

The M in DOM stands for Model, but it could just as easily stand for Map. A model, like a map, is a representation of something. A model train represents a real train. A street map of a city represents the real city. The Document Object Model represents the web page that's currently loaded in the browser window. The browser provides a map (or model) of the page. You can use JavaScript to read this map.

Maps make use of conventions like direction, contours, and scale. In order to read a map, you need to understand these conventions—and it's the same with the Document Object Model. In order to gain information from the model, you need to understand what conventions are being used to represent the document.

The most important convention used by the Document Object Model is the representation of a document as a tree. More specifically, the document is represented as a family tree.

A family tree is another example of a model. A family tree represents a real family, describes the relationships between family members, and uses conventions, like *parent*, *child*, and *sibling*. These can be used to represent some fairly complex relationships: one member of a family can be a parent to others, while also being the child of another family member, and the sibling of yet another family member.

The family tree model works just as well in representing a document written in (X)HTML.

Take a look at this very basic web page:

```
<!DOCTYPE html PUBLIC "-//W3C//DTD XHTML 1.1//EN"
"http://www.w3.org/TR/xhtml11/DTD/xhtml11.dtd">
<html xmlns="http://www.w3.org/1999/xhtml" xml:lang="en">
  <head>
    <meta http-equiv="content-type" content="text/html;
➥ charset=utf-8" />
    <title>Shopping list</title>
  </head>
  <body>
    <h1>What to buy</h1>
    <p title="a gentle reminder">Don't forget to buy this stuff.</p>
    <ul id="purchases">
      <li>A tin of beans</li>
      <li>Cheese</li>
      <li>Milk</li>
    </ul>
  </body>
</html>
```

This can be represented by the model in Figure 3-1.

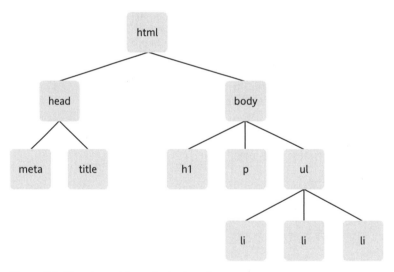

Figure 3-1. The element tree of a basic web page

Let's walk through the web page structure to see what it's made up of, and show why it's represented so well by the model shown previously. After the Doctype declaration, the document begins by opening an <html> tag. All the other elements of the web page are contained within this element, meaning it is a parent. Because all the other elements are inside, the <html> tag has no parent itself. It also has no siblings. If this were a tree, the <html> tag would be the root.

The root element is html. For all intents and purposes, the html element *is* the document.

If we move one level deeper, we find two branches: <head> and <body>. They exist side by side, which makes them siblings. They share the same parent, <html>, but they also both contain children, so they are parents themselves.

The <head> element has two children: <meta> and <title> (siblings of one another). The children of the <body> element are <h1>, <p>, and <ul> (all siblings of one another). If we drill down deeper still, we find that <ul> is also a parent. It has three children, all of them <li> elements.

By using this simple convention of familial relationships, we can access lots of information about the relationship between elements.

For example, what is the relationship between <h1> and <p>? The answer is that they are siblings.

What is the relationship between <body> and <ul>? <body> is the parent of <ul>. <ul> is a child of <body>.

If you can think of the elements of a document in terms of a tree of familial relationships, then you're using the same terms as the DOM. However, instead of using the term "family tree," it's more accurate to call a document a **node tree**.

Nodes

The term **node** comes from networking, where it used to denote a point of connection in a network. A network is a collection of nodes.

In the real world, everything is made up of atoms. Atoms are the nodes of the real world. But atoms can themselves be broken down into smaller, subatomic particles. These subatomic particles are also considered nodes.

It's a similar situation with the Document Object Model. A document is a collection of nodes, with nodes as the branches and leaves on the document tree.

There are a number of different types of nodes. Just as atoms contain subatomic particles, some types of nodes contain other types of nodes.

element nodes

The DOM's equivalent of the atom is the **element node**.

When I described the structure of the shopping list document, I did so in terms of elements such as <body>, <p>, and <ul>. Elements are the basic building blocks of documents on the Web, and it's the arrangement of these elements in a document that gives the document its structure.

The tag provides the name of an element. Paragraph elements have the name p, unordered lists have the name ul, and list items have the name li.

Elements can contain other elements. All the list item elements in our document are contained within an unordered list element. In fact, the only element that isn't contained within another element is the <html> element. It's the root of our node tree.

text nodes

Elements are just one type of node. If a document consisted purely of empty elements, it would have a structure, but the document itself wouldn't contain much content. On the Web, where content is king, most content is provided by text.

In our example, the <p> element contains the text "Don't forget to buy this stuff." This is a **text node**.

In XHTML, text nodes are always enclosed within element nodes. But not all elements contain text nodes. In our shopping list document, the <ul> element doesn't contain any text directly. It contains other element nodes (the <li> elements), and these contain text nodes.

attribute nodes

There are quite a few other types of nodes. Comments are a separate node type, for instance. But I'd just like to mention one more node type here.

Attributes are used to give more specific information about an element. The title attribute, for example, can be used on just about any element to specify exactly what the element contains:

```
<p title="a gentle reminder">Don't forget to buy this stuff.</p>
```

In the Document Object Model, title="a gentle reminder" is an **attribute node**, as shown in Figure 3-2. Because attributes are always placed within opening tags, attribute nodes are always contained within element nodes.

Not all elements contain attributes, but all attributes are contained by elements.

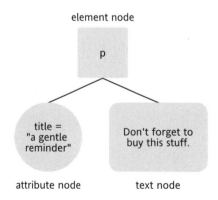

Figure 3-2. An element node that contains an attribute node and a text node

In our example document, you'll see that the unordered list (<ul>) has been marked with the id attribute. You're probably familiar with the id and class attributes from using CSS. Just in case you haven't got that much familiarity with CSS, now we'll briefly recap the very basics of CSS.

Cascading Style Sheets

The DOM isn't the only technology that interacts with the structure of web pages. Cascading Style Sheets are used to instruct a browser how to display the contents of a document.

Like JavaScript, styles can be declared either in the <head> of a document (between <style> tags), or in an external style sheet. The syntax for styling an element with CSS is similar to that of JavaScript functions:

```
selector {
 property: value;
}
```

Style declarations can be used to specify the colors, fonts, and sizes used by the browser to display elements:

```
p {
  color: yellow;
  font-family: "arial", sans-serif;
  font-size: 1.2em;
}
```

Inheritance is a powerful feature of CSS. Like the DOM, CSS view the contents of a document as a node tree. Elements that are nested within the node tree will inherit the style properties of their parents.

For instance, declaring colors or fonts on the body element will automatically apply those styles to all the elements contained within the body:

```
body {
  color: white;
  background-color: black;
}
```

Those colors will be applied not just to content contained directly by the <body> tag, but also by elements nested within the body.

The image at right is a basic web page with styles applied:

When you're applying styles to a document, there are times when you will want to target specific elements. You might want to make one paragraph a certain size and color, but leave other paragraphs unaffected. To get this level of precision, you'll need to insert something into the document itself to mark the paragraph as a special case.

To mark elements for special treatment, you can use one of two attributes: class or id.

class

The class attribute can be applied as often as you like to as many different elements as you like:

```
<p class="special">This paragraph has the special class</p>
<h2 class="special">So does this headline</h2>
```

In a style sheet, styles can then be applied to all the elements of this class:

```
.special {
  font-style: italic;
}
```

You can also target specific types of elements with this class:

```
h2.special {
  text-transform: uppercase;
}
```

id

The id attribute can be used once in a web page to uniquely identify an element:

```
<ul id="purchases">
```

In a style sheet, styles can then be applied specifically to this element:

```
#purchases {
  border: 1px solid white;
  background-color: #333;
  color: #ccc;
  padding: 1em;
}
```

Although the id itself can only be applied once, a style sheet can use the id to apply styles to elements nested within the uniquely identified element:

```
#purchases li {
  font-weight: bold;
}
```

The image at right is an example of styles applied to a list with a unique id:

The id attribute acts as a kind of "hook" that can be targeted by CSS. The DOM can use the same hook.

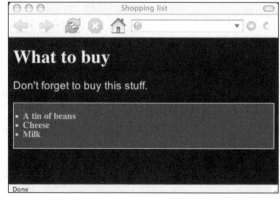

getElementById

The DOM has a method called **getElementById**, which does exactly what it sounds like: it allows you to get straight to the element node with the specified id. Remember that JavaScript is case-sensitive so getElementById must always be written with case preserved. If you write **GetElementById** or **getElementbyid**, you won't get the results you expect.

This method is a function associated with the document object. Functions are always followed by parentheses that contain the function's arguments. getElementById takes just one argument: the id of the element you want to get to, contained in either single or double quotes.

> *document.getElementById(id)*

Here's an example:

> document.getElementById("purchases")

This is referencing the unique element that has been assigned the HTML id attribute "purchases" in the document object. This element also corresponds to an object. You can test this for yourself by using the typeof operator. This will tell you whether something is a string, a number, a function, a Boolean value, or an object.

I don't recommend this way of adding JavaScript to a document but, purely for testing purposes, insert this piece of JavaScript into the shopping list document. Put it right before the closing </body> tag:

```
<!DOCTYPE html PUBLIC "-//W3C//DTD XHTML 1.1//EN"
"http://www.w3.org/TR/xhtml11/DTD/xhtml11.dtd">
<html xmlns="http://www.w3.org/1999/xhtml" xml:lang="en">
  <head>
    <meta http-equiv="content-type" content="text/html;
➥ charset=utf-8" />
    <title>Shopping list</title>
  </head>
  <body>
    <h1>What to buy</h1>
    <p title="a gentle reminder">Don't forget to buy this stuff.</p>
    <ul id="purchases">
      <li>A tin of beans</li>
      <li>Cheese</li>
      <li>Milk</li>
    </ul>
<script type="text/javascript">
alert(typeof document.getElementById("purchases"));
</script>
  </body>
</html>
```

3

When you load the XHTML file in a web browser, you will be greeted with an annoying pop-up box stating the nature of document.getElementById("purchases"). It is an object.

Here, an alert dialog reveals the nature of an element node:

In fact, every single element in a document is an object. Using the DOM, you can "get" at every single one of these elements.

Obviously you shouldn't give a unique id to every single element in a document. That would be overkill. Fortunately, the document object provides another method for getting at elements that don't have unique identifiers.

getElementsByTagName

If you use the method **getElementsByTagName**, you have instant access to an array populated with every occurrence of a specified tag. Like getElementById, this is a function that takes one argument. In this case, the argument is the name of a tag:

```
element.getElementsByTagName(tag)
```

It looks very similar to getElementById, but notice that this time you can get elements, plural. Be careful when you are writing your scripts that you don't inadvertently write *getElementsById* or *getElementByTagName*.

Here it is in action:

```
document.getElementsByTagName("li")
```

This is an array populated with all the list items in the document object. Just as with any other array, you can use the length property to get the total number of elements.

Delete the alert statement you placed between <script> tags earlier and replace it with this:

```
alert(document.getElementsByTagName("li").length);
```

This will tell you the total number of list items in the document: three, in this case. Every value in the array is an object. You can test this yourself by looping through the array and using typeof on each value. For example, try this with a for loop:

```
for (var i=0; i < document.getElementsByTagName("li").length; i++) {
  alert(typeof document.getElementsByTagName("li")[i]);
}
```

Even if there is only one element with the specified tag name, getElementsByTagName still returns an array. The length of the array will simply be 1.

Now you will begin to notice it is starting to become tedious typing out document.getElementsByTagName("li") every time, and that the code is starting to get hard to read. You can reduce the amount of unnecessary typing and improve readability by assigning a variable to contain document.getElementsByTagName("li").

Replace the alert statement between the <script> tags with these statements:

```
var items = document.getElementsByTagName("li");
for (var i=0; i < items.length; i++) {
  alert(typeof items[i]);
}
```

Now you'll get three annoying alert boxes, each one of them saying the same thing: object.

You can also use a wildcard with getElementsByTagName, which means you can make an array with every single element. The wildcard symbol (the asterisk) must be contained in quotes to distinguish it from the multiplication operator. The wildcard will give you the total number of element nodes in a document:

```
alert(document.getElementsByTagName("*").length);
```

You can also combine getElementsByTagName with getElementById. So far, we've only applied getElementsByTagName to the document object, but if you're interested in finding out how many list items are inside the element with the id "purchases", you could apply getElementsByTagName to that specific object:

```
var shopping = document.getElementById("purchases");
var items = shopping.getElementsByTagName("*");
```

Now the items array contains just the elements contained by the "purchases" list. In this case, that happens to be the same as the total number of the list items in the document:

```
alert (items.length);
```

And, if any further proof were needed, you can test that each one is an object:

```
for (var i=0; i < items.length; i++) {
  alert(typeof items[i]);
}
```

Taking stock

By now, you are probably well and truly fed up with seeing alert boxes containing the word "object". I think I've made my point: every element node in a document is an object. Not only that, but every single one of these objects comes with an arsenal of methods, courtesy of the DOM. Using these pre-supplied methods, you can retrieve information about any element in a document. You can even alter the properties of an element.

Here's a quick summary of what you've seen so far:

- A document is a tree of nodes.
- There are different types of nodes: elements, attributes, text, and so on.
- You can get straight to a specific element node using getElementById.
- You can get straight to a collection of element nodes using getElementsByTagName.
- Every one of these nodes is an object.

Now I want to show you some of the properties and methods associated with these objects.

getAttribute

So far, you've seen two different ways of getting to element nodes, using either getElementById or getElementsByTagName. Once you've got the element, you can find out the values of any of its attributes. You can do this with the **getAttribute** method.

getAttribute is a function. It takes only one argument—the attribute that you want to get:

object.getAttribute(attribute)

Unlike the other methods you've seen, you can't use getAttribute on the document object. It can only be used on an element node object.

For example, you can use it in combination with getElementsByTagName to get the title attribute of every <p> element:

```
var paras = document.getElementsByTagName("p");
for (var i=0; i < paras.length; i++ ) {
  alert(paras[i].getAttribute("title"));
}
```

If you include this code at the end of our shopping list document and then load the page in a web browser, you'll be greeted with an alert box containing the text, "a gentle reminder".

In our shopping list, there is only one <p> element and it has a title attribute. If there were more <p> elements and they didn't have title attributes, then getAttribute("title") would return the value **null**. In JavaScript, null means that there is no value. You can test this for yourself by inserting this paragraph right after the existing paragraph:

```
<p>This is just a test</p>
```

Now reload the page. This time, you'll see two alert boxes. The second one is either completely empty or simply says "null", depending on how the browser chooses to display null values.

We can modify our script so that it only pops up a message when a title attribute exists. We will add an if statement to check that the value returned by getAttribute is not null. While we're at it, let's use a few more variables to make the script easier to read:

```
var paras = document.getElementsByTagName("p");
for (var i=0; i< paras.length; i++) {
  var title_text = paras[i].getAttribute("title");
  if (title_text != null) {
    alert(title_text);
  }
}
```

Now if you reload the page, you will only see the alert box that contains the value, "a gentle reminder". Here is an example of this:

We can shorten the code even more. Whenever you want to check that something isn't null, you're really checking to see if it exists. A shorthand way of doing that is to use it as the condition in an if statement. if (something) is a shorthand way of writing if (something != null). The condition of the if statement will be true if something exists. It will be false if something doesn't exist.

We can tighten up our code by simply writing if (title_text) instead of if (title_text != null). While we're at it, we can put the alert statement on the same line as the if statement so that it reads more like English:

```
var paras = document.getElementsByTagName("p");
for (var i=0; i< paras.length; i++) {
  var title_text = paras[i].getAttribute("title");
  if (title_text) alert(title_text);
}
```

setAttribute

All of the methods you've seen so far have dealt with retrieving information. **setAttribute** is a bit different. It allows you to change the value of an attribute node.

Like getAttribute, this method is a function that only works on element nodes. However, setAttribute takes two arguments:

```
object.setAttribute(attribute,value)
```

In this example, I'm going to get the element with the id "purchases", and give it a title attribute with the value "a list of goods":

```
var shopping = document.getElementById("purchases");
shopping.setAttribute("title","a list of goods");
```

You can use getAttribute to test that the title attribute has been set:

```
var shopping = document.getElementById("purchases");
alert(shopping.getAttribute("title"));
shopping.setAttribute("title","a list of goods");
alert(shopping.getAttribute("title"));
```

Loading the page will now give you two alert boxes. The first one, which is executed before setAttribute, is empty or else displays "null". The second one, which is executed after the title attribute has been set, says "a list of goods".

In that example, we set an attribute where previously none had existed. The setAttribute method created the attribute and then set its value. If you use setAttribute on an element node that already has the specified attribute, the old value will be overwritten.

In our shopping list document, the <p> element already has a title attribute with the value "a gentle reminder". You use setAttribute to change this value:

```
var paras = document.getElementsByTagName("p");
for (var i=0; i< paras.length; i++) {
  var title_text = paras[i].getAttribute("title");
  if (title_text) {
    paras[i].setAttribute("title","brand new title text");
    alert(paras[i].getAttribute("title"));
  }
}
```

This will apply the value "brand new title text" to the title attribute of every <p> element in the document that already had a title attribute. In our shopping list document, the value "a gentle reminder" has been overwritten.

It's worth noting that, even when a document has been changed by setAttribute, you won't see that change reflected when you use the view source option in your web browser. This is because the DOM has dynamically updated the contents of the page after it has loaded. The real power of the DOM is that the contents of a page can be updated without refreshing the page in the browser.

What's next?

I've shown you four methods provided by the Document Object Model:

- getElementById
- getElementsByTagName
- getAttribute
- setAttribute

These four methods will be the cornerstones for many of the DOM scripts you're going to write.

The DOM offers many more methods and properties. There's nodeName, nodeValue, childNodes, nextSibling, and parentNode, to name just a few. But I'm not going to explain those just yet—I'll explain each one in turn as and when they're needed. I'm mentioning them now just to whet your appetite.

You've read through a lot of theory in this chapter. I hope by now you're itching to test the power of the DOM using something other than alert boxes. I think it's high time we applied the DOM to a case study.

Next, you're going to build a JavaScript image gallery using the four DOM methods introduced in this chapter.

3

4 A JAVASCRIPT IMAGE GALLERY

It's time to put to the Document Object Model to work. This chapter will show you how to make an image gallery using JavaScript and the DOM.

- Begin with a well-marked-up document
- Write a JavaScript function to display a requested image
- Trigger the function from within the markup
- Expand the function using some new methods

There are a number of ways to put a gallery of images online. You could simply put all the images on one web page, for example. However, if you want to display more than a handful of images, the page is going to get big and bloated fairly quickly. The weight of the markup by itself might not be all that much, but the combined weight of the markup and images can result in a hefty download. Let's face it—nobody likes waiting a long time for pages to download.

A better solution might be to create a web page for each image. Then, instead of having one large page to download, you have lots of reasonably sized pages. But, at the same time, making all of those pages could be very time-consuming. Each page would probably need to have some kind of navigation to show the position of the current image in the gallery.

Using JavaScript, you can create an image gallery that offers the best of both worlds. You can put the navigation for the entire gallery on one page and then download each image as, and when, it's required.

The markup

For this example, I'm going to use a handful of snapshots I've taken with a digital camera. I've scaled them down to the web-friendly size of 400 pixels wide by 300 pixels tall.

I'll start by creating a list of links that point to the images. I haven't arranged the images in any particular order, so I'm going to use an unordered list (<ul>) to do this. If your images are arranged sequentially, then an ordered list (<ol>) is probably the best way to mark them up.

Here's my document:

```
<!DOCTYPE html PUBLIC "-//W3C//DTD XHTML 1.1//EN"
"http://www.w3.org/TR/xhtml11/DTD/xhtml11.dtd">
<html xmlns="http://www.w3.org/1999/xhtml" xml:lang="en">
<head>
  <meta http-equiv="content-type" content="text/html; charset=utf-8" />
  <title>Image Gallery</title>
</head>
<body>
  <h1>Snapshots</h1>
  <ul>
    <li>
      <a href="images/fireworks.jpg" title="A fireworks display">
➥ Fireworks</a>
```

```
      </li>
      <li>
        <a href="images/coffee.jpg" title="A cup of black coffee">
➥ Coffee</a>
      </li>
      <li>
        <a href="images/rose.jpg" title="A red, red rose">Rose</a>
      </li>
      <li>
        <a href="images/bigben.jpg" title="The famous clock">
➥ Big Ben</a>
      </li>
    </ul>
  </body>
</html>
```

I'm going to save that file as `gallery.htm` and place my pictures in a directory called images. My images directory is inside the same directory as `gallery.html`. Each of the links in the unordered list points to a different image. Clicking on one of the links takes you to the image, but in order to get back to the list, you have to use the browser's back button. Here's an illustration of the bare-bones list of links:

This is a perfectly fine web page, but the default behavior isn't ideal. These are the things I want to happen instead:

- When I click a link, I want to remain on the same page.
- When I click a link, I want to see the image on the same page that has my original list of images.

This is how I'm going to do it:

- I'll put a placeholder image on the same page as the list.
- When I click a link, I'll intercept the default behavior.
- I'll replace the placeholder image with the image from the link.

Let's start with the placeholder image. I'm going to use a kind of title card, but you can just as easily use a blank image.

Insert this line right after the list:

```
<img id="placeholder" src="images/placeholder.gif"
➥ alt="my image gallery" />
```

I've added an id attribute to this image, which I can use to style the image from an external style sheet. For instance, I might want to float the image so that it appears next to the link list instead of underneath it. I can also use this id in my JavaScript. An illustration of the placeholder image added to the page is shown next:

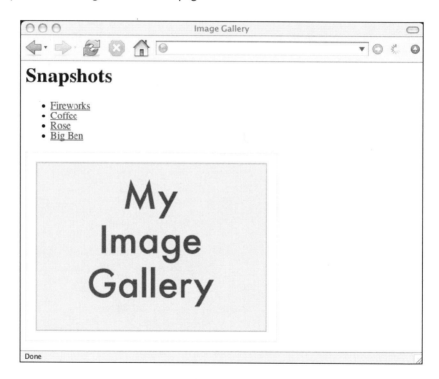

The markup is ready. Now it's time to stir in the JavaScript.

The JavaScript

In order to swap out the placeholder image, I need to change its src attribute. Luckily, the setAttribute method is perfect for this task. I'll write a function using this method that accepts a single argument: a link to an image. My function will then update the src attribute of the placeholder image with this image.

To start, I need a good name for my function. It should be descriptive, but not too verbose. I'm going to call it showPic. I also need a name for the argument that gets passed to the function, which I've decided to call whichpic:

```
function showPic(whichpic)
```

whichpic represents an element node. Specifically, it's an <a> element that leads to an image. I need to extract the path to the image, and I can do this by using the getAttribute method on the whichpic element. By passing "href" as the argument, I can find out what the path to the image is:

```
whichpic.getAttribute("href")
```

I'm going to store this value in a variable so that I can retrieve it later. Let's call the variable source:

```
var source = whichpic.getAttribute("href");
```

The next thing I need to do is get to the placeholder image. This is easily done using getElementById:

```
document.getElementById("placeholder")
```

I'm going to assign this element to a variable so I don't have to type out document.getElementById("placeholder") more than once. I'll call this variable placeholder:

```
var placeholder = document.getElementById("placeholder");
```

Now I've assigned values to two variables, source and placeholder. That will help me keep the script readable.

I'll update the src attribute of the placeholder element using setAttribute. Remember, this method takes two arguments: the attribute you want to set, and the value you want this attribute to have. In this case, I want to set the src attribute so the first argument is "src". The second argument, the value I want the src attribute to have, has already been stored as source:

```
placeholder.setAttribute("src",source);
```

That's a lot easier to read than this:

```
document.getElementById("placeholder").setAttribute("src",
➥ whichpic.getAttribute("href"));
```

4

61

A DOM diversion

It's possible to change the src attribute of an image without using setAttribute.

setAttribute is part of the DOM Level 1 specification, which allows you to set any attribute for any element node. Before DOM Level 1, it was still possible to set the attributes of many, though not all, elements, but it was done differently. You can still change attributes in this way, however.

For instance, to change the value attribute of an input element, you could use the value method:

```
element.value = "the new value"
```

That would have the same effect as this:

```
element.setAttribute("value","the new value");
```

Similarly, there's another way to change the source of an image. I could write my image gallery script to use this method instead of setAttribute:

```
placeholder.src = source;
```

Personally, I prefer to use setAttribute. For one thing, I don't have to remember which pre-DOM methods work on which elements. Though the old methods work fine on images, forms, and some other elements in a document, I can use setAttribute on any element in a document that I'd like.

Also, DOM Level 1 is more portable. While the older methods deal specifically with web documents, DOM methods can be used on any markup. Admittedly, that doesn't apply to what we're doing here, but it's worth bearing in mind. Remember, the DOM is an API that can be applied with many programming languages in many environments. If you ever need to apply the DOM skills you're learning now to situations outside the browser, sticking with DOM Level 1 will avoid any compatibility issues.

Finishing the function

Here's how the finished function looks:

```
function showPic(whichpic) {
  var source = whichpic.getAttribute("href");
  var placeholder = document.getElementById("placeholder");
  placeholder.setAttribute("src",source);
}
```

Now it's time to hook up the JavaScript with the markup.

Applying the JavaScript

I need to make sure that my newly written showPic function is available to my image gallery document. I could place the function between <script> tags in the <head> of the document, but that would be quite short-sighted of me. If I ever want to use the same function on a different page, I'd have to cut and paste the whole thing. It makes a lot more sense to put the function into an external file and simply place a reference to this file in the <head> of every document that needs it.

Save the function in a text file with the extension .js. You can call the file anything you want, but I like to name them after the functions they contain. I would call the file showPic.js.

Just as I've placed all my pictures in a directory called images, it's a good idea to keep all your JavaScript files in one place. Create a directory called scripts and save the showPic.js file there.

Now I need to point the image gallery document to the JavaScript file. Add this line to the <head> of the document (after the <title> tag, for instance):

```
<script type="text/javascript" src="scripts/showPic.js"></script>
```

The showPic function is now available to the image gallery document. As it stands, the function will never be invoked. I need to add the behavior to the links in my list. I'm going to do this by adding an **event handler**.

Event handlers

Event handlers are used to invoke some JavaScript when a certain action happens. If you want some behavior to be triggered when the user moves their cursor over an element, you use the onmouseover event handler. There's a corresponding onmouseout event. For my image gallery, I want to add a behavior when the user clicks on a link. The event handler for this is onclick.

I can't invoke the showPic function without sending it some information. showPic expects one argument: an element node that has an href attribute. When I place the onclick event handler in a link, I want to send that link to the showPic function as the argument.

Luckily, there's a very short but powerful way of doing just that. The keyword this is a shorthand way of saying "this object". In this case, I'm going to use this to mean "this <a> element node":

```
showPic(this)
```

I'm going to add that using the onclick event handler. Here's the syntax for adding JavaScript using an event handler:

```
event = "JavaScript statement(s)"
```

Notice that the JavaScript itself is contained within quotes. You can put as many JavaScript statements as you like between the quotes, as long as they are separated with semicolons.

This will invoke the showPic function with the onclick event handler:

```
onclick = "showPic(this);"
```

However, if I simply add this event handler to a link in my list, I'm going to be faced with a problem. The function will be invoked, but the default behavior for clicking on a link will also be invoked. This means that the user will be taken to the image—exactly what I didn't want to happen. I need to stop the default behavior from being invoked.

Let me explain a bit more about how event handling works. When you attach an event handler to an element, you can trigger JavaScript statements with the event. The JavaScript can return a result that is then passed back to the event handler. For example, you can attach some JavaScript to the onclick event of a link so that it returns a Boolean value of true or false. If you click on the link, and the event handler receives a value of true, it's getting the message "yes, this link has been clicked." If you add some JavaScript to the event handler so that it returns false, then the message being sent back is "no, this link has not been clicked."

You can see this for yourself with this simple test:

```
<a href="http://www.example.com" onclick="return false;">Click me</a>
```

If you click on that link, the default behavior will not be triggered, because the JavaScript is effectively canceling the default behavior.

By adding a return false statement to the JavaScript contained by the onclick event handler, I can stop the user from being taken straight to destination of the link:

```
onclick = "showPic(this); return false;"
```

This is how it would look in the context of the document:

```
<li>
    <a href="images/fireworks.jpg" onclick="showPic(this);
➡ return false;" title="A fireworks display">Fireworks</a>
</li>
```

Now I'll need to add that event handler to every link in my list. That's a tedious task, but later on, I'll show you a way to avoid it completely. For now, I'm going to dive into the markup and add the event handler by hand:

```
<li>
    <a href="images/fireworks.jpg" onclick="showPic(this);
➡ return false;" title="A fireworks display">Fireworks</a>
  </li>
  <li>
    <a href="images/coffee.jpg" onclick="showPic(this);
➡ return false;" title="A cup of black coffee">Coffee</a>
```

```
   </li>
   <li>
     <a href="images/rose.jpg" onclick="showPic(this); return false;"
➥ title="A red, red rose">Rose</a>
   </li>
   <li>
     <a href="images/bigben.jpg" onclick="showPic(this); return false;"
➥ title="The famous clock">Big Ben</a>
   </li>
```

If you load the page in a web browser, you will see a working JavaScript image gallery. Click on a link in the list and you will see the image displayed on the same page:

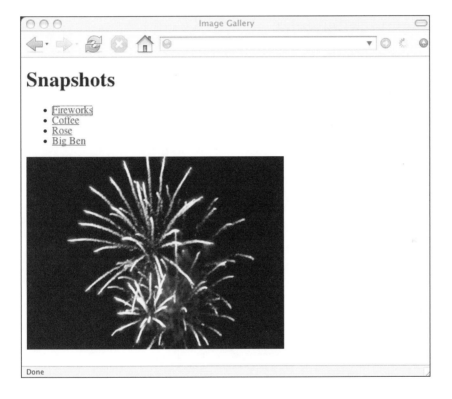

Expanding the function

Swapping out images on a web page isn't really all that impressive. You could do it even prior to WC3 DOM JavaScript. It was the basis for all those rollover scripts that have proven so popular.

What would be really great, you're thinking, would be the ability to update the text on a web page. Using JavaScript and the DOM, you can do just that.

Every link in my list has a title attribute. I'd like to take the value of that attribute and display it on the page along with the image. I can get the value of the title attribute easily enough using getAttribute, and if I add this line to the start of the showPic function, I can store the title value in a variable:

```
var titletext = whichPic.getAttribute("title");
```

Now I need to insert it into the document. To do that, I need to introduce some new DOM properties.

Introducing childNodes

The childNodes property is a way of getting information about the children of any element in a document's node tree.

childNodes returns an array containing all the children of an element node:

```
element.childNodes
```

Let's say you wanted to get all the children of the body element. We can use getElementsByTagName to get at the body element. We know that there is only one body element, so it will be the first (and only) element of the array getElementsByTagName("body"):

```
var body_element = document.getElementsByTagName("body")[0];
```

Now the variable body_element refers to the body element in our document. To access the children of the body element, you just need to use

```
body_element.childNodes
```

That's a lot easier than writing this:

```
document.getElementsByTagName("body")[0].childNodes
```

Actually, in the case of the body element, you can simply use

```
document.body
```

In any case, now that you can get at all the children of the body element, let's take a look at what you can do with that information.

Firstly, you can find out exactly how many children the body element has. Because childNodes returns an array, you can use the length property to find out how many elements it contains:

```
body_element.childNodes.length;
```

Try adding this little function to the showPic.js file:

```
function countBodyChildren() {
  var body_element = document.getElementsByTagName("body")[0];
  alert (body_element.childNodes.length);
}
```

This simple little function will pop up an alert dialog with the total number of the body element's children.

You'll want this function to be executed when the page loads, and you can use the onload event handler to do this. Add this line to the end of the code:

```
window.onload = countBodyChildren;
```

When the document loads, the countBodyChildren function will be invoked.

Refresh the gallery.html file in your web browser. You will be greeted with an alert dialog containing the total number of children of the body element. The result may surprise you.

Introducing the nodeType property

Looking at the structure of the gallery.html file, it would appear that the body element has just three children: the h1 element, the ul element, and the img element. Yet, when we invoke the countBodyChildren function, we get a much higher figure. This is because elements are just one type of node.

The childNodes property returns an array containing all types of nodes, not just element nodes. It will bring back all the attribute nodes and text nodes as well. In fact, just about everything in a document is some kind of node. Even spaces and line breaks are interpreted as nodes and are included in the childNodes array.

That explains why the result produced by countBodyChildren is so high.

Fortunately, we can use the **nodeType** property on any node in a document. This will tell us exactly what kind of node we're dealing with. Unfortunately, it won't tell us in plain English.

The nodeType property is called like this:

node.nodeType

However, instead of returning a string like "element" or "attribute", it returns a number.

Change the alert statement in the countBodyChildren function so that it now gives us the nodeType of body_element:

```
alert(body_element.nodeType);
```

Refresh the browser window that's displaying gallery.html. Now you'll see an alert dialog containing the number one. Element nodes have a nodeType value of 1.

There are twelve possible values for nodeType, but only three of them are going to be of much practical use: the nodeType values for element nodes, attribute nodes, and text nodes. Their nodeType values are 1, 2, and 3 respectively.

- **Element** nodes have a nodeType value of **1**.
- **Attribute** nodes have a nodeType value of **2**.
- **Text** nodes have a nodeType value of **3**.

This means that you can target specific types of nodes in your functions. For instance, you could create a function that only affects element nodes.

Adding a description in the markup

To improve the image gallery function, I want to manipulate a text node. I want to replace its value with a value taken from an attribute node (the title attribute in a link).

First, I need to have somewhere to put the text. I'm going to add a new paragraph to gallery.html. I'll place it right before the img tag. I'm going to give it a unique id so that I can reference it easily from the JavaScript function:

```
<p id="description">Choose an image.</p>
```

I've given the id attribute the value "description", which describes its role fairly accurately. For now, it contains the text "Choose an image." In the following image, you can see that a new paragraph has been added:

I plan to replace this text with text taken from a link's title attribute. I want this to happen at the same time as the placeholder image is replaced with the image taken from the link's href attribute. To achieve this, I need to update the showPic function.

Changing the description with JavaScript

I'm going to update the showPic function so that the text in the description paragraph is replaced with the text from a title attribute in a link.

This is how the showPic function looks right now:

```
function showPic(whichpic) {
  var source = whichpic.getAttribute("href");
  var placeholder = document.getElementById("placeholder");
  placeholder.setAttribute("src",source);
}
```

I'm going to begin my improvements by getting the value of the title attribute of whichpic. I'll store this value in a variable called text. This is easily done using getAttribute:

```
var text = whichpic.getAttribute("title");
```

Now I want to create a new variable so that I have an easy way of referencing the paragraph with the id "description". I'll call this variable description also:

```
var description = document.getElementById("description");
```

I have my variables:

```
function showPic(whichpic) {
  var source = whichpic.getAttribute("href");
  var placeholder = document.getElementById("placeholder");
  placeholder.setAttribute("src",source);
  var text = whichpic.getAttribute("title");
  var description = document.getElementById("description");
}
```

Now it's time to do the text swapping.

Introducing the nodeValue property

If you want to change the value of a text node, there is a DOM property called nodeValue that can be used to get (and set) the value of a node:

```
node.nodeValue
```

4

Here's a tricky little point. If you retrieve the nodeValue for description, you *won't* get the text within the paragraph. You can test this with an alert statement:

```
alert (description.nodeValue);
```

This will return a value of null. The nodeValue of the paragraph element itself is empty. What you actually want is the value of the text within the paragraph.

The text within the paragraph is a different node. This text is the first child node of the paragraph. Therefore, you want to retrieve the nodeValue of this child node.

This alert statement will give you the value you're looking for:

```
alert(description.childNodes[0].nodeValue);
```

This will return a value of "Choose an image." This means that you're accessing the childNodes array and getting the value of the first element (index number zero).

Introducing firstChild and lastChild

There is a shorthand way of writing childNodes[0]. Whenever you want to get the value of the first node in the childNodes array, you can use firstChild:

```
node.firstChild
```

This is equivalent to

```
node.childNodes[0]
```

This is a handy shortcut and it's also a lot easier to read.

The Document Object Model also provides a corresponding lastChild property:

```
node.lastChild
```

This refers to the last node in the childNodes array. If you wanted to access this node without using the lastChild property, you would have to write

```
node.childNodes[node.childNodes.length-1]
```

That's clearly very unwieldy. It's a lot easier to simply use lastChild.

Using nodeValue to update the description

Now we'll go back to the showPic function. I'm going to update the nodeValue of the text node within the description paragraph.

In the case of the description paragraph, only one child node exists. I can use either description.firstChild or description.lastChild. I'm going to use firstChild in this case.

I can rewrite my alert statement so that it now reads

```
alert(description.firstChild.nodeValue);
```

The value is the same ("Choose an image"), but now the code is more readable.

The nodeValue property is very versatile. It can be used to retrieve the value of a node, but it can also be used to set the value of a node. That's exactly what I want to do in this case.

If you recall, I've already set aside a string in the variable text, which I retrieved from the title attribute of the link that has been clicked. I'm now going to update the value of the first child node of the description paragraph:

```
description.firstChild.nodeValue = text;
```

These are the three new lines that I've added to showPic function:

```
var text = whichpic.getAttribute("title");
var description = document.getElementById("description");
description.firstChild.nodeValue = text;
```

In plain English, I'm saying:

- Get the value of the title attribute of the link that has just been clicked and store this value in a variable called text.

- Get the element with the id "description" and store this object as the variable description.

- Update the value of the first child node of the description object with the value of text.

This is how the final function looks:

```
function showPic(whichpic) {
  var source = whichpic.getAttribute("href");
  var placeholder = document.getElementById("placeholder");
  placeholder.setAttribute("src",source);
  var text = whichpic.getAttribute("title");
  var description = document.getElementById("description");
  description.firstChild.nodeValue = text;
}
```

4

If you update the showPic.js file with these new lines and then refresh gallery.html in your browser, you can test the expanded functionality. Clicking on a link to an image now produces two results. The placeholder image is replaced with the new image and the description text is replaced with the title text from the link, as shown in the following image:

You can find my image gallery script and markup at http://friendsofed.com/. All of my images are there, too, but if you want to have some fun with this script, try using your own pictures.

If you want to liven up the image gallery, you can add a style sheet like this one:

```css
body {
  font-family: "Helvetica","Arial",serif;
  color: #333;
  background-color: #ccc;
  margin: 1em 10%;
}
h1 {
  color: #333;
  background-color: transparent;
}
a {
  color: #c60;
```

```
    background-color: transparent;
    font-weight: bold;
    text-decoration: none;
}
ul {
    padding: 0;
}
li {
    float: left;
    padding: 1em;
    list-style: none;
}
```

You can save that CSS in a file called layout.css in a directory called styles. You can then reference this file from a <link> tag in the head of gallery.html:

```
<!DOCTYPE html PUBLIC "-//W3C//DTD XHTML 1.1//EN"
"http://www.w3.org/TR/xhtml11/DTD/xhtml11.dtd">
<html xmlns="http://www.w3.org/1999/xhtml" xml:lang="en">
<head>
  <meta http-equiv="content-type" content="text/html; charset=utf-8" />
  <title>Image Gallery</title>
  <script type="text/javascript" src="scripts/showPic.js"></script>
  <link rel="stylesheet" href="styles/layout.css"
➥ type="text/css" media="screen" />
</head>
<body>
  <h1>Snapshots</h1>
  <ul>
    <li>
      <a href="images/fireworks.jpg" title="A fireworks display"
➥ onclick="showPic(this); return false;">Fireworks</a>
    </li>
    <li>
      <a href="images/coffee.jpg" title="A cup of black coffee"
➥ onclick="showPic(this); return false;">Coffee</a>
    </li>
    <li>
      <a href="images/rose.jpg" title="A red, red rose"
➥ onclick="showPic(this); return false;">Rose</a>
    </li>
    <li>
      <a href="images/bigben.jpg" title="The famous clock"
➥ onclick="showPic(this); return false;">Big Ben</a>
    </li>
  </ul>
  <img id="placeholder" src="images/placeholder.gif"
➥ alt="my image gallery" />
  <p id="description">Choose an image.</p>
</body>
</html>
```

4

73

Here's an example of the image gallery with a simple style sheet attached:

What's next?

In this chapter, you've seen some applied JavaScript. You've also been introduced to some new DOM properties, such as

- childNodes
- nodeType
- nodeValue
- firstChild
- lastChild

You've learned how to put together an image gallery script using some of the methods offered by the Document Object Model. You've also learned how to integrate JavaScript into your web pages using event handlers.

On the surface, this JavaScript image gallery probably appears to be a complete success. However, there's actually quite a lot of room for improvement, which I'll be covering shortly.

In the next chapter, I'll cover the best practices that should be used when writing JavaScript. You'll see that how you achieve a final result is as important as the result itself.

After that, I'm going to show you how to apply those best practices to the image gallery script.

4

5 BEST PRACTICES

What this chapter covers:

- Graceful degradation: ensuring that your web pages still work without JavaScript.
- Unobtrusive JavaScript: separating structure from behavior.
- Backwards compatibility: ensuring that older browsers don't choke on your scripts.

Together, JavaScript and the Document Object Model form a powerful combination. It's important that you use this power wisely. In this chapter, I'm going to show you some best practices that you can use to ensure that your scripts don't do more harm than good.

Please don't let me be misunderstood

JavaScript has something of a bad reputation. Right from its inception, seasoned programmers treated it with skepticism. The convoluted origin of the name JavaScript certainly did not help (see Chapter 1). With a name like JavaScript, it was inevitably compared to the Java programming language and found lacking.

Programmers who were expecting to find the power of Java were disappointed by the simplicity of the first iterations of JavaScript. Despite a superficial lexical similarity, JavaScript was a much simpler language. Most importantly, where Java is very object-oriented, JavaScript was usually written in a procedural way.

JavaScript can also be used in an object-oriented fashion, but the stigma remains. Many programmers turn their noses up at JavaScript for being "just a scripting language."

JavaScript also received a less than enthusiastic welcome from web designers for just the opposite reasons. Whereas programmers bemoaned the language's lack of complexity, designers were intimidated by the thought of having to learn how to write code.

Designers who made quick progress in learning HTML would have been brought up short by objects, functions, arrays, variables, and the other building blocks of JavaScript. The fact that programmers were insisting that JavaScript was laughably simple probably increased the frustration felt by web designers trying to grapple with the language.

Nonetheless, the fact that JavaScript was effectively the only way of adding real-time interactivity in web pages ensured that it would be widely adopted. Unfortunately, in many cases, the way that JavaScript was implemented only served to increase the scorn and resentment designers and programmers felt for the language.

Don't blame the messenger

A low barrier to entry can be a double-edged sword. A technology that people can use speedily and easily will probably be adopted very quickly. However, there is likely to be a correspondingly low level of quality control.

HTML's ease of use is one of the reasons behind the explosive growth of the World Wide Web. Anybody can learn the basics of HTML in a short space of time and create a web page very quickly. It's even possible to use WYSIWYG editors (**W**hat **Y**ou **S**ee **I**s **W**hat **Y**ou **G**et) to make web pages without ever seeing a line of markup.

The downside to this is that most pages on the Web are badly formed and don't validate. Browser manufacturers have to accept this state of affairs by making their software very forgiving and unfussy. Much of the code in browser software is dedicated to handling ambiguous use of HTML and trying to second-guess how authors want their web pages to be rendered.

In theory, there are billions of HTML documents on the Web. In practice, only a small fraction of those documents are made of well-formed, valid markup. This legacy makes the process of advancing web technologies like XHTML and CSS much more difficult.

HTML's low barrier to entry has been a mixed blessing for the World Wide Web.

The situation with JavaScript isn't quite as drastic. If JavaScript code isn't written with the correct syntax, the coder will be alerted because it will cause an error (as opposed to HTML, which, in most cases, will render anyway).

Nonetheless, there is a lot of very bad JavaScript out there on the Web.

Many web designers wanted to reap the benefits of using JavaScript for adding spice to their web pages without spending the time to learn the language. It wasn't long before WYSIWYG editors began offering snippets of code that could be attached to documents.

Even without a WYSIWYG editor, it was still quite easy to find snippets of JavaScript. Many websites and books appeared offering self-contained functions that could be easily added to web pages. Cutting and pasting was the order of the day.

Unfortunately, many of these functions weren't very well thought out. On the surface, they accomplished their tasks and added extra interactivity to web pages. In most cases, however, little thought was given to how these pages behaved when JavaScript was disabled. Poorly implemented scripts sometimes had the effect of inadvertently making JavaScript a requirement for navigating a website. From an accessibility viewpoint, this was clearly a problem. It wasn't long before the words "JavaScript" and "inaccessible" became linked in many people's minds.

In fact, there's nothing inherently inaccessible about JavaScript. It all depends on how it's used. In the words of the old song, "it ain't what you do, it's the way that you do it."

The Flash mob

In truth, there are no bad technologies. There are just bad uses of a technology. The cruel hand that fate had dealt JavaScript reminds me of another much maligned technology: Macromedia's Flash.

Many people today associate Flash with annoying splash pages, overlong download times, and unintuitive navigation. None of these things are intrinsic to Flash. They're simply by-products of poorly implemented Flash movies.

5

It's ironic that Flash has become associated with overlong download times. One of the great strengths of Flash is its ability to create light, compressed vector images and movies. But once it became the norm for Flash sites to have bloated splash intro movies, the trend was hard to reverse.

Similarly, JavaScript can and should be used to make web pages more usable. Yet it has a reputation for decreasing the usability and accessibility of websites.

The problem is one of both inertia and momentum. If a technology is used in a thought-less way from very early on and that technology is then quickly adopted, it becomes very hard to change those initial bad habits.

I'm sure that all the pointless Flash intro movies on splash pages didn't spring up simulta-neously. Instead, it was a case of "monkey see, monkey do." People wanted splash pages because other people had splash pages. Nobody stopped to ask why it was necessary.

JavaScript suffered a similar fate. Badly written functions, particularly those written by WYSIWYG editors, have shown a remarkable tenacity. The code has been copied and pasted. The functions have spread far and wide across the Web, but nobody has ever ques-tioned whether they could have been better.

Question everything

Whenever you use JavaScript to alter the behavior of your web pages, you should question your decisions. First and foremost, you should question whether the extra behavior is really necessary.

JavaScript has been misused in the past to add all sorts of pointless bells and whistles to websites. You can use scripts that move the position of the browser window or even cause the browser window to shake.

Most notoriously of all, there are scripts that cause ad-containing pop-up windows to appear when a page loads. The really nefarious scripts cause these newly spawned win-dows to appear *under* the current browser window. These pop-under ads further cemented JavaScript's reputation as being user-unfriendly. Some people dealt with the problem by disabling JavaScript entirely. The browser manufacturers themselves took steps to deal with the problem by offering built-in pop-up blockers.

Pop-under windows are the epitome of JavaScript abuse. Ostensibly, they are supposed to solve a problem: how to deliver advertising to users. In practice, they only increase user frustration. The onus was on the user to close these windows, something that often turned into an unhappy game of whack-a-mole.

If only someone had asked, "How will this benefit the user?"

Fortunately, this question is being asked more often these days. User-centric web design is on the increase. Any other approach is, in the long term, doomed to failure.

Whenever you are using JavaScript, you should ask yourself how it will affect the user's experience. There's another very important question you should also ask yourself: what if the user doesn't have JavaScript?

Graceful degradation

It's always worth remembering that a visitor to your site might be using a browser that doesn't have JavaScript support. Or maybe the browser supports JavaScript but it has been disabled (perhaps after being exposed to one too many pop-under windows). If you don't consider this possibility, you could inadvertently stop visitors from using your site.

If you use JavaScript correctly, your site will still be navigable by users who don't have JavaScript. This is called **graceful degradation**. When a technology degrades gracefully, the functionality may be reduced but it doesn't fail completely.

Take the example of opening a link in a new window. Don't worry: I'm not talking about spawning a new window when the page loads. I'm talking about creating a pop-up window when the user clicks on a link.

This can be quite a useful feature. Many e-commerce websites will have links to terms of service or delivery rates from within the checkout process. Rather than having the user leave the current screen, a pop-up window can display the relevant information without interrupting the shopping experience.

> *Popping up a new window should only be used when it's absolutely required. There are accessibility issues involved: for example, some screen-reading software doesn't indicate that a new window has been opened. It's a good idea to make it clear in the link text that a new browser window will be opened.*

JavaScript uses the open() method of the window object to create new browser windows. The method takes three arguments:

```
window.open(url,name,features)
```

All of the arguments are optional. The first argument is the URL for the document you want to open in a new window. If this is missing, an empty browser window will be created.

The second argument is the name that you can give this newly created window. You can use this name in your code to communicate with your newly created window.

The final argument accepted by the method is a comma-separated list of features that you want your new window to have. These include the size of the window (width and height) and aspects of the browser chrome that you want to enable or disable (including toolbars, menu bar, location, and so on). You don't have to list all of the features, and anyway, it's a good idea not to disable too many features.

5

This method is a good example of using the Browser Object Model (BOM). Nothing about the functionality affects the contents of the document (that's what the Document Object Model is for). The method is purely concerned with the browsing environment (in this case, the window object).

Here's an example of a typical function that uses window.open():

```
function popUp(winURL) {
  window.open(winURL,"popup","width=320,height=480");
}
```

This will open up a new window (called "popup") that's 320 pixels wide by 480 pixels tall. Because I'm setting the name of the window in the function, any time a new URL is passed to the function, the function will replace the existing spawned window rather than creating a second one.

I can save this function in an external file and link to it from a <script> tag within the <head> of a web page. By itself, this function doesn't have any usability implications. What matters is how I use it.

The javascript: pseudo-protocol

One way of calling the popUp function is to use what's known as a **pseudo-protocol**.

Real protocols are used to send packets of information between computers on the Internet. Examples are **http://**, **ftp://**, and so on. A pseudo-protocol is a non-standard take on this idea. The **javascript:** pseudo-protocol is supposed to be used to invoke JavaScript from within a link.

Here's how the javascript: pseudo-protocol would be used to call the popUp function:

```
<a href="javascript:popUp('http://www.example.com/');">Example</a>
```

This will work just fine in browsers that understand the javascript: pseudo-protocol. Older browsers, however, will attempt to follow the link and fail. Even in browsers that understand the pseudo-protocol, the link becomes useless if JavaScript has been disabled.

In short, using the javascript: pseudo-protocol is usually a very bad way of referencing JavaScript from within your markup.

Inline event handlers

You've already seen event handlers in action with the image gallery script. The image swapping function was invoked from within an <a> tag by adding the onclick event handler as an attribute of the same tag.

The same technique will work for the popUp function. If you use an onclick event handler from within a link to spawn a new window, then the href attribute might seem irrelevant.

After all, all the important information about where the link leads is now contained in the onclick attribute. That's why you'll often see links like this:

```
<a href="#" onclick="popUp('http://www.example.com/');
➥ return false;">Example<a>
```

The return false has been included so that the link isn't actually followed. The "#" symbol is used for internal links within documents. (In this case, it's an internal link to nowhere.) In some browsers, this will simply lead to the top of the current document. Using a value of "#" for the href attribute is an attempt to create a blank link. The real work is done by the onclick attribute.

This technique is just as bad as using the javascript: pseudo-protocol. It doesn't degrade gracefully. If JavaScript is disabled, the link is useless.

Who cares?

You might be wondering about this theoretical situation I keep mentioning. Is it really worth making sure that your site works for this kind of user?

Imagine a visitor to your website who browses the Web with both images and JavaScript disabled. You might imagine that this visitor is very much in the minority, and you'd be right. But this visitor is important.

The visitor that you've just imagined is a **searchbot**. A searchbot is an automated program that spiders the web in order to add pages to a search engine's index. All the major search engines have programs like this. Right now, very few searchbots understand JavaScript.

If your JavaScript doesn't degrade gracefully, your search engine rankings might be seriously damaged.

In the case of the popUp function, it's relatively easy to ensure that the JavaScript degrades gracefully. As long as there is a real URL in the href attribute, then the link can be followed:

```
<a href="http://www.example.com/"
➥ onclick="popUp('http://www.example.com'); return false;">Example</a>
```

That's quite long-winded bit of code because the URL appears twice. Fortunately, there's a shortcut that can be used within the JavaScript. The word this can be used to refer to the current element. Using a combination of this and getAttribute, you can extract the value of the href attribute:

```
<a href="http://www.example.com/"
➥ onclick="popUp(this.getAttribute('href')); return
false;">Example</a>
```

Actually, that doesn't save all that much space. There's an even shorter way of referencing the href of the current link by using the pre-standardized DOM property, this.href:

```
<a href="http://www.example.com/"
➥ onclick="popUp(this.href); return false;">Example</a>
```

5

In either case, the important point is that the value of the href attribute is now a valid one. This is far better than using either href="javascript:..." or href="#".

So you see, if JavaScript isn't enabled (or if the visitor is a searchbot), the link can still be followed if you've used a real URL in the href attribute. The functionality is reduced (because the link doesn't open in a new window), but it doesn't fail completely. This is a classic example of graceful degradation.

This technique is certainly the best one I've covered so far, but it is not without its problems. The most obvious problem is the need to insert JavaScript into the markup whenever you want to open a window. It would be far better if all the JavaScript, including the event handlers, were contained in an external file.

The lessons of CSS

Earlier I referred to both JavaScript and Flash as examples of technologies that were often implemented badly in the wild, anarchic days when they were first unleashed. We can learn a lot from the mistakes of the past.

There are other technologies that were implemented in a thoughtful, considered manner right from their inception. We can learn even more from these.

Cascading Style Sheets are a wonderful technology. They allow for great control over every aspect of a site's design. Ostensibly, there's nothing new about this. It's always been possible to dictate a design using <table> and <font> tags. The great advantage of CSS is that you can separate the structure of a web document (the markup) from the design (the CSS).

It's entirely possible to use CSS in an inefficient manner. You could just add style attributes in almost every element of your web document, for example. But the real benefits of CSS become apparent when all your styles are contained in external files.

CSS arrived on the scene much later than Flash and JavaScript. Perhaps as a result of the trauma caused by badly implemented Flash and JavaScript, web designers used CSS in a thoughtful, constructive way from day one.

The separation of structure and style makes life easier for everyone. If your job is writing content, you no longer have to worry about messing up the design. Instead of swimming through a tag soup of <table> and <font> tags, you can now concentrate on marking up your content correctly. If your job is creating the design for a site, you can now concentrate on controlling colors, fonts, and positioning using external style sheets without touching the content. At most, you'll need to add the occasional class or id attribute.

A great advantage of this separation of structure and style is that it guarantees graceful degradation. Browsers that are capable of interpreting CSS will display the web pages in all their styled glory. Older browsers, or browsers with CSS disabled, will still be able to view the content of the pages, in a correctly structured way. The Googlebot doesn't understand CSS, but it has no problems navigating around sites that use CSS for layout.

When it comes to applying JavaScript, we can learn a lot from CSS.

Progressive enhancement

"Content is king" is an oft-used adage in web design. It's true. Without any content, there's little point in trying to create a website.

That said, you can't simply put your content online without first describing what it is. The content needs to be wrapped up in a markup language like HTML or XHTML. Marking up content correctly is the first and perhaps the most important step in creating a website. A revised version of the web design adage might be "well-marked-up content is king."

When a markup language is used correctly, it describes the content semantically. The markup provides information such as "this is an item in a list" or "this is a paragraph." They are all pieces of content, but tags like <li> and <p> distinguish them.

Once the content has been marked up, you can dictate how the content should look by using CSS. The instructions in the CSS form a presentation layer. This layer can then be draped over the structure of the markup. If the presentation layer is removed, the content is still accessible (although now it's a king with no clothes).

Applying layers of extra information like this is called **progressive enhancement**. Web pages that are built using progressive enhancement will almost certainly degrade gracefully.

Like CSS, all the functionality provided by JavaScript and the DOM should be treated as an extra layer of instructions. Where CSS contain information about presentation, JavaScript code contains information about behavior. Ideally, this behavior layer should be applied in the same way as the presentation layer.

CSS work best when they are contained in external files, separate from the markup. It's entirely possible to use CSS in an inefficient manner and mix them in with the markup, like this:

```
<p style="font-weight: bold; color: red;">
Be careful!
</p>
```

It makes more sense to keep the style information in an external file that can be called via a <link> tag in the head of the document:

```
.warning {
  font-weight: bold;
  color: red;
}
```

The class attribute can then be used as a hook to tie the style to the markup:

```
<p class="warning">
Be careful!
</p>
```

This is far more readable. It's also a lot easier to change the styles. Imagine you had a hundred documents with the warning class peppered throughout. Now suppose you wanted to change how warnings are displayed. Maybe you'd prefer them to be blue instead of red.

As long as your presentation is separated from your structure, you can change the style easily:

```
.warning {
  font-weight: bold;
  color: blue;
}
```

If your style declarations were intermingled with your markup, you would have to do a lot of searching and replacing.

It's clear that CSS work best when they are unobtrusive. What works for the presentation layer will also work for the behavior layer.

Unobtrusive JavaScript

The JavaScript you've seen so far has already been separated from the markup to a certain degree. The functions that do all the work are contained in external files. The problem lies with inline event handlers.

Using an attribute like onclick in the markup is just as inefficient as using the style attribute. It would be much better if we could use a hook, like class or id, to tether the behavior to the markup without intermingling it. This is how the markup could indicate that a link should have the popUp function performed when it is clicked:

```
<a href="http://www.example.com/" class="popup">Example</a>
```

Fortunately, this is entirely possible. Events don't have to be handled in the markup. You can attach an event to an element in an external JavaScript file:

```
element.event = action...
```

The tricky part is figuring out which elements should have the event attached. That's where hooks like class and id come in handy.

If you want to attach an event to an element with a unique id, you can simply use getElementById:

```
getElementById(id).event = action
```

With multiple elements, you can use a combination of getElementsByTagName and getAttribute to attach events to elements with specific attributes.

Here's the plan in plain English:

1. Make an array of all the links in the document.
2. Loop through this array.
3. If a link has the class "popup", execute this behavior when the link is clicked:
   A. Pass the value of the link's href attribute to the popUp function.
   B. Cancel the default behavior so that the link isn't followed in the original window.

This is how it looks in JavaScript:

```
var links = document.getElementsByTagName("a");
for (var i=0; i<links.length; i++) {
  if (links[i].getAttribute("class") == "popup") {
    links[i].onclick = function() {
      popUp(this.getAttribute("href"));
      return false;
    }
  }
}
```

Now the connection between the links and the behavior that should occur when the links are clicked has been moved out of the markup and into the external JavaScript. This is unobtrusive JavaScript.

There's just one problem. If I put that code in my external JavaScript file, it won't work. The first line reads:

```
var links = document.getElementsByTagName("a");
```

This code will be executed as soon as the JavaScript file loads. The JavaScript file is called from a <script> tag in the <head> of my document and the JavaScript file will load before the document. Because the document is incomplete, the model of the document is also incomplete. Without a complete Document Object Model, methods like getElementsByTagName simply won't work.

I need to execute the code once the document has finished loading. Fortunately, the complete loading of a document is an event with a corresponding event handler.

The document loads within the browser window. The document object is a property of the window object. When the onload event is triggered by the window object, the document object then exists.

I'm going to wrap up my JavaScript inside a function called prepareLinks, and I'm going to attach this function to the onload event of the window object. This way I know that the Document Object Model will be working:

```
window.onload = prepareLinks;
function prepareLinks() {
  var links = document.getElementsByTagName("a");
  for (var i=0; i<links.length; i++) {
    if (links[i].getAttribute("class") == "popup") {
      links[i].onclick = function() {
        popUp(this.getAttribute("href"));
        return false;
      }
    }
  }
}
```

Don't forget to include the popUp function as well:

```
function popUp(winURL) {
  window.open(winURL,"popup","width=320,height=480");
}
```

This is a very simple example, but it demonstrates how behavior can be successfully separated from structure. Later on, I'll show you more elegant ways to attach events when the document loads.

Backwards compatibility

As I keep mentioning, it's important to consider that visitors to your website might not have JavaScript enabled. However, there are degrees of JavaScript support.

Most browsers support JavaScript to some degree, and most modern browsers have excellent support for the Document Object Model. Older browsers, however, might not be able to understand DOM methods and properties.

So even if a user visits your site with a browser that supports some JavaScript, some of your scripts may not work.

The simplest solution to this problem is to quiz the browser on its level of JavaScript support. This is a bit like those signs at amusement parks that read, "You must be this tall to ride." The DOM Scripting equivalent would be, "You must understand this much JavaScript to execute these statements."

This is quite easy to accomplish. If you wrap a method in an `if` statement, the statement will evaluate to either true or false, depending on whether the method exists. This is called **object detection**. Methods, like almost everything else in JavaScript, can be treated as objects. This makes it quite easy to exclude browsers that don't support a specific DOM method:

```
if (method) {
statements
}
```

If I have a function that uses getElementById, I can test whether or not that method is supported before attempting to use it. The method won't actually be executed so there's no need for the usual parentheses. I'm just testing to see whether it exists or not:

```
function myFunction() {
  if (document.getElementById) {
    statements using getElementById
  }
}
```

If a browser doesn't understand getElementById, it will never even get to the statements using that method.

The only disadvantage in the way I've written that function is that it adds another set of curly braces. If I do that every time I want to test for a particular method or property, then I'm going to end up with the most important statements being wrapped in layers and layers of curly braces. That won't be much fun to read.

It would be much more convenient to say, "If you don't understand this method, leave now."

To turn "if you do understand" into "if you don't understand", all that's needed is the "not" operator, represented by an exclamation point:

```
if (!method)
```

You can use return to achieve the "leave now" part. Seeing as the function is ending prematurely, it makes sense that the Boolean value being returned is false. This is how it would look in a test for getElementById:

```
if (!getElementById) {
  return false;
}
```

Because just one statement needs to be executed (return false), you can shorten the test even further by putting it on one line:

```
if (!getElementById) return false;
```

If you need to test for the existence of more than one method or property, you can join them together using the "or" logical operator, represented by two vertical pipe symbols:

```
if (!getElementById || !getElementsByTagName) return false;
```

If this were a sign in an amusement park, it would read, "If you don't understand getElementById or getElementsByTagName, you can't ride."

I can put this into practice with my page load script that attaches the onclick event to certain links. It uses getElementsByTagName, so I want to be sure that the browser understands that method:

```
window.onload = function() {
  if (!document.getElementsByTagName) return false;
  var lnks = document.getElementsByTagName("a");
  for (var i=0; i<lnks.length; i++) {
    if (lnks[i].getAttribute("class") == "popup") {
      lnks[i].onclick = function() {
        popUp(this.getAttribute("href"));
        return false;
      }
    }
  }
}
```

By just adding this one line, I can be sure that older browsers won't choke on my code. This is assuring backwards compatibility. Because I've used progressive enhancement to add behavior to my web page, I can be sure that the functionality will degrade gracefully in older browsers. Browsers that understand some JavaScript, but not the DOM, can still access my content.

Browser sniffing

Testing for the existence of a specific property or method that you're about to use in your code is the safest and surest way of ensuring backwards compatibility. There is another technique that was very popular during the dark days of the browser wars.

Browser sniffing involves extracting information provided by the browser vendor. In theory, browsers supply information (readable by JavaScript) about their make and model. You can attempt to achieve backwards compatibility by parsing this information, but it's a very risky technique.

For one thing, the browsers sometimes lie. For historical reasons, some browsers report themselves as being a different user-agent. Other browsers allow the user to change this information at will.

As the number of different browsers being used increases, browser-sniffing scripts become more and more complex. They need to test for all possible combinations of vendor and version number in order to ensure that they work cross-platform. This is a Sisyphean task that can result in extremely convoluted and messy code.

Many browser-sniffing scripts test for an exact match on a browser's version number. If a new version is released, these scripts will need to be updated.

Thankfully, the practice of browser sniffing is being replaced with the simpler and more robust technique of object detection.

What's next?

In this chapter, I've introduced some important concepts and practices that should be at the heart of any DOM scripting you do:

- Graceful degradation
- Unobtrusive JavaScript
- Backwards compatibility

You've seen how we can learn from other technologies like Flash and CSS to ensure that JavaScript is used wisely. A cautious, questioning attitude certainly seems to be a desirable trait when you're writing scripts.

I'd like to take that attitude and apply it to the example from the last chapter. In the next chapter, I'm going to re-examine the JavaScript image gallery, identify its flaws, and take steps to remedy them.

6 IMAGE GALLERY REVISITED

What this chapter covers:

- Removing inline event handlers
- Building in backwards compatibility
- Ensuring accessibility

In Chapter 4, we made a JavaScript image gallery. In Chapter 5, we talked about good coding practices. In this chapter, I'm going to apply those practices to the image gallery.

"Question everything" is a good ethos for conspiracy theorists and web designers alike. Whether it's CSS, JavaScript, or visual design, a good web designer will always ask, "Is there a better way of doing this?"

As you saw in the last chapter, the questions relating to DOM scripting are all about graceful degradation, backwards compatibility, and unobtrusive JavaScript. The answers to these questions can affect the usability and accessibility of your web pages.

A quick recap

In Chapter 4, I put together a script for switching out the src attribute of an image, effectively making a single-page image gallery. Here's how the finished function looked:

```
function showPic(whichpic) {
   var source = whichpic.getAttribute("href");
   var placeholder = document.getElementById("placeholder");
   placeholder.setAttribute("src",source);
   var text = whichpic.getAttribute("title");
   var description = document.getElementById("description");
   description.firstChild.nodeValue = text;
}
```

Here's the relevant part of the XHTML file that calls the function:

```
<ul>
<li>
    <a href="images/fireworks.jpg" onclick="showPic(this);
➥return false;" title="A fireworks display">Fireworks</a>
  </li>
  <li>
    <a href="images/coffee.jpg" onclick="showPic(this); return false;"
➥title="A cup of black coffee">Coffee</a>
  </li>
  <li>
    <a href="images/rose.jpg" onclick="showPic(this); return false;"
➥title="A red, red rose">Rose</a>
  </li>
  <li>
    <a href="images/bigben.jpg" onclick="showPic(this); return false;"
```

```
➥title="The famous clock">Big Ben</a>
   </li>
</ul>
<p id="description">Choose an image.</p>
<img id="placeholder" src="images/placeholder.gif"
➥alt="my image gallery" />
```

Now I'm going to take a questioning look at this solution, with a view toward improving it.

Does it degrade gracefully?

My first question is, "What happens when JavaScript is disabled?"

As it turns out, my image gallery script does degrade gracefully. If JavaScript is disabled, the user can still view all the images in the gallery. All the links in the list still work, too:

```
<li>
   <a href="images/fireworks.jpg" onclick="showPic(this);
➥return false;" title="A fireworks display">Fireworks</a>
</li>
```

Without any JavaScript intervention, the browser naturally follows each link. The user sees the image as a new page instead of simply changing part of the existing page. The user experience isn't quite as seamless as the JavaScript alternative, but the important thing is that all the content is accessible.

It would be a very different story if I had chosen to use the javascript: pseudo-protocol. The links would then be written like this:

```
<li>
   <a href="javascript:showPic(' images/coffee.jpg'); return false;"
➥title="A cup of black coffee">Coffee</a>
</li>
```

If I had written the links like that, then the link list would be useless to anyone without JavaScript.

Similarly, it would have been just as disastrous to use the href="#" convention. Sadly, this technique is often used when scripts are being "plugged into" web pages. Like the javascript: pseudo-protocol, it would have killed the image gallery for users surfing without JavaScript:

```
<li>
   <a href="#" onclick="showPic(' images/rose.jpg'); return false;"
➥title="A red, red rose">Rose</a>
</li>
```

6

By using real values for the href attribute, the image gallery degrades gracefully. Anyone viewing the pictures without the benefit of JavaScript will have to use their browser's back button to return to the list of links, but that's better than not being able to view the images at all.

The image gallery passes the first test.

Is the JavaScript unobtrusive?

My next question concerns how the JavaScript has been added to the markup, and it's this: Is there separation between structure and behavior? In other words, has the behavior layer (the JavaScript) been applied *over* the structure (the XHTML), rather than mixed in with it?

In this case, the answer is a resounding no.

Event handlers have been inserted directly into the markup:

```
<li>
  <a href="images/bigben.jpg" onclick="showPic(this); return false;"
➥title="The famous clock">Big Ben</a>
</li>
```

Ideally, I should attach the onclick event in the external JavaScript file. That would leave the markup unsullied:

```
<li>
  <a href="images/bigben.jpg" title="The famous clock">Big Ben</a>
</li>
```

The JavaScript is still going to need some sort of "hook," or marker, so that it can recognize which links require the new behavior. There are a few different ways I could do this.

I could add a class attribute to each link in the list:

```
<li>
  <a href="images/bigben.jpg" class="gallerypic"
➥title="The famous clock">Big Ben</a>
</li>
```

But that technique is less than ideal. Adding a class to each link is almost as cumbersome as adding inline event handlers.

All the links have one thing in common. They are contained within a list. It's much simpler to give the entire list a unique ID:

```
<ul id="imagegallery">
<li>
    <a href="images/fireworks.jpg" title="A fireworks display">
➥Fireworks</a>
```

```
        </li>
        <li>
          <a href="images/coffee.jpg" title="A cup of black coffee">
  ➥Coffee</a>
        </li>
        <li>
          <a href="images/rose.jpg" title="A red, red rose">Rose</a>
        </li>
        <li>
          <a href="images/bigben.jpg" title="The famous clock">Big Ben</a>
        </li>
      </ul>
```

As you will soon see, this single hook will be enough for the JavaScript.

Adding the event handler

Now I need to write a short little function to attach the behavior for the onclick event. I'll call the function prepareGallery.

In plain English, this is what I'm going to do:

- Check whether this browser understands getElementsByTagName.
- Check whether this browser understands getElementById.
- Check whether an element with the ID "imagegallery" exists.
- Loop through all the links in the "imagegallery" element.
- Set the onclick event so that when the link is clicked:
  - The link is passed to the showPic function.
  - The default behavior is cancelled so that the link isn't followed.

I'll begin by defining the prepareGallery function. The function won't be taking any arguments so there won't be anything between the parentheses after the function name:

```
function prepareGallery() {
```

Checkpoints

The first thing I want to do is to find out if the browser can understand the DOM method getElementsByTagName. I'll be using this method in the function, and I want to be sure that older browsers won't execute the function if they don't understand the method:

```
if (!document.getElementsByTagName) return false;
```

This is saying, "If getElementsByTagName isn't defined, leave now." Browsers that understand that particular DOM method will continue on.

Now I'm going to do the same thing for getElementById, which will also be used by the function:

```
if (!document.getElementById) return false;
```

I could combine the two checks into one: "If either method isn't understood, go no further":

```
if (!document.getElementsByTagName || !document.getElementById)
➥return false;
```

But that begins to look a bit unwieldy and is perhaps less readable. In fact, putting these tests on single lines isn't necessarily the best idea from a readability point of view. You might prefer to put the return statement on its own line:

```
if (!document.getElementsByTagName)
  return false;
if (!document.getElementById)
  return false;
```

In that case, I recommend enclosing the return statements within curly braces:

```
if (!document.getElementsByTagName) {
  return false;
}
if (!document.getElementById) {
  return false;
}
```

This is perhaps the clearest, most readable solution.

Whether you do these tests on single or multiple lines is entirely up to you. Use whichever one you find easiest to follow.

Once these general tests have been passed, there's a more specific test. This function is going to deal with links inside an element identified as "imagegallery". If this element can't be found, then the script should go no further.

Once again, I'm going to use the "not" operator for this test:

```
if (!document.getElementById("imagegallery")) return false;
```

Or, if your prefer:

```
if (!document.getElementById("imagegallery")) {
  return false;
}
```

This is a safety check. Right now, I know that there is an "imagegallery" list in the document that's calling the JavaScript file. But that could change in the future. If, for some reason, I decided to remove the image gallery from the page, I can rest assured that related JavaScript errors won't suddenly occur. It all comes back to the importance of the separation of content from behavior. If I add behavior to a page using JavaScript, that JavaScript shouldn't make assumptions about the structure of the page.

A short note about structured programming

There is a school of thought known as **structured programming**. One of its doctrines states that functions should have a single point of entry and a single exit point.

I am violating this principle by having multiple return false statements at the beginning of my function. These are all exit points. According to a principle of structured programming, there should only ever be one exit point.

In theory, I agree with this principle. In practice, it could make code very difficult to read. If I rewrote my safety checks to avoid multiple exit points, the main point of my function would be buried quite deep in a sea of curly braces:

```
function prepareGallery() {
  if (document.getElementsByTagName) {
    if (document.getElementById) {
      if (document.getElementById("imagegallery")) {
        statements go here...
      }
    }
  }
}
```

I think it is acceptable to have multiple exit points as long as they occur early on in the function.

For the sake of readability, I'm going to keep the return false statements at the start of the prepareGallery function:

```
function prepareGallery() {
  if (!document.getElementsByTagName) return false;
  if (!document.getElementById) return false;
  if (!document.getElementById("imagegallery")) return false;
```

Now that all the tests and checks have been passed, I'm going to move on to the functionality.

What's in a name?

First of all, I'm going to make things a little easier for myself. Instead of writing out document.getElementById("imagegallery") all the time, it's going to make life a lot simpler if I just use a variable name like gallery:

```
var gallery = document.getElementById("imagegallery");
```

I could have chosen anything for the variable name, but gallery has some meaning. It's a lot easier to read code that uses recognizable words for variable names.

> *Be careful when you're choosing your variable names. There are some words that are reserved by JavaScript. You can't give a variable the same name as a JavaScript function or method. Avoid using words like* alert, var, *and* if.

I want to loop through all the links in the "imagegallery" element. I'll be using getElementsByTagName to do this. Because I now have the variable gallery at my disposal, I can simply write this:

```
gallery.getElementsByTagName("a")
```

instead of the more long-winded version:

```
document.getElementById("imagegallery").getElementsByTagName("a")
```

Once again, I'm going to make life a little easier for myself. I'm going to assign this node list to a nice short variable. I'll use the word links:

```
var links = gallery.getElementsByTagName("a");
```

This is how the prepareGallery function is looking so far:

```
function prepareGallery() {
    if (!document.getElementsByTagName) return false;
    if (!document.getElementById) return false;
    if (!document.getElementById("imagegallery")) return false;
    var gallery = document.getElementById("imagegallery");
    var links = gallery.getElementsByTagName("a");
```

Everything is set up now. I have put safety checks in place, and I have assigned variables.

Looping the loop

I want to loop through all the individual elements in the links set. I'm going to use a for loop to do this.

I'll begin by setting a counter to zero. The loop will be executed for each element in links, and the counter will be incremented by one. Here's the initialization of the counter:

```
var i = 0;
```

I've chosen the name i purely for traditional reasons. Using the name i for incrementing variables is a programming convention in many languages.

The test condition comes next:

```
i < links.length;
```

The loop will be executed as long as the value of i is less than the length property of the links array. The length property contains the total number of elements in an array. So, if links contains four elements, then the loop will be executed as long as i is less than four.

Finally, the counter is incremented by one:

```
i++;
```

This is a shorthand way of saying:

```
i = i+1;
```

The value of i is increased by one every time the loop is executed. As soon as its value is no longer less than links.length, the loop will finish. If links contains four elements, the loop will stop once the value of i equals four. The loop will have run four times. Remember that i began with a value of zero.

Here's how the for loop opens:

```
for ( var i=0; i < links.length; i++) {
```

Changing behavior

I want to change the behavior of each element in the links array. Actually, it would be more correct to refer to links as a **node list** rather than an array. It is a set of nodes. Each node in the set has its own properties and methods.

I'm interested in the onclick method. This is how I attach a behavior for that method:

```
links[i].onclick = function() {
```

This is called an anonymous function. It is a way of creating a function on the fly. In this case, the function is created when the onclick event handler is triggered, Whatever statements I put in next will be executed when the link is clicked.

The value of links[i] will change as the value of i increases. It begins as links[0] and, if there are four elements in the links set, it will finish as links[3].

The value I'm going to pass to the showPic function is the this keyword. It refers to the element that is currently having the onclick method attached to it. So this refers to links[i], which in turn refers to a specific node in the links node list:

```
showPic(this);
```

There's one more thing I need to do. I need to cancel the default behavior. If the showPic function is successfully executed, I don't want the browser to carry out the default action for clicking on a link. Just as before, I want to cancel this default action so that the link isn't followed:

```
return false;
```

By returning the Boolean value false, a message is sent back to the browser saying, "Act as if this link wasn't clicked."

I just need to close up this function within a function by adding a closing curly brace. This is how it looks:

```
links[i].onclick = function() {
  showPic(this);
  return false;
}
```

6

Closing it up

Now I need to finish the for loop by adding the closing curly brace:

```
for ( var i=0; i < links.length; i++) {
  links[i].onclick = function() {
    showPic(this);
    return false;
  }
}
```

All that remains for me to do is to close the function with one more curly brace.

This is how the final prepareGallery function looks:

```
function prepareGallery() {
  if (!document.getElementsByTagName) return false;
  if (!document.getElementById) return false;
  if (!document.getElementById("imagegallery")) return false;
  var gallery = document.getElementById("imagegallery");
  var links = gallery.getElementsByTagName("a");
  for ( var i=0; i < links.length; i++) {
    links[i].onclick = function() {
      showPic(this);
      return false;
    }
  }
}
```

When this function is called, the onclick events will be attached to the links in the element identified as "imagegallery".

Share the load

I need to execute the prepareGallery function in order to attach the onclick events.

If I simply execute the function right away, it won't work. If the JavaScript is executed before the document has finished loading, the Document Object Model will be incomplete. By the third line of the function (the test for the existence of "imagegallery"), things won't go according to plan.

I want to execute the function only when the page has finished loading. When the page loads, an event is triggered. This event is onload and it is attached to the window object. If I attach the prepareGallery function to this event, then everything will go smoothly:

```
window.onload = prepareGallery;
```

That's quite straightforward, but it is also potentially a little shortsighted.

Suppose I have two functions: firstFunction and secondFunction. What if I want to execute both of them when the page loads? If I attach them, one after the other, to the onload event, only the last specified function will actually be executed:

```
window.onload = firstFunction;
window.onload = secondFunction;
```

secondFunction will replace firstFunction. On the face of it, you would think that an event handler can hold only one instruction.

But here's a workaround: I could create an anonymous function to hold the other two and then execute that third function when the page loads:

```
window.onload = function() {
  firstFunction();
  secondFunction();
}
```

This works fine, and it's the simplest solution when you have a small number of functions.

There's another solution that scales very nicely, no matter how many functions you want to execute when the page loads. It takes a few more lines to set it up initially but, once it's in place, attaching functions to window.onload is an easy task.

This function is called addLoadEvent, and it was written by Simon Willison (http://simon.incutio.com/). It takes a single argument: the name of the function that you want to execute when the page loads.

Here's what addLoadEvent does:

- Stores the existing window.onload as a variable called oldonload.
- If this hasn't yet had a function attached to it, then simply add the new function in the usual way.
- If there is already a function attached, add the new function after the existing instructions.

Here's how the function looks:

```
function addLoadEvent(func) {
  var oldonload = window.onload;
  if (typeof window.onload != 'function') {
    window.onload = func;
  } else {
    window.onload = function() {
      oldonload();
      func();
    }
  }
}
```

6

This effectively creates a queue of functions to be executed when the page loads. To add functions to this queue, I just need to write:

```
addLoadEvent(firstFunction);
addLoadEvent(secondFunction);
```

I've found this function to be enormously useful when my code starts to get complex. No matter how many individual functions I want to execute when the page loads, I just need to add a single line for each one.

For the prepareGallery function, this might be overkill. After all, only one function needs to be executed when the page loads. Still, it's good to plan for future expansion. If I include the addLoadEvent function, this is all I need to write:

```
addLoadEvent(prepareGallery);
```

At this stage, I think the prepareGallery function is as foolproof as I can make it. It's time for me to turn my questioning gaze on the original showPic function.

Assuming too much

One of the first things I notice when I look at the showPic function is that I'm not running any checks or tests.

The showPic function is being called from prepareGallery. That function has already tested for the existence of DOM methods like getElementById and getElementsByTagName, so I know that the browser won't choke on this code.

Still, I'm making a lot of assumptions. The code contains instructions for elements identified as "placeholder" and "description", but it never checks to see if these elements actually exist:

```
function showPic(whichpic) {
  var source = whichpic.getAttribute("href");
  var placeholder = document.getElementById("placeholder");
  placeholder.setAttribute("src",source);
  var text = whichpic.getAttribute("title");
  var description = document.getElementById("description");
  description.firstChild.nodeValue = text;
}
```

I need to introduce some checks for these elements.

Two things are happening in this function. The image identified as "placeholder" is having its src attribute changed, and the element identified as "description" is having the nodeValue of its firstChild changed. The first action is the real task of the function. The second action is a nice added extra. For that reason, I'm going to run the checks separately. If the "placeholder" image exists but the "description" element doesn't, then I still want the image to be swapped out.

Just as with the prepareGallery function, it's a simple matter to check for the existence of an element:

```
if (!document.getElementById("placeholder")) return false;
```

I can then go on to do the image swapping:

```
var source = whichpic.getAttribute("href");
var placeholder = document.getElementById("placeholder");
placeholder.setAttribute("src",source);
```

The main task has been accomplished. At this point, I can check for the existence of the "description" element:

```
if (!document.getElementById("description")) return false;
```

Only then do I go on to change the text:

```
var text = whichpic.getAttribute("title");
var description = document.getElementById("description");
description.firstChild.nodeValue = text;
```

This is how the updated function looks with the checks built in:

```
function showPic(whichpic) {
  if (!document.getElementById("placeholder")) return false;
  var source = whichpic.getAttribute("href");
  var placeholder = document.getElementById("placeholder");
  placeholder.setAttribute("src",source);
  if (!document.getElementById("description")) return false;
  var text = whichpic.getAttribute("title");
  var description = document.getElementById("description");
  description.firstChild.nodeValue = text;
}
```

That's better. The script no longer assumes the existence of elements in the markup. If, for some reason, the "placeholder" image isn't in the document, there won't be any JavaScript errors.

But there's a problem. Remove the "placeholder" image from the markup and refresh the page in a browser. Click on any link in the "imagegallery" list. You'll see that nothing happens.

This means that the script isn't degrading gracefully. In this situation, it would be better to follow the link in the browser than have nothing happen at all.

The problem lies with the prepareGallery function. It makes the assumption that the showPic function will work fine, and it cancels the default action:

```
links[i].onclick = function() {
  showPic(this);
  return false;
}
```

6

The decision to return a value of false (thereby canceling the default action of following the link in the browser) should really be made in the showPic function.

This is a little counterintuitive, but here's what I want the showPic function to do:

- If the image is successfully swapped out, the function should return false.
- If the function is unsuccessful, I want it to return true.

To do this, I just need to change my first test. If the "placeholder" image doesn't exist, the function should return true instead of false:

```
if (!document.getElementById("placeholder")) return true;
```

I'm going to leave the second test as it is. If the "description" element doesn't get updated, I still want to cancel the default action:

```
if (!document.getElementById("description")) return false;
```

Most importantly, if the function executes completely, I need to cancel the default action. I'll do this by adding one line to the end of the showPic function:

```
return false;
```

If the showPic function doesn't succeed, it returns a value of true. If the function does succeed in its main task, it returns a value of false:

```
function showPic(whichpic) {
  if (!document.getElementById("placeholder")) return true;
  var source = whichpic.getAttribute("href");
  var placeholder = document.getElementById("placeholder");
  placeholder.setAttribute("src",source);
  if (!document.getElementById("description")) return false;
  var text = whichpic.getAttribute("title");
  var description = document.getElementById("description");
  description.firstChild.nodeValue = text;
  return false;
}
```

Now I need to update the prepareGallery function so that it uses the returned Boolean value.

```
links[i].onclick = function() {
  return showPic(this);
}
```

If showPic returns false, then that is what will get sent back to the browser when the link is clicked. The default action won't occur. The link won't be followed by the browser.

If showPic returns true, the link will be followed by the browser.

The prepareGallery function now looks like this:

```
function prepareGallery() {
  if (!document.getElementsByTagName) return false;
  if (!document.getElementById) return false;
  if (!document.getElementById("imagegallery")) return false;
  var gallery = document.getElementById("imagegallery");
  var links = gallery.getElementsByTagName("a");
  for ( var i=0; i < links.length; i++) {
    links[i].onclick = function() {
      return showPic(this);
    }
  }
}
```

That solves the problem with our test case. If the "placeholder" image doesn't exist, the browser simply follows the links to the images. You can go ahead and put the "placeholder" image back into the markup.

Fine-tuning

The functions are looking a lot better now. They may have grown in size, but they now assume much less about the markup.

I can still see some assumptions being made in the showPic function that I may need to tackle.

For instance, I am assuming that the link has a title attribute:

```
var text = whichpic.getAttribute("title");
```

To find out if there is a title attribute, I can test to see if it isn't equal to null:

```
if (whichpic.getAttribute("title") != null)
```

This if statement will evaluate to true if there is a title attribute. It will return a value of false if there is no title attribute, because the value of whichpic.getAttribute("title") will be equal to null.

I can save some space by simply writing:

```
if (whichpic.getAttribue("title"))
```

The if statement will still return a value of true as long as there is a title attribute.

As a simple fallback, I could set the value of text to be empty if there is no title attribute:

```
if (whichpic.getAttribute("title")) {
  var text = whichpic.getAttribute("title");
} else {
  var text = "";
}
```

Here's another way of doing the same thing:

```
var text = whichPic.getAttribute("title") ?
➥whichPic.getAttribute("title") : "";
```

The getAttribute test is followed by a question mark. This is called a **ternary operator**. Two possible values for the variable text are provided after the question mark. The first value will be assigned if getAttribute("title") returns a value. The second value will be returned if getAttribute("title") returns a value of null:

```
variable = condition ? if true : if false;
```

If a title attribute exists, the variable text will contain whichPic.getAttribute("title"). If there is no title attribute, the variable text will be an empty string, "".

A ternary operator is just another way of performing if/else statements. It's shorter, but if you find it confusing, you can always use the more verbose if/else statement.

Try removing the title attribute from one of the links in the "imagegallery" list. If you click on that link, the "description" element will be filled with an empty string.

If I wanted to be really thorough, I could introduce checks for just about everything.

For example, I'm checking for the existence of an element called "placeholder", but I'm just assuming that it is an image. I could run a further check, using the nodeName property, to verify this:

```
if (placeholder.nodeName != "IMG") return true;
```

Notice that in HTML documents, nodeName always a returns an uppercase value, even if the element is lowercase in the markup.

There are further checks I could introduce. I'm assuming that the firstChild of the "description" element is a text node, but I should really check to make sure.

I can use the nodeType property for this test. If you recall, text nodes have a nodeType value of 3:

```
if (description.firstChild.nodeType == 3) {
  description.firstChild.nodeValue = text;
}
```

This is how the showPic function would look with these extra tests:

```
function showPic(whichpic) {
  if (!document.getElementById("placeholder")) return true;
  var source = whichpic.getAttribute("href");
  var placeholder = document.getElementById("placeholder");
  if (placeholder.nodeName != "IMG") return true;
  placeholder.setAttribute("src",source);
  if (!document.getElementById("description")) return false;
  var text = whichPic.getAttribute("title") ?
➥whichPic.getAttribute("title") : "";
```

```
  var description = document.getElementById("description");
  if (description.firstChild.nodeType == 3) {
    description.firstChild.nodeValue = text;
  }
  return false;
}
```

The function is much more verbose when it's done in this way. In a real-world situation, you may decide that all these checks aren't necessary. They are intended to account for situations where the markup might be beyond your control. Ideally, your scripts shouldn't assume too much about the content and structure of the markup.

That said, these kinds of decisions need to be made on a case-by-case basis.

Keyboard access

There is one last piece of fine-tuning that often arises with any scripts that are attached to the onclick event handler.

Take a look at the heart of the prepareGallery function:

```
links[i].onclick = function() {
  return showPic(this);
}
```

This works fine. When the link is clicked, the showPic function is executed. It looks like I'm assuming that the user will be clicking on the link with a mouse.

But remember, not everybody navigates using a mouse. People with visual disabilities, for example, aren't going to move a small icon around their screen. Instead, they are likely to navigate using a keyboard.

You don't need a mouse to browse the web. You can use the *TAB* key on your keyboard to move from link to link. Pressing the *RETURN* key will activate the currently selected link.

There is an event handler specifically for the action of pressing any key on the keyboard. It is called onkeypress.

If I want to execute the same behavior for onkeypress as onclick, I could simply duplicate the instructions:

```
links[i].onclick = function() {
  return showPic(this);
}
links[i].onkeypress = function() {
  return showPic(this);
}
```

There's an easier way to ensure that onkeypress imitates onclick, however:

```
links[i].onkeypress = links[i].onclick;
```

This assigns all the functionality from the onclick event to the onkeypress event as well:

```
links[i].onclick = function() {
  return showPic(this);
}
links[i].onkeypress = links[i].onclick;
```

That brings us right back to the benefits of unobtrusive JavaScript.

By keeping all your functions and event handlers in external files, you can change them without tinkering with the markup. You can always revisit your scripts and refine them, knowing that those refinements will automatically be applied to every web page that references the JavaScript file.

If I were still using inline event handlers, I would have needed to make a lot of changes to my markup as the JavaScript functionality changed. I used to have inline event handlers like this:

```
<li>
  <a href="images/fireworks.jpg" onclick="showPic(this);
➥return false;" title="A fireworks display">Fireworks</a>
</li>
```

When I changed the showPic function to return either true or false, I would have needed to update the event handlers accordingly:

```
<li>
  <a href="images/fireworks.jpg" onclick="return showPic(this);"
➥title="A fireworks display">Fireworks</a>
</li>
```

If my image gallery were more than a few links long, this would have been quite tiresome.

Suppose I wanted to add the onkeypress event handler. I would have to go through all the links and add another inline event handler to each one:

```
<li>
  <a href="images/fireworks.jpg" onclick="return showPic(this);"
➥onkeypress="return showPic(this);"
➥title="A fireworks display">Fireworks</a>
</li>
```

That would have been a lot of drudgery. It's so much simpler to tweak and adjust a few lines of JavaScript in an external file.

Beware of onkeypress

As it turns out, I'm not going to add the onkeypress event handler at all. This event handler is quite problematic. It is triggered whenever a key is pressed. In some browsers, that includes the *TAB* key! That means that a user navigating with a keyboard can never tab past a link if a function associated with onkeypress returns false. That's exactly what's happening with the image gallery. The showPic function, if it is successful, returns false.

So where does that leave users navigating with a keyboard?

Fortunately, the onclick event handler turns out to be smarter than it sounds. With a name like onclick, it gives the impression of being tied to the action of clicking a button on a mouse. In fact, in nearly all browsers, the onclick event handler is also triggered if you press RETURN while tabbing from link to link. It would be more accurate if it were named something like onactivate.

There is a lot of confusion surrounding onclick and onkeypress, which is hardly surprising given the terminology. Some accessibility guidelines recommend using onkeypress whenever you use onclick. In reality, this could cause more harm than good.

Avoid using onkeypress. The onclick event handler is all that's needed. In spite of its name, onclick supports keyboard access perfectly well.

The finished functions look like this:

```
function prepareGallery() {
  if (!document.getElementsByTagName) return false;
  if (!document.getElementById) return false;
  if (!document.getElementById("imagegallery")) return false;
  var gallery = document.getElementById("imagegallery");
  var links = gallery.getElementsByTagName("a");
  for ( var i=0; i < links.length; i++) {
    links[i].onclick = function() {
      return showPic(this);
    }
  }
}
function showPic(whichpic) {
  if (!document.getElementById("placeholder")) return true;
  var source = whichpic.getAttribute("href");
  var placeholder = document.getElementById("placeholder");
  if (placeholder.nodeName != "IMG") return true;
  placeholder.setAttribute("src",source);
  if (!document.getElementById("description")) return false;
  var text = whichPic.getAttribute("title") ?
➥whichPic.getAttribute("title") : "";
  var description = document.getElementById("description");
  if (description.firstChild.nodeType == 3) {
    description.firstChild.nodeValue = text;
  }
  return false;
}
```

You can download the completed functions from this book's page from the Friends of ED website, http://www.friendsofed.com/.

6

Sharing hooks with CSS

There's another benefit to unobtrusive JavaScript. Since removing the inline event handlers from my markup, I've added one hook for my JavaScript:

```
<ul id="imagegallery">
```

There's no reason why I can't also use that hook for my CSS.

For instance, I might not want the list to have bullet points. I can use the "imagegallery" identifier to specify this in the CSS:

```
#imagegallery {
  list-style: none;
}
```

I can put this CSS in an external file, say layout.css, and reference it from the <head> of my gallery.html file:

```
<link rel="stylesheet" href="styles/layout.css" type="text/css"
➥ media="screen" />
```

Using CSS, I can even make the list run horizontally instead of vertically:

```
#imagegallery li {
  display: inline;
}
```

Here's what my page looks like now:

This also works if I decide to use thumbnail images instead of text for my links:

```
<ul id="imagegallery">
  <li>
    <a href="images/fireworks.jpg" title="A fireworks display">
      <img src="images/thumbnail_fireworks.jpg" alt="Fireworks" />
    </a>
  </li>
  <li>
    <a href="images/coffee.jpg" title="A cup of black coffee" >
      <img src="images/thumbnail_coffee.jpg" alt="Coffee" />
    </a>
  </li>
  <li>
    <a href="images/rose.jpg" title="A red, red rose">
      <img src="images/thumbnail_rose.jpg" alt="Rose" />
    </a>
  </li>
  <li>
    <a href="images/bigben.jpg" title="The famous clock">
      <img src="images/thumbnail_bigben.jpg" alt="Big Ben" />
    </a>
  </li>
</ul>
```

Here's my web page with thumbnails rather than text:

The complete layout.css file looks like this:

```css
body {
  font-family: "Helvetica","Arial",serif;
  color: #333;
  background-color: #ccc;
  margin: 1em 10%;
}
h1 {
  color: #333;
  background-color: transparent;
}
a {
  color: #c60;
  background-color: transparent;
  font-weight: bold;
  text-decoration: none;
}
ul {
  padding: 0;
}
li {
  float: left;
  padding: 1em;
  list-style: none;
}
#imagegallery {
  list-style: none;
}
#imagegallery li {
  display: inline;
}
#imagegallery li a img {
  border: 0;
}
```

Applying that style sheet will give the image gallery a nice sheen:

DOM Core and HTML-DOM

So far, I've been using a small set of methods to accomplish everything I want to do, including

- getElementById
- getElementsByTagName
- getAttribute
- setAttribute

These methods are all part of the **DOM Core**. They aren't specific to JavaScript, and they can be used by any programming language with DOM support. They aren't just for web pages, either. These methods can be used on documents written in any markup language (XML, for instance).

When you are using JavaScript and the DOM with (X)HTML files, you have many more properties at your disposal. These properties belong to the **HTML-DOM**, which has been around longer than the DOM Core.

For instance, the HTML-DOM provides a forms object. That means that instead of writing:

```
document.getElementsByTagName("form")
```

You can use:

```
document.forms
```

Similarly, the HTML-DOM provides properties to represent attributes of elements. Images, for instance, have a src property. Instead of writing:

```
element.getAttribute("src")
```

You can write:

```
element.src
```

These methods and properties are interchangeable. It doesn't really matter whether you decide to use the DOM Core exclusively or if you use the HTML-DOM. As you can see, the HTML-DOM is generally shorter. However, it's worth remembering that it is specific to web documents, so you'll need to bear that in mind if you ever find yourself using the DOM with other kinds of documents.

If I were to use the HTML-DOM, I could shorten a few lines from the showPic function.

This line uses the DOM Core to retrieve the href attribute of the whichpic element and assign its value to the variable source:

```
var source = whichpic.getAttribute("href");
```

Here's the same thing using HTML-DOM:

```
var source = whichpic.href;
```

Here's another example of the DOM Core. This time, the src attribute of the placeholder element is being set to the value of the variable source:

```
placeholder.setAttribute("src",source);
```

Here it is using HTML-DOM:

```
placeholder.src = source;
```

Even if you decide to use DOM Core methods exclusively, you should still be aware of the HTML-DOM. You're bound to come across these shorthand methods when you're looking at the source code for other people's scripts. It's good to at least be able to recognize them.

For the most part, I'm going to stick to using DOM Core. I find it easier to use a small arsenal of DOM methods, even if that means slightly more verbose code. However, you don't have to do the same. Wherever possible, I'll point out where you can use HTML-DOM to shorten your code.

What's next?

In this chapter I've made plenty of tweaks to the image gallery. The markup is now tidier. I've introduced some basic CSS. Most of all, I've improved the JavaScript. Here are some of the main things I accomplished:

- Wherever possible, I've tried to avoid making unwarranted assumptions in my code. I've introduced lots of tests and checks. The JavaScript is more likely to degrade gracefully in unforeseen situations.

- I've ensured the accessibility of the JavaScript by avoiding the onkeypress event handler.

- Perhaps most importantly of all, I've moved the event handling from the markup to the JavaScript. This is unobtrusive JavaScript.

Here's my final product after all of the tweaks I've made through this chapter:

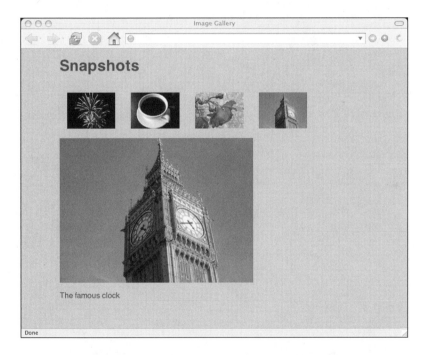

And my mantra: the more separation there is between structure and behavior, the better.

Something about the markup of the image gallery is still bothering me. I have two elements, "placeholder" and "description", that exist solely for the showPic function to use. For visitors without JavaScript, these elements are, at best, meaningless. At worst, they could be downright confusing.

Ideally, these elements should only appear in the document if the visitor has a DOM-capable browser. In the next chapter, I'm going to show you how you can use the DOM to create elements and insert them into your markup.

7 CREATING MARKUP ON THE FLY

What this chapter covers:

- A quick look at the "old school" techniques: document.write and innerHTML
- An in-depth look at the DOM methods createElement, createTextNode, appendChild, and insertBefore

The DOM methods you've seen so far have all been applied to previously existing markup. In this chapter, I'm going to show you some DOM methods that can alter the structure of a web page by creating new elements and modifying existing ones.

Most of the DOM methods you've seen so far have been very useful for identifying elements. Both getElementById and getElementsByTagName allow you to quickly and easily target specific element nodes in a document. These elements can then be manipulated using methods and properties like setAttribute (to change the value of an attribute) or nodeValue (to change the text contained by an element node).

That's how the image gallery works. The showPic function identifies two elements, with the IDs "placeholder" and "description", and then updates their contents. The src attribute of the "placeholder" element is changed using setAttribute. The text within "description" is changed using nodeValue. In both cases, changes are being made to elements that already exist.

This is the way that the majority of JavaScript functions work. The structure of the web page is created with markup. JavaScript is then used to change some of the details without altering the underlying structure.

It is also possible to use JavaScript to change the structure and contents of a web page.

document.write

The write method of the document object provides a quick and easy way to insert a string into a document.

Save this markup as a file. Call it something like test.html:

```
<!DOCTYPE html PUBLIC "-//W3C//DTD XHTML 1.1//EN"
"http://www.w3.org/TR/xhtml11/DTD/xhtml11.dtd">
<html xmlns="http://www.w3.org/1999/xhtml" xml:lang="en">
<head>
  <meta http-equiv="content-type" content="text/html; charset=utf-8" />
  <title>Test</title>
</head>
<body>
  <script type="text/javascript">
    document.write("<p>This is inserted.</p>");
  </script>
</body>
</html>
```

If you load `test.html` in a web browser, you will see a paragraph of text that reads, "This is inserted."

The major drawback to using document.write is that it goes against the principle of **unobtrusive JavaScript**. Even if you place the document.write statement in an external function, you'll still need to insert <script> tags into the body of your markup in order to call the function.

Here's a function that takes a string as its argument. This function concatenates an opening <p> tag, the string, and a closing </p> tag. This concatenated string is stored in a variable called str, which is then written out:

```
function insertParagraph(text) {
  var str = "<p>";
  str += text;
  str += "</p>";
  document.write(str);
}
```

You can store this function in an external file called `example.js`. In order to call this function, you have to insert <script> tags into your markup:

```
<!DOCTYPE html PUBLIC "-//W3C//DTD XHTML 1.1//EN"
"http://www.w3.org/TR/xhtml11/DTD/xhtml11.dtd">
<html xmlns="http://www.w3.org/1999/xhtml" xml:lang="en">
<head>
  <meta http-equiv="content-type" content="text/html; charset=utf-8" />
  <title>Test</title>
  <script type="text/javascript" src="example.js">
  </script>
</head>
<body>
  <script type="text/javascript">
    insertParagraph("This is inserted.");
  </script>
</body>
</html>
```

7

121

Mixing up JavaScript and markup like this is a bad idea. Editing the markup becomes trickier and the benefits of separating behavior from structure are lost.

You could also very easily introduce validation errors. For instance, in the first example, it appears as though a <p> tag has been opened after a <script> tag, which is invalid. In fact, the "<p>" and "</p>" form part of the string being inserted into the document.

If you are writing XHTML documents that are being served up with the mime-type application/xhtml+xml, then document.write simply won't work.

In some ways, using document.write is a bit like using <font> tags to specify font size and color. Both techniques work fine in HTML documents, but neither of them is very elegant.

It's always a good idea to separate structure, behavior, and style. It's much better to specify and maintain styling information by using external CSS files instead of <font> tags. It's also much better to control behavior with external JavaScript files. You should avoid using <script> tags in your <body>. That rules out using document.write.

innerHTML

Most browsers today include support for a property called innerHTML. This property is not part of the DOM specification from the W3C. It was first introduced by Microsoft, in Internet Explorer 4, and has since been adopted by other browsers. However, it is unlikely that it will ever become part of the standardized DOM.

innerHTML can be used to read and write the HTML in an element. Insert this piece of markup into the <body> of test.html:

```
<div id="testdiv">
<p>This is <em>my</em> content.</p>
</div>
```

This is how the Document Object Model sees the markup inside "testdiv", as shown in Figure 7-1:

The div element with the id attribute "testdiv" contains an element node, the p element. This p element, in turn, has a number of child nodes. There are two text nodes. These text nodes have the values "This is" and "content." There's also an element node, em, which itself contains a text node with the value "my".

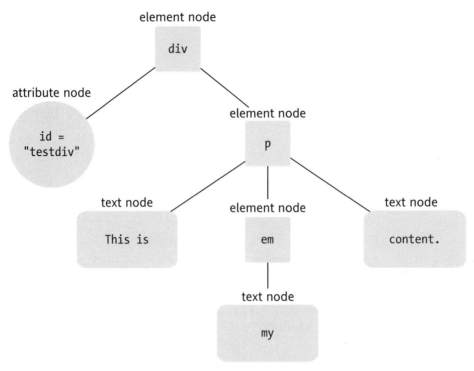

Figure 7-1. The contents of an element node in DOM terms

The DOM provides a very detailed picture of the markup. Using DOM methods and properties, you can access any of those nodes individually.

The innerHTML property takes a much simpler view. This is how it sees the markup inside "testdiv", as shown in Figure 7-2:

There is a string of HTML with the value "<p>This is my content.</p>".

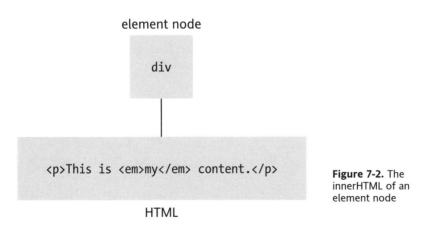

Figure 7-2. The innerHTML of an element node

You can test this by updating example.js with a new function:

```
window.onload = function() {
  var testdiv = document.getElementById("testdiv");
  alert(testdiv.innerHTML);
}
```

Refresh test.html in a web browser. You will see an alert dialog with the innerHTML value of "testdiv".

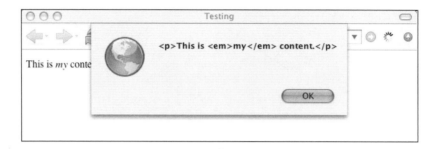

Clearly, innerHTML doesn't offer the fine detail that you can get from DOM methods and properties. Using the standardized DOM is like using a scalpel. Using innerHTML is like using a sledgehammer.

There are times when you might want to use a sledgehammer. If you have a chunk of HTML that you'd like to insert verbatim into a web page, innerHTML can do that. It is a read/write method, which means you can use it not only to *get* the HTML inside an element, but also to *set* the HTML inside an element.

Edit the test.html file so that the element with the ID "testdiv" is empty:

```
<div id="testdiv">
</div>
```

If you put this JavaScript into example.js, you can insert a chunk of HTML into the <div>:

```
window.onload = function() {
  var testdiv = document.getElementById("testdiv");
  testdiv.innerHTML = "<p>I inserted <em>this</em> content.</p>";
}
```

To view the result, refresh test.html in a web browser.

This technique makes no distinction between inserting a chunk of HTML and replacing a chunk of HTML. It doesn't matter if the testdiv element has HTML inside it or not: once you use innerHTML, its entire contents will be replaced.

In the test.html file, change the contents of the element identified as "testdiv" back to what it was:

```
<div id="testdiv">
<p>This is <em>my</em> content.</p>
</div>
```

Leave the example.js file as it is. If you refresh test.html in a web browser, the result will be the same as before. The HTML contained within the testdiv element has been set by innerHTML. The HTML that was previously there has been obliterated.

Pros and cons

The innerHTML property can be quite useful when you want a quick and easy way to insert a chunk of HTML into a document. Unfortunately, innerHTML doesn't return any references to the content you insert. If you want to manipulate the inserted content, you'll need the precision offered by DOM methods.

innerHTML compares favorably to document.write. Using innerHTML, you can keep your JavaScript separate from your markup. There's no need to insert <script> tags into the <body> of your document.

Like document.write, innerHTML is HTML-specific. You won't be able to use it on any other kind of markup document. That means if you are serving up XHTML with the correct mime-type, innerHTML won't work.

It's also worth remembering that innerHTML is a proprietary method, not a web standard. I think it's a good idea to avoid any kind of proprietary JavaScript, so that we don't repeat the bad old days of the browser wars. Back then, as I discussed in Chapter 1, competing browsers had different Document Object Models. As it turns out, innerHTML is well supported. Nonetheless, its future existence is far from certain.

In any case, the standardized DOM can be used instead of innerHTML. It may take slightly more code to achieve the same results but, as you'll see, it offers more precision and power.

DOM methods

Methods such as getElementById and getElementsByTagName are extremely useful for retrieving information about the structure and content of a document.

The Document Object Model is a representation of the document. The information contained in the DOM reflects the information in the document. Once you know how to ask the right questions (using the right methods), you can get the details of any node in the DOM.

The DOM is a two-way street. You can query the contents of a document, but you can also update the contents of a document. If you change the DOM tree, you will change the document as viewed in a browser.

You've already seen this voodoo in action with setAttribute. Using that method, you can alter an attribute node in the DOM. This change is reflected in the document displayed in the browser.

You haven't physically changed the document. If you open up the document in a text editor instead of a browser, you won't see a changed attribute. The changes to the document can only be seen when a browser renders the document. This is because the browser is really displaying the DOM tree. As far as the browser is concerned, the DOM tree *is* the document.

Once you understand this, the idea of creating markup on the fly isn't quite so strange. You aren't really creating markup, you're updating the Document Object Model. The key to doing this is to think in the same terms as the DOM.

According to the Document Object Model, a document is a tree of nodes. If you want add to this tree, you need to insert new nodes.

If you want to add markup to a document, you need to insert element nodes.

createElement

The test.html file should contain an empty <div> with the id value of "testdiv":

```
<div id="testdiv">
</div>
```

I want to insert a paragraph into "testdiv". To use the language of the DOM, I want to add a p element node as a child node of the div element node (which already has one child node: an id attribute node with the value "testdiv").

This is a two-step process:

1. Create the new element.
2. Insert the element into the node tree.

You can achieve the first step by using a DOM method called **createElement**.

This is the syntax:

document.createElement(nodeName)

This statement will create a paragraph element:

```
document.createElement("p");
```

By itself, this method won't prove very useful. You will want to insert the newly created element node into the document. To do this, you'll need to be able to refer to the newly created node. Whenever you use createElement, it's a good idea to assign the newly created element to a variable:

```
var para = document.createElement("p");
```

The variable para now contains a reference to the p element you've just created.

Right now, this newly created paragraph element is floating in JavaScript limbo. The element exists, but it isn't part of the DOM node tree. This is a DocumentFragment. It isn't displayed in the browser. Nonetheless, it has DOM properties, just like any other node.

The homeless paragraph element has a nodeType value and a nodeName value. You can test this for yourself by putting this into example.js:

```
window.onload = function() {
  var para = document.createElement("p");
  var info = "nodeName: ";
  info+= para.nodeName;
  info+= " nodeType: ";
  info+= para.nodeType;
  alert(info);
}
```

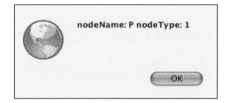

The node exists. It has the nodeName property with the value "P". It also has a nodeType property with the value 1, which means it's an element node. But this node is not connected to the node tree of the document, test.html.

appendChild

The simplest way to insert a newly created node into the node tree of a document is to make it a child of an existing node in that document.

In test.html, a new paragraph should be inserted into the element node identified as "testdiv". In other words, the paragraph element should be a child node of the "testdiv" element. You can do this with a method called **appendChild**.

This is the syntax for appendChild:

parent.appendChild(child)

In the case of test.html, the child is the paragraph you just created with createElement. The parent is the "testdiv" element node. You'll need to reference this node using a DOM method. The simplest way to reference the node is to use getElementById.

As usual, you can make life simpler for yourself, and make your code easier to read, by assigning the element to a variable:

```
var testdiv = document.getElementById("testdiv");
```

The variable testdiv contains a reference to the element with the id "testdiv".

You already have a variable, para, which contains a reference to the newly created paragraph node:

```
var para = document.createElement("p");
```

You can insert para into testdiv using appendChild:

```
testdiv.appendChild(para);
```

The newly created paragraph element is now a child of the "testdiv" element. It has been moved from JavaScript limbo and inserted into the node tree of test.html.

You don't have to use variables when you use appendChild. You could just write:

```
document.getElementById("testdiv").appendChild(
➥ document.createElement("p"));
```

As you can see, that's quite confusing to read. It's worth the extra few lines to write:

```
var para = document.createElement("p");
var testdiv = document.getElementById("testdiv");
testdiv.appendChild(para);
```

createTextNode

You have now created an element node and inserted it into the node tree of the document.

The node you have created is an empty paragraph element. If you want to put some text into that paragraph, you can't use createElement. That only works for creating element nodes. You need to create a text node. You can do this using a method called **createTextNode**.

> Don't let the names of these methods confuse you. It would be simpler if the methods were called createElementNode and createTextNode, or simply createElement and createText. Instead, the names are createElement and createTextNode.

The syntax for createTextNode is very similar to the syntax for createElement:

document.createTextNode(text)

This is how you would create the text "Hello world":

```
document.createTextNode("Hello world");
```

Again, it's a good idea to assign a variable to contain the newly created node:

```
var txt = document.createTextNode("Hello world");
```

The variable txt contains a reference to the newly created text node. This node is floating free in JavaScript. It hasn't been tethered to the node tree of a document.

You can use appendChild to make the text the child node of an existing element. You could insert the text into the paragraph element you created. The variable para is a reference to the paragraph element. The variable txt is a reference to the newly created text node:

```
para.appendChild(txt);
```

The text node with the value "Hello world" is now a child node of the paragraph element.

Try writing this into the example.js file:

```
window.onload = function() {
  var para = document.createElement("p");
  var testdiv = document.getElementById("testdiv");
  testdiv.appendChild(para);
  var txt = document.createTextNode("Hello world");
  para.appendChild(txt);
}
```

If you reload test.html, you will see the text "Hello world" in the browser window:

7

In this example, nodes were created and appended in this order:

1. Create a paragraph element node.
2. Append this paragraph to an element node in the document.
3. Create a text node.
4. Append this text node to the paragraph.

You can also use appendChild to join nodes that aren't yet part of the document tree. That means you could rewrite the steps in this order:

1. Create a paragraph element node.
2. Create a text node.
3. Append this text node to the paragraph.
4. Append this paragraph to an element node in the document.

This is how the reorganized function would look:

```
window.onload = function() {
  var para = document.createElement("p");
  var txt = document.createTextNode("Hello world");
  para.appendChild(txt);
  var testdiv = document.getElementById("testdiv");
  testdiv.appendChild(para);
}
```

The end result is the same. Write this version in the example.js file and reload the test.html document in a web browser. You will see the text "Hello world", just as before.

A more complex combination

When I was demonstrating innerHTML, I used the following piece of markup:

```
<p>This is <em>my</em> content.</p>
```

This is a bit more complex than simply creating a paragraph containing some text. To insert this markup into test.html using DOM methods, you'll need to first break it down into nodes.

As shown in Figure 7-3, an element node "p" contains:

- a text node, "This is "
- an element node, "em"
  - containing a text node, "my"
- a text node, " content."

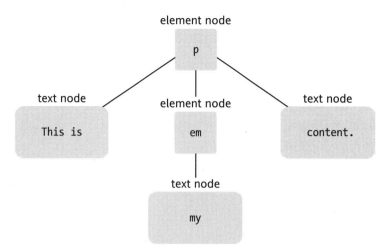

element node

p

text node

This is

element node

em

text node

content.

text node

my

Figure 7-3. A piece of HTML represented as nodes

Once you know the nodes you need to create, you can draw up a plan of action:

1. Create an element node "p" assigned to the variable para.

2. Create a text node assigned to the variable txt1.

3. Append txt1 to para.

4. Create an element node "em" assigned to the variable emphasis.

5. Create a text node assigned to the variable txt2.

6. Append txt2 to emphasis.

7. Append emphasis to para.

8. Create a text node assigned to the variable txt3.

9. Append txt3 to para.

10. Append para to the element "testdiv" in the document.

You can then translate the plan into JavaScript:

```
window.onload = function() {
  var para = document.createElement("p");
  var txt1 = document.createTextNode("This is ");
  para.appendChild(txt1);
  var emphasis = document.createElement("em");
  var txt2 = document.createTextNode("my");
  emphasis.appendChild(txt2);
  para.appendChild(emphasis);
  var txt3 = document.createTextNode(" content.");
  para.appendChild(txt3);
  var testdiv = document.getElementById("testdiv");
  testdiv.appendChild(para);
}
```

7

131

Write that code into example.js and reload test.html in a browser.

You can use a different approach if you like. You could do all the creating first and then do all the appending. In that case, your plan of action would look this:

1. Create an element node "p" assigned to the variable para.
2. Create a text node assigned to the variable txt1.
3. Create an element node "em" assigned to the variable emphasis.
4. Create a text node assigned to the variable txt2.
5. Create a text node assigned to the variable txt3.
6. Append txt1 to para.
7. Append txt2 to emphasis.
8. Append emphasis to para.
9. Append txt3 to para.
10. Append para to the element "testdiv" in the document.

That plan translates into this JavaScript code:

```javascript
window.onload = function() {
  var para = document.createElement("p");
  var txt1 = document.createTextNode("This is ");
  var emphasis = document.createElement("em");
  var txt2 = document.createTextNode("my");
  var txt3 = document.createTextNode(" content.");
  para.appendChild(txt1);
  emphasis.appendChild(txt2);
  para.appendChild(emphasis);
  para.appendChild(txt3);
  var testdiv = document.getElementById("testdiv");
  testdiv.appendChild(para);
}
```

If you write that code into the example.js file and then refresh test.html, you will see the same result as before.

As you can see, there's always more than one way of adding to the node tree of a document. Even if you decide to never use document.write or innerHTML, you still have a lot of choice and flexibility in how you implement the DOM methods for creating and appending nodes.

Revisiting the image gallery

Leave aside test.html and example.js. I'd like to show you a practical example of creating markup on the fly.

In the last chapter, I made a lot of improvements to the image gallery script. The JavaScript is unobtrusive, it degrades gracefully, and I made some accessibility enhancements.

There's still something that bothers me though. Take a look at the markup I'm using in
gallery.html:

```
<!DOCTYPE html PUBLIC "-//W3C//DTD XHTML 1.1//EN"
"http://www.w3.org/TR/xhtml11/DTD/xhtml11.dtd">
<html xmlns="http://www.w3.org/1999/xhtml" xml:lang="en">
<head>
  <meta http-equiv="content-type" content="text/html; charset=utf-8" />
  <title>Image Gallery</title>
  <script type="text/javascript" src="scripts/showPic.js"></script>
  <link rel="stylesheet" href="styles/layout.css" type="text/css"
➥ media="screen" />
</head>
<body>
  <h1>Snapshots</h1>
  <ul id="imagegallery">
    <li>
      <a href="images/fireworks.jpg" title="A fireworks display">
        <img src="images/thumbnail_fireworks.jpg" alt="Fireworks" />
      </a>
    </li>
    <li>
      <a href="images/coffee.jpg" title="A cup of black coffee" >
        <img src="images/thumbnail_coffee.jpg" alt="Coffee" />
      </a>
    </li>
    <li>
      <a href="images/rose.jpg" title="A red, red rose">
        <img src="images/thumbnail_rose.jpg" alt="Rose" />
      </a>
    </li>
    <li>
      <a href="images/bigben.jpg" title="The famous clock">
        <img src="images/thumbnail_bigben.jpg" alt="Big Ben" />
      </a>
    </li>
  </ul>
  <img id="placeholder" src="images/placeholder.gif"
➥ alt="my image gallery" />
  <p id="description">Choose an image.</p>
</body>
</html>
```

The XHTML file contains an image and a paragraph solely for the use of the showPic script.
I would prefer to separate the structure and the behavior entirely. If these elements exist
just to be manipulated by DOM methods, then it makes sense to also create them using
DOM methods.

The first step is straightforward: remove those elements from the gallery.html document. For the next step, I want to create those elements using JavaScript.

7

133

I'm going to write a function called preparePlaceholder and place it into the showPic.js file. I'm going to call this function when the document loads. This is what the function is going to do:

1. Create an image element node.
2. Give this node an id attribute.
3. Give this node a src attribute.
4. Give this node an alt attribute.
5. Create a paragraph element node.
6. Give this node an id attribute.
7. Create a text node.
8. Append the text node to the paragraph element.
9. Insert the image and paragraph into the document.

Creating the elements and giving them attributes is relatively straightforward. I can use a combination of createElement, createTextNode, and setAttribute:

```
var placeholder = document.createElement("img");
placeholder.setAttribute("id","placeholder");
placeholder.setAttribute("src","images/placeholder.gif");
placeholder.setAttribute("alt","my image gallery");
var description = document.createElement("p");
description.setAttribute("id","description");
var desctext = document.createTextNode("Choose an image");
```

I can then put the text node inside the paragraph node using appendChild:

```
description.appendChild(desctext);
```

The final step is to insert the newly created elements into the document. As it happens, the gallery list is currently the last element in the document. If I append the placeholder and description elements to the body element, they will then appear after the gallery list. I can reference the body tag as the first (and only) element with the tag name "body":

```
document.getElementsByTagName("body")[0].appendChild(placeholder);
document.getElementsByTagName("body")[0].appendChild(description);
```

Alternatively, I could use the HTML-DOM shortcut body:

```
document.body.appendChild(placeholder);
document.body.appendChild(description);
```

In either case, the placeholder and description elements will be inserted before the closing </body> tag.

This works, but only because the image gallery list is the last element in the body. What if there was some more content after the image gallery list? What I'd really like to do is insert the newly created elements after the image gallery list, no matter where the list appears in the document.

insertBefore

There is a DOM method called **insertBefore**. You can use it to insert a new element before an existing element. You must specify three things:

1. the new element you want to insert,

2. the target element before which you want to insert it,

3. the parent of both elements.

Here's the syntax:

```
parentElement.insertBefore(newElement,targetElement)
```

You might not know what the parent element is. That's okay. You can always use the parentNode property of the target element. The parent of any element node must be another element node (attribute nodes and text nodes can't have element nodes as children).

For instance, this is how I could insert the placeholder element before the image gallery list, which has the id "imagegallery":

```
var gallery = document.getElementById("imagegallery");
gallery.parentNode.insertBefore(placeholder,gallery);
```

At the moment, the parentNode of gallery is the body element. The placeholder element will be inserted as a new child of the body element. It will be inserted before its sibling element, gallery.

I can also insert the description element as a sibling of the gallery element:

```
gallery.parentNode.insertBefore(description,gallery);
```

The placeholder image and description paragraph are inserted before the image gallery list:

That's all well and good, but I want to add the newly created elements *after* the image gallery, not before it.

Seeing as there is an insertBefore method, you might expect to be able to use a corresponding "insert after" method. Unfortunately, no such DOM method exists.

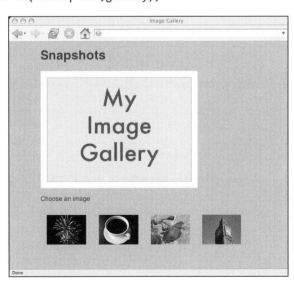

7

Writing the insertAfter function

I don't know why there is no insertAfter method. It seems to me that it would be very useful.

Although the DOM hasn't provided a method called insertAfter, it has provided all the tools you need to insert a node after another node. You can use existing DOM methods and properties to create a function called insertAfter:

```
function insertAfter(newElement,targetElement) {
  var parent = targetElement.parentNode;
  if (parent.lastChild == targetElement) {
    parent.appendChild(newElement);
  } else {
    parent.insertBefore(newElement,targetElement.nextSibling);
  }
}
```

This function is using quite a few DOM methods and properties:

- parentNode property
- lastChild property
- appendChild method
- insertBefore method
- nextSibling property

This is what the function is doing, step by step:

First, the function takes two arguments: the new element and the target element after which the new element should be inserted. These are passed as the variables newElement and targetElement:

```
function insertAfter(newElement,targetElement)
```

Get the parentNode property of the target element and assign it to the variable parent:

```
var parent = targetElement.parentNode
```

Find out if the target element happens to be the last child of parent. Compare the lastChild property of parent with the target element:

```
if (parent.lastChild == targetElement)
```

If this is true, then append the new element to parent using appendChild. The new element will be inserted straight after the target element:

```
parent.appendChild(newElement)
```

Otherwise, the new element needs to be inserted between the target element and the next child of parent. The next node after the target element is the nextSibling property of the target element. Use the insertBefore method to place the new element before the target element's next sibling:

```
parent.insertBefore(newElement.targetElement.nextSibling)
```

On the face of it, that's quite a complex little function. If you break it down into its individual components, it's relatively straightforward. Don't worry if isn't completely clear to you right now. As you become more familiar with the DOM methods and properties that insertAfter uses, it will make more sense.

Like addLoadEvent, this is a very handy function to include in your scripts.

Using the insertAfter function

I can use the insertAfter function in the preparePlaceholder function. First of all, I need a reference to the image gallery list:

```
var gallery = document.getElementById("imagegallery");
```

Now I can insert placeholder, which refers to the newly created image, right after gallery:

```
insertAfter(placeholder,gallery);
```

The "placeholder" image is now part of the node tree of gallery.html. I want to insert the "description" paragraph right after it. I already have the variable description for this node. I can use the insertAfter function again to insert description after placeholder:

```
insertAfter(description, placeholder);
```

With those lines added, this is how the preparePlaceholder function looks:

```
function preparePlaceholder() {
  var placeholder = document.createElement("img");
  placeholder.setAttribute("id","placeholder");
  placeholder.setAttribute("src","images/placeholder.gif");
  placeholder.setAttribute("alt","my image gallery");
  var description = document.createElement("p");
  description.setAttribute("id","description");
  var desctext = document.createTextNode("Choose an image");
  description.appendChild(desctext);
  var gallery = document.getElementById("imagegallery");
  insertAfter(placeholder,gallery);
  insertAfter(description,placeholder);
}
```

There's just one problem with the function: I haven't tested whether or not the browser supports the DOM methods I'm using. To ensure that the function degrades gracefully, I need to add just a few extra lines:

```
function preparePlaceholder() {
  if (!document.createElement) return false;
  if (!document.createTextNode) return false;
  if (!document.getElementById) return false;
  if (!document.getElementById("imagegallery")) return false;
```

7

```
    var placeholder = document.createElement("img");
    placeholder.setAttribute("id","placeholder");
    placeholder.setAttribute("src","images/placeholder.gif");
    placeholder.setAttribute("alt","my image gallery");
    var description = document.createElement("p");
    description.setAttribute("id","description");
    var desctext = document.createTextNode("Choose an image");
    description.appendChild(desctext);
    var gallery = document.getElementById("imagegallery");
    insertAfter(placeholder,gallery);
    insertAfter(description,placeholder);
}
```

The finished image gallery

The showPic.js file now contains five different functions:

- addLoadEvent
- insertAfter
- preparePlaceholder
- prepareGallery
- showPic

Both addLoadEvent and insertAfter are general-purpose functions that you can use in many situations.

The preparePlaceholder function creates an image element and a paragraph element. The function then inserts these newly created elements into the node tree, right after the image gallery list.

The prepareGallery function handles events. The function loops through all the links in the image gallery list. When one of these links is activated, the showPic function is called.

The showPic swaps out the placeholder image for one of the images linked from the gallery list.

To initiate the functionality, the two functions preparePlaceholder and prepareGallery are called using the addLoadEvent function:

```
addLoadEvent(preparePlaceholder);
addLoadEvent(prepareGallery);
```

This is how the finished showPic.js file looks:

```
function addLoadEvent(func) {
  var oldonload = window.onload;
  if (typeof window.onload != 'function') {
    window.onload = func;
```

```
  } else {
    window.onload = function() {
      oldonload();
      func();
    }
  }
}

function insertAfter(newElement,targetElement) {
  var parent = targetElement.parentNode;
  if (parent.lastChild == targetElement) {
    parent.appendChild(newElement);
  } else {
    parent.insertBefore(newElement,targetElement.nextSibling);
  }
}

function preparePlaceholder() {
  if (!document.createElement) return false;
  if (!document.createTextNode) return false;
  if (!document.getElementById) return false;
  if (!document.getElementById("imagegallery")) return false;
  var placeholder = document.createElement("img");
  placeholder.setAttribute("id","placeholder");
  placeholder.setAttribute("src","images/placeholder.gif");
  placeholder.setAttribute("alt","my image gallery");
  var description = document.createElement("p");
  description.setAttribute("id","description");
  var desctext = document.createTextNode("Choose an image");
  description.appendChild(desctext);
  var gallery = document.getElementById("imagegallery");
  insertAfter(placeholder,gallery);
  insertAfter(description,placeholder);
}

function prepareGallery() {
  if (!document.getElementsByTagName) return false;
  if (!document.getElementById) return false;
  if (!document.getElementById("imagegallery")) return false;
  var gallery = document.getElementById("imagegallery");
  var links = gallery.getElementsByTagName("a");
  for ( var i=0; i < links.length; i++) {
    links[i].onclick = function() {
      return showPic(this);
      }
    links[i].onkeypress = links[i].onclick;
  }
}
```

7

```
function showPic(whichpic) {
  if (!document.getElementById("placeholder")) return true;
  var source = whichpic.getAttribute("href");
  var placeholder = document.getElementById("placeholder");
  placeholder.setAttribute("src",source);
  if (!document.getElementById("description")) return false;
  if (whichpic.getAttribute("title")) {
    var text = whichpic.getAttribute("title");
  } else {
    var text = "";
  }
  var description = document.getElementById("description");
  if (description.firstChild.nodeType == 3) {
    description.firstChild.nodeValue = text;
  }
  return false;
}

addLoadEvent(preparePlaceholder);
addLoadEvent(prepareGallery);
```

While the JavaScript file has grown, the amount of markup has diminished. The gallery.html file now contains just a single "hook", which is being used by the JavaScript and the CSS. This "hook" is the id attribute of the image gallery list:

```
<!DOCTYPE html PUBLIC "-//W3C//DTD XHTML 1.1//EN"
"http://www.w3.org/TR/xhtml11/DTD/xhtml11.dtd">
<html xmlns="http://www.w3.org/1999/xhtml" xml:lang="en">
<head>
  <meta http-equiv="content-type" content="text/html;
➥ charset=utf-8" />
  <title>Image Gallery</title>
  <script type="text/javascript" src="scripts/showPic.js"></script>
  <link rel="stylesheet" href="styles/layout.css" type="text/css"
➥ media="screen" />
</head>
<body>
  <h1>Snapshots</h1>
  <ul id="imagegallery">
    <li>
      <a href="images/fireworks.jpg" title="A fireworks display">
        <img src="images/thumbnail_fireworks.jpg" alt="Fireworks" />
      </a>
    </li>
    <li>
      <a href="images/coffee.jpg" title="A cup of black coffee" >
        <img src="images/thumbnail_coffee.jpg" alt="Coffee" />
      </a>
    </li>
```

```
        <li>
          <a href="images/rose.jpg" title="A red, red rose">
            <img src="images/thumbnail_rose.jpg" alt="Rose" />
          </a>
        </li>
        <li>
          <a href="images/bigben.jpg" title="The famous clock">
            <img src="images/thumbnail_bigben.jpg" alt="Big Ben" />
          </a>
        </li>
      </ul>
    </body>
  </html>
```

The structure, style, and behavior are now separated.

Load gallery.html in a web browser. You will see the "placeholder" image and the "description" paragraph. They have been inserted after the "imagegallery" list.

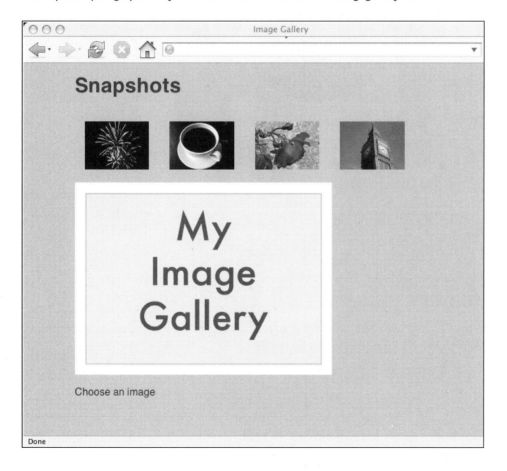

The JavaScript has created markup on the fly and added the markup to the document.

The JavaScript has also prepared all the links in the image gallery list. Click on any of the thumbnails to see the image gallery in action.

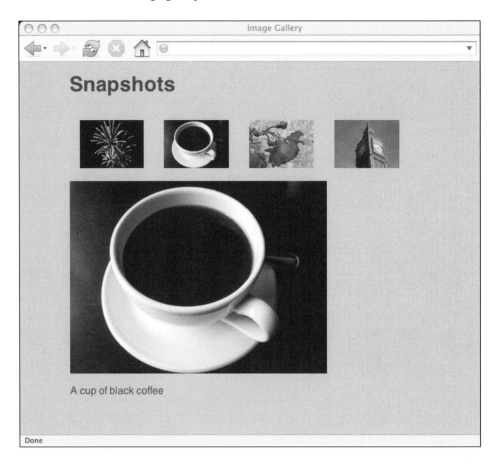

Summary

In this chapter, you've seen different ways of adding markup to a document in the web browser. I've shown you some quick examples of the "old school" techniques:

- document.write
- innerHTML

I've given you more in-depth examples using the DOM methods. The key to using these methods is to see a web document as a tree of nodes.

- createElement
- createTextNode
- appendChild
- insertBefore

Whenever you use createElement or createTextNode, you are creating a node that floats around in JavaScript limbo. Using appendChild and insertBefore, you can take these DocumentFragments and insert them into the node tree of a document.

You've seen the image gallery example refined. Along the way, you've seen the construction of a very handy function called insertAfter. You'll be able to use this function in lots of situations where you need to add markup to a document.

What's next?

In the next chapter, I'd like to give you some more examples of adding markup to documents. I'm going to show you how to create little nuggets of useful information that you can add to a document on the fly.

7

8 ENHANCING CONTENT

What this chapter covers:

- A function that creates a list of abbreviations used in a document
- A function that adds links to the sources of quotes in a document
- A function that creates a list of access keys available in a document

In the last chapter, I showed that you could use the DOM to create markup on the fly. In this chapter, you're going to put those techniques into practice. You will use the DOM to create discrete chunks of markup that can be added to a web page.

What not to do

You can use JavaScript to insert content into a document. However, just because you can do something doesn't mean you should.

In theory, you could use JavaScript to add important content to a web page. That would be a very bad idea, because there would be no room for graceful degradation. Visitors lacking the necessary JavaScript support will never see the content. At the time of writing, that includes searchbots.

If you find yourself using the DOM to insert important content into a web page, you should probably re-examine your process. You may find that you are using the DOM inappropriately.

Always consider the issues of progressive enhancement and graceful degradation.

The principle of **progressive enhancement** is based on the idea that you should begin with your core content. The content is structured using markup. The marked-up content is then enhanced. The enhancement might be stylistic, using CSS, or it might be behavioral, using DOM Scripting.

If you are adding core content with the DOM, you are adding it too late. The content should be part of the initial document.

The corollary to progressive enhancement is **graceful degradation**. If you have progressively enhanced your content, then it follows that your stylistic and behavioral enhancements will degrade gracefully. Visitors to your web site who lack the means to benefit from your CSS and DOM Scripting will still be able to get to your core content.

If you add important content using JavaScript, it won't degrade gracefully. No JavaScript, no content.

This may seem like a restriction, but it isn't. There are plenty of other uses for generating content with the DOM.

Making the invisible visible

Web designers today have a great amount of control over how web pages are displayed. CSS are very powerful tools for styling the content contained between (X)HTML tags. The techniques go far beyond simply changing the fonts and colors used to display content. Using CSS, you can make block-level elements display as if they were inline. That's what I've done with the list containing the thumbnail images in the markup for the JavaScript image gallery. The list items, contained within <li> tags, would normally be displayed on separate lines. By specifying a value of inline for the display property of each list item, the list items appear horizontally instead of vertically.

The reverse is also possible. By declaring display:block for an element that is normally inline, you can put that element on its own line. You can even use CSS to hide content completely. By specifying display:none, you can completely remove elements from the flow of the document. These elements are still part of the DOM's node tree—the browser simply doesn't display them.

Even CSS has its limits. For the time being at least, it only works on the content between tags. The only attributes that CSS pays any significant attention to at the moment are id and class.

Whereas content is placed between tags, semantic information is supplied within the tags themselves. Placing information in attributes is an important part of marking up content.

Web browsers don't display the content of most attributes. When exceptional attributes are displayed, the presentation can vary from browser to browser. Some browsers display the contents of the title attribute as a tool tip. Others display it in the status bar. Some browsers display the contents of the alt attribute as a tool tip, which has led to widespread abuse of an attribute intended to provide an *alternative* description of an image.

When it comes to displaying attributes, you're at the mercy of the browser right now. With a little bit of DOM Scripting, you can wrest control back into your own hands.

I'd like to show you a few variations on the concept of creating "widgets" for web pages using the DOM. The first two examples follow the same basic principle:

1. Retrieve information that is hidden in attributes.
2. Create markup to wrap around this information.
3. Insert this markup into the document.

This approach is different to simply creating content with the Document Object Model. In this scenario, the content already exists in the markup. You will be using JavaScript and the DOM to duplicate content and present it in a different structure.

8

The content

As always, the starting point for any web page is the content.

Take the following text as your starting point:

```
What is the Document Object Model?
The W3C defines the DOM as:
A platform- and language-neutral interface that will allow programs
and scripts to dynamically access and update the
content, structure  and style of documents.
It is an API that can be used to navigate HTML and XML documents.
```

This is how I would probably mark it up:

```
<h1>What is the Document Object Model?</h1>
<p>
The <abbr title="World Wide Web Consortium">W3C</abbr> defines
➥the <abbr title="Document Object Model">DOM</abbr> as:
</p>
<blockquote cite="http://www.w3.org/DOM/">
  <p>
A platform- and language-neutral interface that will allow programs
➥and scripts to dynamically access and update the
➥content, structure and style of documents.
  </p>
</blockquote>
<p>
It is an <abbr title="Application Programming Interface">API</abbr>
➥that can be used to navigate <abbr title="HyperText Markup Language">
➥HTML</abbr> and <abbr title="eXtensible Markup Language">XML
➥</abbr> documents.
</p>
```

There are quite a few abbreviations in there. I've marked them up using the <abbr> tag.

> *There's a lot of confusion surrounding the difference between the <abbr> tag and the <acronym> tag. An **abbreviation** is any shortened version of a word or phrase. An **acronym** is an abbreviation that is spoken as a single word. DOM is an acronym if you are saying it as a word, "dom", rather than saying each letter, "D.O.M." All acronyms are abbreviations, but not all abbreviations are acronyms. The <acronym> tag will probably be deprecated in future versions of XHTML.*

Now that you have your content structured in a fragment of markup, you can put it into context. This fragment goes inside a <body> tag. This body element, along with a corresponding head element, goes inside the <html> tag.

HTML or XHTML?

It's up to you whether to use HTML or XHTML. The important thing is that, whichever document type you choose, the markup validates to the specified doctype declaration. Personally, I like to use XHTML. It is stricter about the markup it allows, so it encourages me to write cleaner markup.

For instance, with HTML you can write tags and attributes in uppercase or lowercase: <p> or <P>, while XHTML insists on lowercase for all tags and attributes.

HTML also allows you to leave off the closing tags sometimes. You can omit closing </p> and </li> tags. This may seem to offer flexibility, but it actually makes it harder to track down problems when browsers render your documents in unexpected ways. By using a stricter doctype, validation tools can become more useful in tracking down errors.

If you use XHTML, remember that all tags must be closed. That includes standalone elements like <img> and <br>, which must be written with a closing slash: <img /> and <br />. For backwards compatibility with very old browsers, you should put a space before the closing slash.

XHTML is basically HTML rewritten as XML. Technically, web browsers should treat XHTML documents as XML rather than HTML. In practice, you need to send the correct mime-type, application/xhtml+xml, in the headers of your document. Some browsers don't understand this mime-type so it is usually only sent after some server-side browser sniffing.

If you are using XHTML with the correct mime-type, remember that some HTML-DOM methods and properties, like document.write and innerHTML, will no longer work. The core DOM methods will continue to work just fine. They will work on any valid XML document, not just XHTML.

If you decide to use HTML, you can still keep your markup nice and clean. You can still write all your tags and attributes in lowercase. You can add closing tags for </p> and </li>, even if they aren't required. From there, it's a short step to writing XHTML.

But remember, HTML will eventually be deprecated. You'll probably end up migrating to XHTML at some stage so, if you haven't yet begun, I'd encourage you to at least consider it.

In any case, the important point is to choose a doctype for your documents and stick to it.

8

The markup

This is how the content looks when it is marked up as a complete XHTML document:

```
<!DOCTYPE html PUBLIC "-//W3C//DTD XHTML 1.1//EN"
"http://www.w3.org/TR/xhtml11/DTD/xhtml11.dtd">
<html xmlns="http://www.w3.org/1999/xhtml" xml:lang="en">
  <head>
    <meta http-equiv="content-type" content="text/html;
➥charset=utf-8" />
```

```
    <title>Explaining the Document Object Model</title>
  </head>
  <body>
    <h1>What is the Document Object Model?</h1>
    <p>
The <abbr title="World Wide Web Consortium">W3C</abbr> defines
➥the <abbr title="Document Object Model">DOM</abbr> as:
    </p>
    <blockquote cite="http://www.w3.org/DOM/">
      <p>
A platform- and language-neutral interface that will allow programs
➥and scripts to dynamically access and update the
➥content, structure and style of documents.
      </p>
    </blockquote>
    <p>
It is an <abbr title="Application Programming Interface">API</abbr>
➥that can be used to navigate <abbr title="HyperText Markup Language">
➥HTML</abbr> and <abbr title="eXtensible Markup Language">XML
➥</abbr> documents.
    </p>
  </body>
</html>
```

Save this page as explanation.html.

If you load the page in a web browser, you will see the how the browser displays the marked-up content.

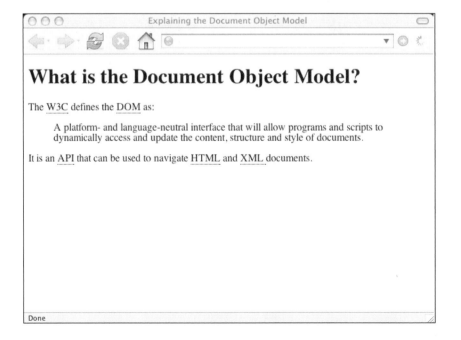

The CSS

Some browsers will render the abbreviations with dotted underlines. Others will show them italicized.

Even though there is no style sheet attached to this document, styles are still being applied. Every browser applies its own default styling.

You can override the browser's default styles by applying your own style sheet. Here's an example:

```
body {
  font-family: "Helvetica","Arial",sans-serif;
  font-size: 10pt;
}
abbr {
  text-decoration: none;
  border: 0;
  font-style: normal;
}
```

Save this as typography.css and put it in a folder called styles.

Now add this line to the <head> of explanation.html:

```
<link rel="stylesheet" type="text/css" media="screen"
➥href="styles/typography.css" />
```

If you load explanation.html in a web browser, you should see a difference. The text is now displayed with a different font, and abbreviations no longer stand out.

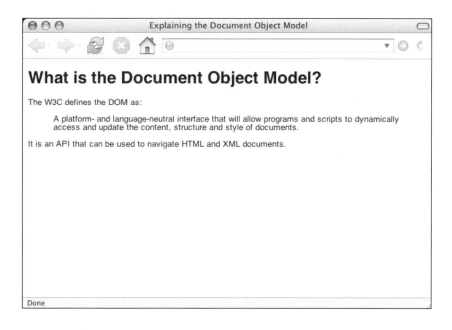

The JavaScript

The title attributes for the abbreviations in the document are hidden. Some browsers will display the titles as tool tips when you mouse over the abbreviations. The default browser behavior for abbreviations is as unpredictable as the default browser styling.

In the same way that you can override the default styles with CSS, you can override the default behavior with the DOM.

Displaying abbreviations

It would be nice to gather all the title values from the <abbr> tags and display them on the page. A **definition list** would be the perfect way to display the titles and the values contained in the <abbr> tags. This is how the definition list would be written:

```
<dl>
  <dt>W3C</dt>
  <dd>World Wide Web Consortium</dd>
  <dt>DOM</dt>
  <dd>Document Object Model</dd>
  <dt>API</dt>
  <dd>Application Programming Interface</dd>
  <dt>HTML</dt>
  <dd>HyperText Markup Language</dd>
  <dt>XML</dt>
  <dd>eXtensible Markup Language</dd>
</dl>
```

You can create this list using the DOM. This is how:

1. Loop through all the abbr elements in the document.
2. Store the title attributes from each abbr element.
3. Store the values from each abbr element.
4. Create a definition list element.
5. Loop through the stored titles and values.
6. Create a definition title element.
7. Insert the value into the definition title.
8. Create a definition description element.
9. Insert the title into the definition description.
10. Append the definition title to the definition list.
11. Append the definition description to the definition list.
12. Append the definition list to the body of the document.

You'll need to write a function to do this. You can call it displayAbbreviations. Write the function to a file called displayAbbreviations.js and store it in a folder called scripts.

Writing the displayAbbreviations function

Begin by defining the function. It doesn't need to take any arguments, so the parentheses will be empty:

```
function displayAbbreviations() {
```

Before you can begin looping through all the abbreviations in the document, you must first find them. This is easily done with getElementsByTagName. Pass this method the value "abbr". The method will return a node set containing all the abbr element nodes in the document. As mentioned in previous chapters, a node set is an array of nodes. Store this array in a variable called abbreviations:

```
var abbreviations = document.getElementsByTagName("abbr");
```

Now you can start looping through the abbreviations array. But before you do that, it's worth running a little test.

We know that there are abbreviations in this particular document. But that won't be the case for all documents, and if you want to use this function for other documents, you should probably check to see if the document contains any abbreviations before going further.

You can find out how many abbreviations are in the document by querying the length property of the abbreviations array. If abbreviations.length is less than one, there are no abbr elements in the document. If that is the case, the function should finish now by returning a Boolean value:

```
if (abbreviations.length < 1) return false;
```

If there are no abbr elements in the document, the function will finish at this point.

The next step is to store information from each abbr element. You'll need to store the text within the <abbr> tags as well as the value of each title attribute. When you want to store a series of values like this, an array is the ideal storage medium.

Define a new array called defs:

```
var defs = new Array();
```

Now loop through the abbreviations array:

```
for (var i=0; i<abbreviations.length; i++) {
```

To get the definition provided by the current abbreviation, use the getAttribute method on the title attribute. Store the value in a variable called definition:

```
var definition = abbreviations[i].getAttribute("title");
```

8

To get the abbreviation within the abbr tag, use the nodeValue property. You want the value of the text node within the abbr element. In all the occurrences of the abbr element in explanation.html, the text node is the first (and only) node within the element. In other words, the text node is the first child of the abbr element node:

```
abbreviations[i].firstChild
```

However, it's possible that the text node could be nested within other elements. Consider this piece of markup:

```
<abbr title="Document Object Model"><em>DOM</em></abbr>
```

In this case, the first child of the abbr element node is the em element node. The text node is the second (and last) node within the abbr element. Instead of using the firstChild property, it's safer to use the lastChild property:

```
abbreviations[i].lastChild
```

Get the nodeValue property of this text node and assign to the variable key:

```
var key = abbreviations[i].lastChild.nodeValue;
```

Now you have two variables: definition and key. These are the values that you want to store in the defs array. You can store both values by setting one of them as the key and the other as the value:

```
defs[key] = definition;
```

The first element of the defs array has the key "W3C" and the value "World Wide Web Consortium". The second element of the defs array has the key "DOM" and the value "Document Object Model" and so on.

This is the finished loop:

```
for (var i=0; i<abbreviations.length; i++) {
  var definition = abbreviations[i].getAttribute("title");
  var key = abbreviations[i].lastChild.nodeValue;
  defs[key] = definition;
}
```

If you'd like to improve the readability of the loop, you could assign the value of abbreviations[i], the current iteration of the abbreviations array, to a variable called current_abbr:

```
for (var i=0; i<abbreviations.length; i++) {
  var current_abbr = abbreviations[i];
  var definition = current_abbr.getAttribute("title");
  var key = current_abbr.lastChild.nodeValue;
  defs[key] = definition;
}
```

If you find that the current_abbr variable helps you to follow the code more easily, then I recommend you use it. Adding one extra line is a small price to pay.

In theory, you could write the entire loop in one line but that would be very hard to read:

```
for (var i=0; i<abbreviations.length; i++) {
  defs[abbreviations[i].lastChild.nodeValue] =
➥abbreviations[i].getAttribute("title");
  }
```

There's always more than one way of doing things in JavaScript. You've just seen three different ways of writing the same loop. Choose the one that makes most sense to you. If it seems confusing to you when you write it, there's a good chance that it will confuse you even more when you come back to it later.

Now that you have your definitions stored in the defs array, you can create the markup in which to display them.

Creating the markup

A definition list is the ideal way to structure a list of abbreviations and their meaning. A definition list (<dl>) contains a series of definition titles (<dt>) and definition descriptions (<dd>):

```
<dl>
  <dt>Title 1</dt>
  <dd>Description 1</dd>
  <dt>Title 2</dt>
  <dd>Description 2</dd>
</dl>
```

Create the definition list using the createElement method. Assign the newly created element to a variable called dlist:

```
var dlist = document.createElement("dl");
```

The new dl element you've created is a DocumentFragment floating in JavaScript limbo for now. Later, you'll be able to insert it into the document by referencing the dlist variable.

It's time for another loop. This time, you'll be looping through the defs array that you created earlier. Once again, you'll be using a for loop, but this time it will be slightly different.

for/in loop

You can use a for/in loop to temporarily assign the key of an array to a variable:

```
for (variable in array)
```

On the first iteration of the for loop, the variable has the value of the key of the first element in the array. Next time around, the variable has the value of the key of the second element in the array. The loop will run through all the keys of the array:

This is how you can loop through the associative array, defs:

```
for (key in defs) {
```

8

This means, "For each key in the defs associative array, assign its value to the variable key." You can then use the variable key in the subsequent block of code. Because you have the key for the current iteration of the defs array, you can retrieve the corresponding value:

```
var definition = defs[key];
```

On the first iteration of the for/in loop, the variable key has the value "W3C" and the variable definition has the value "World Wide Web Consortium". The next time around, key has the value "DOM" and definition has the value "Document Object Model".

On each iteration of the loop, you'll need to create a dt element and a dd element. You'll also need to create text nodes to put inside them.

Start by creating the dt element:

```
var dtitle = document.createElement("dt");
```

Create a text node with the value of key:

```
var dtitle_text = document.createTextNode(key);
```

You have created two nodes. The element node you created is assigned to the variable dtitle. The text node you created is assigned to the variable dtitle_text. Use the appendChild method to put the text node inside the element node:

```
dtitle.appendChild(dtitle_text);
```

Repeat the process for the dd element:

```
var ddesc = document.createElement("dd");
```

This time, create a text node with the value of the variable definition:

```
var ddesc_text = document.createTextNode(definition);
```

Again, append the text node to the element node:

```
ddesc.appendChild(ddesc_text);
```

Now you have two element nodes: dtitle and ddesc. These element nodes contain the text nodes dtitle_text and ddesc_text.

Before finishing the loop, append your newly created dt and dd elements to the dl element you created earlier. The dl element has been assigned to the variable dlist:

```
dlist.appendChild(dtitle);
dlist.appendChild(ddesc);
```

Here is the finished for/in loop:

```
for (key in defs) {
  var definition = defs[key];
  var dtitle = document.createElement("dt");
```

```
    var dtitle_text = document.createTextNode(key);
    dtitle.appendChild(dtitle_text);
    var ddesc = document.createElement("dd");
    var ddesc_text = document.createTextNode(definition);
    ddesc.appendChild(ddesc_text);
    dlist.appendChild(dtitle);
    dlist.appendChild(ddesc);
}
```

At this stage, your definition list is complete. It exists in JavaScript as a DocumentFragment. All that remains for you to do is to insert it into the document.

Rather than inserting the list of abbreviations unannounced, it would be a good idea to place them under a descriptive heading.

Create an h2 element node:

```
var header = document.createElement("h2");
```

Create a text node with the value "Abbreviations":

```
var header_text = document.createTextNode("Abbreviations");
```

Place the text node inside the element node:

```
header.appendChild(header_text);
```

In a complicated document, you'd probably want to insert the newly created elements into a specific part of the document, probably identified with an id. In the case of explanation.html, which is quite a straightforward document, you can just append them to the body tag.

There are two ways you could reference the body tag. Using the DOM Core, you can reference the first (and only) body tag in the document:

```
document.getElementsByTagName("body")[0]
```

Using the HTML-DOM, you can simply reference the body property of the document:

```
document.body
```

First, insert the header:

```
document.body.appendChild(header);
```

Then insert the definition list:

```
document.body.appendChild(dlist);
```

The displayAbbreviations function is done:

```
function displayAbbreviations() {
  var abbreviations = document.getElementsByTagName("abbr");
  if (abbreviations.length < 1) return false;
  var defs = new Array();
  for (var i=0; i<abbreviations.length; i++) {
    var current_abbr = abbreviations[i];
    var definition = current_abbr.getAttribute("title");
    var key = current_abbr.lastChild.nodeValue;
    defs[key] = definition;
  }
  var dlist = document.createElement("dl");
  for (key in defs) {
    var definition = defs[key];
    var dtitle = document.createElement("dt");
    var dtitle_text = document.createTextNode(key);
    dtitle.appendChild(dtitle_text);
    var ddesc = document.createElement("dd");
    var ddesc_text = document.createTextNode(definition);
    ddesc.appendChild(ddesc_text);
    dlist.appendChild(dtitle);
    dlist.appendChild(ddesc);
  }
  var header = document.createElement("h2");
  var header_text = document.createTextNode("Abbreviations");
  header.appendChild(header_text);
  document.body.appendChild(header);
  document.body.appendChild(dlist);
}
```

As usual, there's some room for improvement.

At the start of the script, you should check to make sure that the browser will understand the DOM methods you will be using. The function uses getElementsByTagName, createElement, and createTextNode. You can test for each of these individually:

```
if (!document.getElementsyTagName) return false;
if (!document.createElement) return false;
if (!document.createTextNode) return false;
```

Alternatively, you could combine the tests into one statement:

```
if (!document.getElementsByTagName || !document.createElement
➥|| !document.createTextNode) return false;
```

Choose whichever one makes most sense to you.

The displayAbbreviations function is reasonably lengthy. It's a good idea to insert some comments along the way.

```
function displayAbbreviations() {
  if (!document.getElementsByTagName || !document.createElement
➥|| !document.createTextNode) return false;
// get all the abbreviations
  var abbreviations = document.getElementsByTagName("abbr");
  if (abbreviations.length < 1) return false;
  var defs = new Array();
// loop through the abbreviations
  for (var i=0; i<abbreviations.length; i++) {
    var current_abbr = abbreviations[i];
    var definition = current_abbr.getAttribute("title");
    var key = current_abbr.lastChild.nodeValue;
    defs[key] = definition;
  }
// create the definition list
  var dlist = document.createElement("dl");
// loop through the definitions
  for (key in defs) {
    var definition = defs[key];
// create the definition title
    var dtitle = document.createElement("dt");
    var dtitle_text = document.createTextNode(key);
    dtitle.appendChild(dtitle_text);
// create the definition description
    var ddesc = document.createElement("dd");
    var ddesc_text = document.createTextNode(definition);
    ddesc.appendChild(ddesc_text);
// add them to the definition list
    dlist.appendChild(dtitle);
    dlist.appendChild(ddesc);
  }
// create a headline
  var header = document.createElement("h2");
  var header_text = document.createTextNode("Abbreviations");
  header.appendChild(header_text);
// add the headline to the body
  document.body.appendChild(header);
// add the definition list to the body
  document.body.appendChild(dlist);
}
```

The function should be called when the page loads. You can use the `window.onload` event to do this:

```
window.onload = displayAbbreviations;
```

8

It would be better to use the addLoadEvent function in case you need to add more events to window.onload. Write the addLoadEvent function to a new JavaScript file, addLoadEvent.js. Store the file in the scripts folder:

```
function addLoadEvent(func) {
  var oldonload = window.onload;
  if (typeof window.onload != 'function') {
    window.onload = func;
  } else {
    window.onload = function() {
      oldonload();
      func();
    }
  }
}
```

In the displayAbbreviations.js file, add this line:

```
addLoadEvent(displayAbbreviations);
```

Your JavaScript files are ready. You'll need to reference both files from <script> tags in the head of explanation.html:

```
<script type="text/javascript" src="scripts/addLoadEvent.js"></script>
<script type="text/javascript"
➥src="scripts/displayAbbreviations.js"></script>
```

This is the markup for explanation.html:

```
<!DOCTYPE html PUBLIC "-//W3C//DTD XHTML 1.1//EN"
"http://www.w3.org/TR/xhtml11/DTD/xhtml11.dtd">
<html xmlns="http://www.w3.org/1999/xhtml" xml:lang="en">
  <head>
    <meta http-equiv="content-type" content="text/html; charset=utf-8" />
    <title>Explaining the Document Object Model</title>
    <link rel="stylesheet" type="text/css" media="screen"
➥href="styles/typography.css" />
    <script type="text/javascript" src="scripts/addLoadEvent.js">
    </script>
    <script type="text/javascript" src="scripts/displayAbbreviations.js">
    </script>
  </head>
<body>
    <h1>What is the Document Object Model?</h1>
    <p>
The <abbr title="World Wide Web Consortium">W3C</abbr> defines
➥the <abbr title="Document Object Model">DOM</abbr> as:
    </p>
    <blockquote cite="http://www.w3.org/DOM/">
      <p>
```

```
        A platform- and language-neutral interface that will allow programs
      ➥and scripts to dynamically access and update the
      ➥content, structure and style of documents.
            </p>
          </blockquote>
          <p>
      It is an <abbr title="Application Programming Interface">API</abbr>
      ➥that can be used to navigate <abbr title="HyperText Markup Language">
      ➥HTML</abbr> and <abbr title="eXtensible Markup Language">XML
      </abbr> documents.
            </p>
        </body>
      </html>
```

Load `explanation.html` in a web browser to see the effects of the `displayAbbreviations` function.

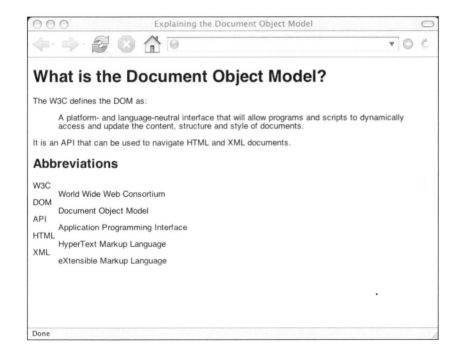

A browser bomb

Up until now, I've avoided mentioning any specific browsers. As long as you are using any DOM-compliant browser, all of the scripts you've seen so far will work. Unfortunately, the displayAbbreviations function is the exception to the rule.

The displayAbbreviations function works fine—unless you try it in Internet Explorer for Windows. If you load `explanation.html` in Internet Explorer, you won't see a list of abbreviations and you will probably get a JavaScript error message.

This seems like very strange behavior. After all, the function begins with some object detection to ensure that only DOM-capable browsers will execute the code. Internet Explorer is clearly capable of understanding methods like getElementsByTagName and getElementById.

The problem goes back to the browser wars I described in Chapter 1. The abbr and acronym elements were used as weapons by Netscape and Microsoft. In the heat of battle, Microsoft decided not to implement the abbr element.

The browser wars are long over. Microsoft won its battle against Netscape. Yet, Internet Explorer still doesn't support the abbr element. When the browser loads a page and builds its Document Object Model, it refuses to recognize any <abbr> tags as element nodes! The displayAbbreviations function fails because it attempts to extract attribute and text nodes from abbr element nodes, and Internet Explorer refuses to accord these abbr nodes the status of being elements.

We seem to have unwittingly stepped on an unexploded bomb left over from a long-finished battle.

There are two possible solutions:

1. Use acronym elements instead of abbr elements.

2. Ensure that displayAbbreviations degrades gracefully in Internet Explorer.

The first option doesn't appeal to me, because I don't want to sacrifice semantically correct markup just to satisfy a stubborn browser.

The second option is quite easy to accomplish. By adding just a couple of extra lines, Internet Explorer or any other browser that doesn't want to recognize the abbr element will simply exit the function early.

First add a single line to the loop that gathers the title attributes and text values from the abbr elements:

```
for (var i=0; i<abbreviations.length; i++) {
  var current_abbr = abbreviations[i];
  if (current_abbr.childNodes.length < 1) continue;
  var definition = current_abbr.getAttribute("title");
  var key = current_abbr.lastChild.nodeValue;
  defs[key] = definition;
}
```

This is effectively saying, "If the current element has no child nodes, carry on to the next iteration of the loop." Internet Explorer will count up the child nodes for each abbr element and incorrectly come up with the number zero each time. This new statement ensures that it doesn't attempt to go any further in the loop.

When Internet Explorer gets to the loop in displayAbbreviations that builds the definition list, it won't create any dt or dd elements because the defs array is empty. I'm going to add one line after that loop. If the definition list has no child nodes, exit the function:

```
                    // create the definition list
                    var dlist = document.createElement("dl");
                    // loop through the definitions
                    for (key in defs) {
                      var definition = defs[key];
                    // create the definition title
                      var dtitle = document.createElement("dt");
                      var dtitle_text = document.createTextNode(key);
                      dtitle.appendChild(dtitle_text);
                    // create the definition description
                      var ddesc = document.createElement("dd");
                      var ddesc_text = document.createTextNode(definition);
                      ddesc.appendChild(ddesc_text);
                    // add them to the definition list
                      dlist.appendChild(dtitle);
                      dlist.appendChild(ddesc);
                    }
                    if (dlist.childNodes.length < 1) return false;
```

Again, this runs counter to the principles of structured programming because there is now an additional exit point in the middle of the function. But this is probably the simplest way of dealing with Internet Explorer's quirk without altering the existing function significantly.

The finished function looks like this:

```
                    function displayAbbreviations() {
                      if (!document.getElementsByTagName || !document.createElement
                    ➥|| !document.createTextNode) return false;
                    // get all the abbreviations
                      var abbreviations = document.getElementsByTagName("abbr");
                      if (abbreviations.length < 1) return false;
                      var defs = new Array();
                    // loop through the abbreviations
                      for (var i=0; i<abbreviations.length; i++) {
                        var current_abbr = abbreviations[i];
                        if (current_abbr.childNodes.length < 1) continue;
                        var definition = current_abbr.getAttribute("title");
                        var key = current_abbr.lastChild.nodeValue;
                        defs[key] = definition;
                      }
                    // create the definition list
                      var dlist = document.createElement("dl");
                    // loop through the definitions
                      for (key in defs) {
                        var definition = defs[key];
                    // create the definition title
                        var dtitle = document.createElement("dt");
                        var dtitle_text = document.createTextNode(key);
                        dtitle.appendChild(dtitle_text);
```

8

163

```
// create the definition description
    var ddesc = document.createElement("dd");
    var ddesc_text = document.createTextNode(definition);
    ddesc.appendChild(ddesc_text);
// add them to the definition list
    dlist.appendChild(dtitle);
    dlist.appendChild(ddesc);
  }
  if (dlist.childNodes.length < 1) return false;
// create a headline
  var header = document.createElement("h2");
  var header_text = document.createTextNode("Abbreviations");
  header.appendChild(header_text);
// add the headline to the body
  document.body.appendChild(header);
// add the definition list to the body
  document.body.appendChild(dlist);
}
```

The two new lines will ensure that there will be no errors even if the abbr element isn't understood. They act as safety checks, much like the object detection at the start of the script.

Notice that even though the problem was caused by a specific browser, there's still no need to use browser sniffing code. Sniffing for a specific browser name and number is bound to cause problems and result in very convoluted code.

We have successfully defused a nasty surprise left over from the legacy of the browser wars. If nothing else, it serves as a reminder of the importance of standards. Because their browser doesn't support the abbr element, users of Internet Explorer won't get the benefit of seeing a generated list of abbreviations. But they will still be able to view the core content. The definition list of abbreviations provides a nice enhancement, but it is by no means a vital part of the page. If it were, it would have been included in the markup to begin with.

You can find the finished displayAbbreviations.js file on the downloads page for this book, at the friends of ED website, http://friendsofed.com/.

Displaying citations

The displayAbbreviations function is a good example of content enhancement (at least in any browser other than Internet Explorer). It takes content that is already part of the document structure and displays it in a clearer way. The information contained in the title attributes of the abbr tags appears directly in the browser.

Take a look at this piece of markup in explanation.html:

```
<blockquote cite="http://www.w3.org/DOM/">
  <p>
A platform- and language-neutral interface that will allow programs
➥and scripts to dynamically access and update the
```

```
➥content, structure and style of documents.
  </p>
</blockquote>
```

The blockquote element contains an attribute called cite. This is an optional attribute you can use to specify a URL where the contents of the blockquote can be found.

In theory, this is a useful way of linking quotes with relevant web pages. In practice, browsers tend to ignore the cite attribute completely. The information is there but it isn't being acted upon. Using JavaScript and the DOM, you can take that information and display it in a more meaningful way.

Here is a plan of action for displaying these kind of citations as links:

1. Loop through all the blockquote elements in the document.

2. Get the value of the cite attribute from the blockquote.

3. Create a link with the text "source".

4. Give this link the value of the cite attribute from the blockquote.

5. Insert this link at the end of the quoted text.

You can turn this plan into a JavaScript function called displayCitations and store it in a file called displayCitations.js.

Writing the displayCitations function

Let's look at how we create the function. It won't be taking any arguments so the parentheses after the function name are empty:

```
function displayCitations() {
```

The first step is to gather all the blockquote elements in the document. Use getElementsByTagName and store the resultant node set as the variable quotes:

```
var quotes = document.getElementsByTagName("blockquote");
```

Now start looping through this set:

```
for (var i=0; i<quotes.length; i ++) {
```

Inside the loop, you're only interested in quotes that have a cite attribute. You can perform a simple test to see if the current quote in the loop has this attribute.

Run the test on the current element of the quotes node set. That's quotes[i]. Use getAttribute to perform the test on this node. If the result of getAttribute("cite") is true, there is a cite attribute. If the result of !getAttribute("cite") is true, there is no cite attribute. If that's the case, the keyword continue will cause the loop to jump forward to the next iteration. All the subsequent statements inside the loop will be ignored during the current iteration:

```
if (!quotes[i].getAttribute("cite")) {
   continue;
}
```

8

165

You could also write it like this:

```
if (!quotes[i].getAttribute("cite")) continue;
```

The following statements will be performed only on blockquote element nodes that have cite attribute nodes.

First of all, get the value of the cite attribute of the current blockquote and store it in a variable called url:

```
var url = quotes[i].getAttribute("cite");
```

The next step involves figuring out where to put the link. At first, this might seem very straightforward.

Finding your element

A blockquote element must contain block level elements, such as paragraphs, to contain the text being quoted. You want to place the link at the end of the last child element node contained by the blockquote element. The obvious thing to do is find the lastChild property of the current blockquote element:

```
quotes[i].lastChild
```

But if you do this, you could potentially run into a problem. Take a look at the markup again:

```
<blockquote cite="http://www.w3.org/DOM/">
  <p>
A platform- and language-neutral interface that will allow programs
➥and scripts to dynamically access and update the
➥content, structure and style of documents.
  </p>
</blockquote>
```

At first glance, it appears as though the last child of the blockquote element is the p element. You might expect the lastChild property to return the p element node. In reality, this won't necessarily be the case.

It's true that the paragraph is the last *element* node contained by the blockquote element. However, between the end of the p element and the end of the blockquote element, there is a line break. Some browsers will treat this line break as a text node. That means that the lastChild property of the blockquote element node isn't the p element node, it's a text node.

> *A common mistake in DOM Scripting is assuming that a node is an element node. When in doubt, always check the* nodeType *value. There are certain methods that can only be performed on element nodes. If you try to perform them on text nodes, you could get an error.*

It would be great if there was a DOM property called lastChildElement in addition to the existing lastChild property. Unfortunately, there isn't. However, using existing DOM methods, you can write some statements to perform the required task.

You can find all the element nodes within the current blockquote. If you use getElementsByTagName with the wildcard character (*), it will return every element regardless of its tag name:

```
var quoteElements = quotes[i].getElementsByTagName("*");
```

The variable quoteElements is an array containing all the element nodes contained by the current blockquote element, quotes[i].

To find the last element node contained by the blockquote, retrieve the last element in the quoteElements array. The last element of the array has an index which is one less than the length of the array. Remember that arrays begin counting from zero. That's why the index of the last element isn't equal to the length of the array; it is equal to the length of the array minus one:

```
var elem = quoteElements[quoteElements.length - 1];
```

The variable elem refers to the last element node within the blockquote.

Getting back to your loop in the displayCitations function, this is what you've got so far:

```
for (var i=0; i<quotes.length; i++) {
  if (!quotes[i].getAttribute("cite")) continue;
  var url = quotes[i].getAttribute("cite");
  var quoteChildren = quotes[i].getElementsByTagName('*');
  var elem = quoteChildren[quoteChildren.length - 1];
```

Rather than assuming that quoteChildren will return an array of element nodes, run a little check to see if its length is less than one. If that's the case, use the continue keyword again to break out of the current loop:

```
for (var i=0; i<quotes.length; i++) {
  if (!quotes[i].getAttribute("cite")) continue;
  var url = quotes[i].getAttribute("cite");
  var quoteChildren = quotes[i].getElementsByTagName('*');
  if (quoteChildren.length < 1) continue;
  var elem = quoteChildren[quoteChildren.length - 1];
```

You have all the values you need to create a link. The variable url contains the information required for the href value of the link you will make. The elem variable contains the node where you want to place the link.

Create the link by using createElement to make an a element:

```
var link = document.createElement("a");
```

Now create the text that will go within the link. Use the createTextNode method to create some text with the value "source":

```
var link_text = document.createTextNode("source");
```

The newly created a element has been assigned to the variable link. The newly created text node has been assigned to the variable link_text.

Put the text inside the link using the appendChild method:

```
link.appendChild(link_text);
```

Add the href attribute to the link. Set it to the value of the variable url using setAttribute:

```
link.setAttribute("href",url);
```

The link is ready. You could insert it into the document as is. You could also wrap it in another element like sup so that the link appears as superscript.

Create a sup element node, giving it the variable superscript:

```
var superscript = document.createElement("sup");
```

Place the link inside this element:

```
superscript.appendChild(link);
```

You now have a DocumentFragment created in JavaScript that isn't connected to the document:

```
<sup><a href="http://www.w3.org/DOM/">source</a></sup>
```

Insert this markup into the document by making it the last child of elem. The variable elem refers to the last element node contained by the blockquote so the superscripted link will be inserted directly after the quoted text:

```
elem.appendChild(superscript);
```

Close the loop with a closing curly brace, and finish the function by adding a closing curly brace.

Here's the finished displayAbbreviations function:

```
function displayCitations() {
  var quotes = document.getElementsByTagName("blockquote");
  for (var i=0; i<quotes.length; i++) {
    if (!quotes[i].getAttribute("cite")) continue;
    var url = quotes[i].getAttribute("cite");
    var quoteChildren = quotes[i].getElementsByTagName('*');
    if (quoteChildren.length < 1) continue;
    var elem = quoteChildren[quoteChildren.length - 1];
```

```
            var link = document.createElement("a");
            var link_text = document.createTextNode("source");
            link.appendChild(link_text);
            link.setAttribute("href",url);
            var superscript = document.createElement("sup");
            superscript.appendChild(link);
            elem.appendChild(superscript);
        }
    }
```

As always, there's room for improvement. Add a test at the start of the function to ensure that the browser will understand the DOM methods you're using. You can also add some comments to the make the code clearer:

```
function displayCitations() {
    if (!document.getElementsByTagName || !document.createElement
    || !document.createTextNode) return false;
    // get all the blockquotes
    var quotes = document.getElementsByTagName("blockquote");
    // loop through all the blockquotes
    for (var i=0; i<quotes.length; i++) {
    // if there is no cite attribute, continue the loop
        if (!quotes[i].getAttribute("cite")) continue;
    // store the cite attribute
        var url = quotes[i].getAttribute("cite");
    // get all the element nodes in the blockquote
        var quoteChildren = quotes[i].getElementsByTagName('*');
    // if there are no element node, continue the loop
        if (quoteChildren.length < 1) continue;
    // get the last element node in the blockquote
        var elem = quoteChildren[quoteChildren.length - 1];
    // create the markup
        var link = document.createElement("a");
        var link_text = document.createTextNode("source");
        link.appendChild(link_text);
        link.setAttribute("href",url);
        var superscript = document.createElement("sup");
        superscript.appendChild(link);
    // add the markup to the last element node in the blockquote
        elem.appendChild(superscript);
    }
}
```

Call the displayCitations function using the addLoadEvent function:

```
addLoadEvent(displayCitations);
```

8

Call the displayCitations.js file from explanation.html by adding a new set of <script> tags to the head of the document:

```
<!DOCTYPE html PUBLIC "-//W3C//DTD XHTML 1.1//EN"
"http://www.w3.org/TR/xhtml11/DTD/xhtml11.dtd">
<html xmlns="http://www.w3.org/1999/xhtml" xml:lang="en">
  <head>
    <meta http-equiv="content-type"
➥content="text/html; charset=utf-8" />
    <title>Explaining the Document Object Model</title>
    <link rel="stylesheet" type="text/css" media="screen"
➥href="styles/typography.css" />
    <script type="text/javascript" src="scripts/addLoadEvent.js">
    </script>
    <script type="text/javascript"
➥src="scripts/displayAbbreviations.js">
    </script>
    <script type="text/javascript" src="scripts/displayCitations.js">
    </script>
  </head>
<body>
    <h1>What is the Document Object Model?</h1>
    <p>
The <abbr title="World Wide Web Consortium">W3C</abbr> defines
➥the <abbr title="Document Object Model">DOM</abbr> as:
    </p>
    <blockquote cite="http://www.w3.org/DOM/">
      <p>
A platform- and language-neutral interface that will allow programs
➥and scripts to dynamically access and update the
➥content, structure and style of documents.
      </p>
    </blockquote>
    <p>
It is an <abbr title="Application Programming Interface">API</abbr>
➥that can be used to navigate <abbr title="HyperText Markup Language">
➥HTML</abbr> and <abbr title="eXtensible Markup Language">XML
➥</abbr> documents.
    </p>
  </body>
</html>
```

Load explanation.html in a web browser to see the result.

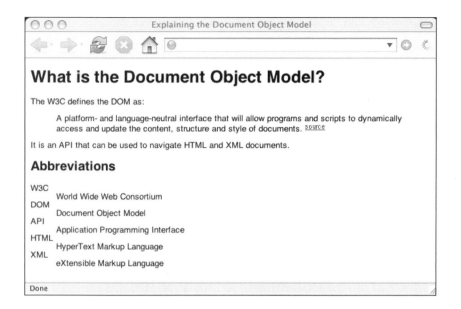

Displaying access keys

The two functions that you've written, displayAbbreviations and displayCitations, have a lot in common. They both begin by creating a node set of a certain element (abbr or blockquote). Then they loop through this node set, creating some markup during each iteration of the loop. This markup is then inserted into the document.

I'd like to show you one more example that follows this pattern. You can write a function to display all the access keys used in a document.

The markup

The accesskey attribute associates an element, such as a link, with a specific key on a keyboard. This can be useful for people who don't navigate with a mouse. If you are visually impaired, for instance, it's very handy to have keyboard shortcuts.

On many Windows browsers, you can press *ALT* + accesskey; on many Mac browsers, you can press *CTRL* + accesskey.

Here's an example of an accesskey attribute:

```
<a href="index.html" accesskey="1">Home</a>
```

It's usually not a good idea to use too many access keys. There is a danger that they could clash with the keyboard shortcuts built into the browser.

A loose convention has arisen for some basic accesskey settings. Have a look at http://www.clagnut.com/blog/193/. An accesskey value of one is used for a link back to the home page of a site. An accesskey value of two is used for "skip navigation" links. An accesskey value of four is used for a link to a search form or page. An accesskey value of nine is used for a link to contact information. An accesskey value of zero is used for a link to an accessibility statement.

8

Here's an example of a site navigation list that uses access keys:

```
<ul id="navigation">
  <li><a href="index.html" accesskey="1">Home</a></li>
  <li><a href="search.html" accesskey="4">Search</a></li>
  <li><a href="contact.html" accesskey="0">Contact</a></li>
</ul>
```

Add that markup right after the opening of the <body> tag in explanation.html.

If you load explanation.html in a web browser, you will see the links in the list. But you won't see anything to indicate that there are accesskey attributes present.

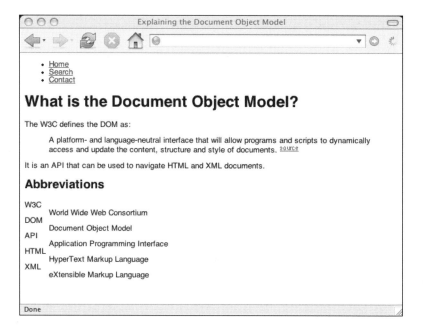

While many browsers support the functionality of the accesskey attribute, it is left to you to indicate which access keys have been assigned. This is often done in an **accessibility statement**, a page that lists the accessibility features of a website.

Using the DOM, you can create a list of access keys on the fly. Here's how:

1. Get a node set of all the links in the document.

2. Loop through all these links.

3. If a link has an accesskey attribute, store its value.

4. Store the link text as well.

5. Create a list.

6. For each link with an access key, create a list item.

7. Add the list item to the list.

8. Add the list to the document.

Let's go through these steps one by one.

The JavaScript

Name the function displayAccesskeys and store it in a file called displayAccesskeys.js.

This function works very similarly to the displayAbbreviations function. The accesskey values and the corresponding link texts are stored in an associative array. A for/in loop is then used to loop through this array and create list items.

Rather than going through each line, I'm going to show you the finished function. The comments give an indication of what's happening at each stage:

```
function displayAccesskeys() {
  if (!document.getElementsByTagName || !document.createElement ||
➡!document.createTextNode) return false;
// get all the links in the document
  var links = document.getElementsByTagName("a");
// create an array to store the access keys
  var akeys = new Array();
// loop through the links
  for (var i=0; i<links.length; i++) {
    var current_link = links[i];
// if there is no accesskey attribute, continue the loop
    if (!current_link.getAttribute("accesskey")) continue;
// get the value of the accesskey
    var key = current_link.getAttribute("accesskey");
// get the value of the link text
    var text = current_link.lastChild.nodeValue;
// add them to the array
    akeys[key] = text;
  }
// create the list
  var list = document.createElement("ul");
// loop through the access keys
  for (key in akeys) {
    var text = akeys[key];
//  create the string to put in the list item
    var str = key + ": "+text;
// create the list item
    var item = document.createElement("li");
    var item_text = document.createTextNode(str);
    item.appendChild(item_text);
// add the list item to the list
    list.appendChild(item);
  }
// create a headline
  var header = document.createElement("h3");
  var header_text = document.createTextNode("Accesskeys");
  header.appendChild(header_text);
// add the headline to the body
```

8

```
  document.body.appendChild(header);
// add the list to the body
  document.body.appendChild(list);
}
addLoadEvent(displayAccesskeys);
```

Reference the `displayAccesskeys.js` file with a new set of `<script>` tags in `explanation.html`:

```
<script type="text/javascript"
src="scripts/displayAccesskeys.js"></script>
```

Load `explanation.html` in a web browser to see the newly created list of access keys.

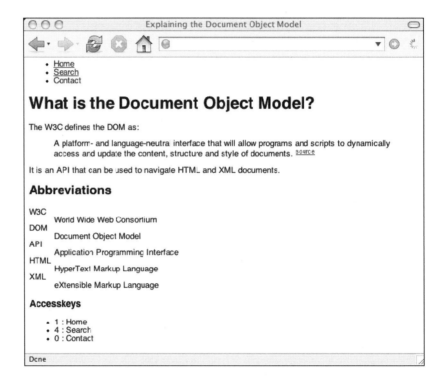

Summary

In the course of this chapter, you've created a number of useful DOM scripts that you can attach to just about any web page. They all perform different tasks, but the underlying principle is the same for each one. The JavaScript functions examine the document structure, extract information from it, and then insert that information back into the document in a clear and meaningful way.

These functions can improve the clarity and usability of web pages:

- Displaying a definition list of abbreviations used in a document.
- Linking to the source of quoted texts.
- Displaying a list of access keys used in a document.

You can alter these scripts if you like. Instead of displaying the source of quoted text with each blockquote, you could display them all as a list at the end of the document, just like footnotes. Alternatively, you could indicate what accesskey has been assigned to a link by appending the accesskey directly to the link text.

You could write whole new scripts. You could create a table of contents for a document. Loop through all the h1 or h2 elements in a document and put them into a list. Attach that list to the start of the document. You could even make each item in the list an internal link to the corresponding header.

You can create useful scripts like these using just a handful of DOM methods and properties. Having well-structured markup is an important prerequisite when you are enhancing content with DOM scripts.

These are the most useful methods for retrieving information from a document:

- getElementById
- getElementsByTagName
- getAttribute

These are the most useful methods for attaching information to a document:

- createElement
- createTextNode
- appendChild
- insertBefore
- setAttribute

By combining those methods, you can create very powerful DOM scripts.

Always remember to use JavaScript to enhance the content of your documents rather than creating any core content directly with the DOM.

What's next?

So far, you've been using JavaScript and the Document Object Model to manipulate or create markup. In the next chapter, you're going to see a whole new side to the DOM. I'm going to show you how you can use the DOM to manipulate styles, such as colors, fonts, and so on.

Not only can the DOM alter the structure of a web page, it can update the CSS attached to elements in the page.

9 CSS-DOM

What this chapter covers:

- Introducing the style property
- How to retrieve style information
- How to change styles

In this chapter, the presentation layer and the behavior layer will meet head-on. You'll see how the DOM can be used to get and set styles by reading and writing CSS.

Three sheets to the Web

Content on the Web can be wrapped up in three successive layers that are readable by web browsers:

- Structure
- Presentation
- Behavior

Structure

First and foremost, the **structural layer** is created with a markup language, such as HTML or XHTML. The **tags**, or words contained in angle brackets, describe the semantic meaning of content. For example, the <p> tag conveys the information, "This content is a paragraph." But the tag doesn't include any information about how the content should be displayed:

```
<p>An example of a paragraph</p>
```

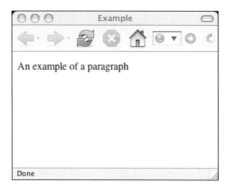

Presentation

The presentation layer, achieved with Cascading Style Sheets, describes how the content should be displayed. You can use CSS to declare, "Paragraphs should be colored grey and use Arial or some other sans-serif font":

```
p {
  color: grey;
  font-family: "Arial", sans-serif;
}
```

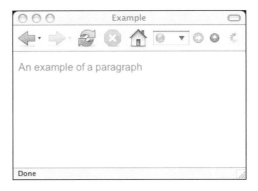

Behavior

Finally, the behavior layer describes how the content should react to events. This is where JavaScript and the DOM rule the roost. Using the DOM, you can specify, "When the user clicks on a paragraph, display an alert dialog":

```
var paras = document.getElementsByTagName("p");
for (var i=0; i<paras.length; i++) {
  paras[i].onclick = function() {
    alert("You clicked on a paragraph.");
  }
}
```

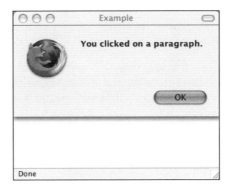

Presentation and behavior are always present, even if you don't give any specific instructions. Web browsers will apply their own default styles and event handlers. Browsers will apply margins to paragraph elements. Many browsers will display the contents of title attributes as tool tips when the user hovers over an element.

Separation

A good rule of thumb in any design discipline is to use the right tool for the task at hand. For web design, that means:

- Use (X)HTML to structure your documents.
- Use CSS to attach presentational information.
- Use DOM Scripting to apply behavioral instructions.

However, there is a certain amount of potential crossover between these three technologies. You've already seen one example of this. Using the DOM, you can alter the structure of a web page. Methods like createElement and appendChild allow you to create and add markup on the fly.

Another example of technologies crossing over can be found in CSS. Pseudo-classes like :hover and :focus allow you to change the appearance of elements based on user-triggered events. Changing the appearance of elements certainly belongs in the presentation layer, but reacting to user-triggered events is part of the behavior layer. This is a situation where presentation and behavior overlap, creating a grey area.

It's true that CSS are stepping on the DOM's toes with pseudo-classes. But the Document Object Model can step right back. You can use the DOM to attach presentational information to elements.

The style property

Every element in a document is an object. Every one of these objects has a whole collection of properties. Some properties contain information about the element's position in the node tree. Properties like parentNode, nextSibling, previousSibling, childNodes, firstChild, and lastChild all supply information about related nodes in the document.

Other properties, like nodeType and nodeName, contain information about the element itself. Querying the nodeName property of an element will return a string like "p".

There's another property called **style**. Every element node has this property. It contains information about the styles attached to the element. Querying this property doesn't return a simple string; it returns an object. Style information is stored as properties of this style object:

```
element.style.property
```

Here's an example of a paragraph with some inline styling attached:

```
<p id="example" style="color: grey; font-family: 'Arial',sans-serif;">
An example of a paragraph
</p>
```

Using the style property, you can retrieve this stylistic information.

First of all, you need to be able to reference the element. I've given the paragraph a unique id value of "example". Pass this id to the getElementById method. Assign a variable, para, so that you have a handle on the element that's easy to reference:

```
var para = document.getElementById("example");
```

Before retrieving any information about the presentation of this element, I want to show you that the style property is in fact an object. You can use the typeof keyword to retrieve this information. Compare the results of applying typeof to a property like nodeName and applying typeof to the style property.

Write out this XHTML and save the file. Call it example.html. Then load it in a web browser:

```
<!DOCTYPE html PUBLIC "-//W3C//DTD XHTML 1.1//EN"
"http://www.w3.org/TR/xhtml11/DTD/xhtml11.dtd">
<html xmlns="http://www.w3.org/1999/xhtml" xml:lang="en">
<head>
  <meta http-equiv="content-type" content="text/html; charset=utf-8" />
  <title>Example</title>
  <script type="text/javascript">
window.onload = function() {
  var para = document.getElementById("example");
  alert(typeof para.nodeName);
  alert(typeof para.style);
}
  </script>
</head>
<body>
  <p id="example" style="color: grey; font-family:
➥ 'Arial',sans-serif;">
An example of a paragraph
  </p>
</body>
</html>
```

The first alert statement returns "string". The nodeName property is a string:

181

On the other hand, the second alert statement returns "object". The style property is an object:

So, not only is every element an object, every element has a property called style, which is also an object.

Getting styles

You can retrieve the styles attached to para. To find out what color has been applied to an element, use the color property of the style object:

element.style.color

Here's an alert statement that will give the color property of the style object, which is a property of the para element:

alert("The color is " + **para.style.color**);

The color property of this element's style property is grey:

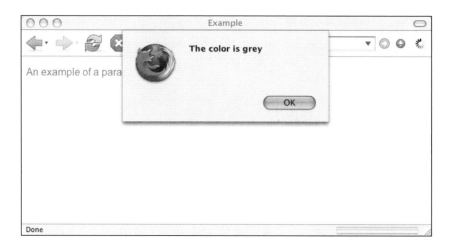

The other property that has been set with CSS is "font-family". This is retrieved in a slightly different way from color. You can't simply query "font-family" as a property of style. The dash between the word "font" and "family" is the same character as the subtraction operator. JavaScript will interpret this as a minus sign. You will get an error if you try to retrieve a property called "font-family":

    element.style.font-family

JavaScript will look at everything up to the minus sign as, "The font property of the style property of the element." It will then attempt to subtract a variable called family. That wasn't your intention at all!

Operators like the minus sign and the plus sign are reserved characters that can't be used in function names or variable names. That means they also can't be used for the names of methods or properties (remember that methods and properties are really just functions and variables attached to an object).

The DOM solves this problem by camel-casing style properties that have more than one word. The CSS property "font-family" becomes the DOM property fontFamily:

    element.style.fontFamily

Write an alert statement in example.html to retrieve the fontFamily property of the style property of the para element:

```
<!DOCTYPE html PUBLIC "-//W3C//DTD XHTML 1.1//EN"
"http://www.w3.org/TR/xhtml11/DTD/xhtml11.dtd">
<html xmlns="http://www.w3.org/1999/xhtml" xml:lang="en">
<head>
  <meta http-equiv="content-type" content="text/html; charset=utf-8" />
  <title>Example</title>
  <script type="text/javascript">
window.onload = function() {
  var para = document.getElementById("example");
  alert("The font family is " + para.style.fontFamily);
}
  </script>
</head>
<body>
  <p id="example" style="color: grey;
➥ font-family: 'Arial',sans-serif;">
An example of a paragraph
  </p>
</body>
</html>
```

Reload example.html in a web browser:

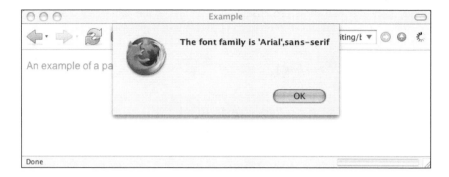

The value of the DOM fontFamily property is the same as the CSS "font-family" property. In this case, it's

    'Arial',sans-serif

The camel-casing convention applies to just about any CSS property that contains one or more dashes. The CSS property "background-color" becomes the DOM property backgroundColor. The CSS property "font-weight" is fontWeight in the DOM. The DOM property marginTopWidth is equivalent to "margin-top-width" in CSS.

Style properties aren't always returned with the same measurements and units with which they were set.

In the example paragraph, the CSS "color" property has been set with the word "grey". The DOM color property returns a value of "grey". Edit the paragraph so that the CSS "color" property is set with the hexadecimal value #999999:

    <p id="example" style="**color: #999999;** font-family: 'Arial',sans-serif">

Now edit the JavaScript so that the DOM color property is output in an alert statement:

    alert("The color is " + **para.style.color**);

In some browsers, the color property will be returned in RGB (Red Green Blue): 153,153,153:

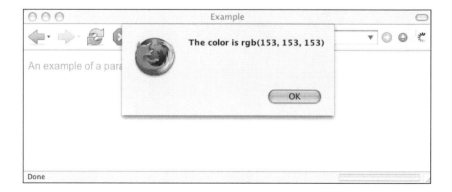

This is an exceptional circumstance. Usually values are returned in the same units with which they are set. If you set the CSS "font-size" property in ems, the corresponding DOM fontSize property will also be in ems:

```
<!DOCTYPE html PUBLIC "-//W3C//DTD XHTML 1.1//EN"
"http://www.w3.org/TR/xhtml11/DTD/xhtml11.dtd">
<html xmlns="http://www.w3.org/1999/xhtml" xml:lang="en">
<head>
  <meta http-equiv="content-type" content="text/html; charset=utf-8" />
  <title>Example</title>
  <script type="text/javascript">
window.onload = function() {
  var para = document.getElementById("example");
  alert("The font size is " + para.style.fontSize);
}
  </script>
</head>
<body>
  <p id="example" style="color: grey; font-family: 'Arial',sans-serif;
➡ font-size: 1em;">
An example of a paragraph
  </p>
</body>
</html>
```

Here, the fontSize property has been set using the em unit:

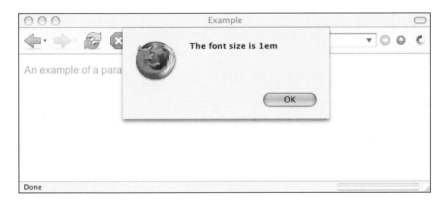

If an element's CSS "font-size" property has a value of "1em", the DOM fontSize property will return a value of "1em". If "12px" is applied with CSS, the DOM will return "12px".

Using CSS shorthand properties, you can combine a number of styles into one declaration. If you declare "font: 12px 'Arial',sans-serif", the CSS "font-size" property is set to "12px" and the CSS "font-family" will have a value of "'Arial',sans-serif":

```
<p id="example" style="color: grey; font: 12px 'Arial',sans-serif;">
```

The DOM is able to parse shorthand properties like "font". If you query the fontSize property, you will get a value of "12px":

```
alert("The font size is " + para.style.fontSize);
```

Here, the fontSize property has been set using pixels:

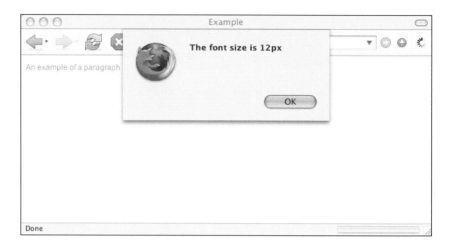

Inline only

There's a big caveat to retrieving stylistic information with the style property.

The style property only returns inline style information. If you apply styling information by inserting style attributes into your markup, you can query that information using the DOM style property:

```
<p id="example" style="color: grey; font: 12px 'Arial',sans-serif;">
```

This is not a very good way of applying styles. Presentational information is mixed in with structure. It's much better to apply styles in an external style sheet:

```
p#example {
  color: grey;
  font: 12px 'Arial', sans-serif;
}
```

Save that CSS in a file called styles.css. Now update example.html, removing the inline styling to leave the following instead:

```
<p id="example">
An example of a paragraph
</p>
```

Add a link element to the head of example.html, pointing to the styles.css file:

```
<link rel="stylesheet" type="text/css" media="screen"
➥ href="styles.css" />
```

The style information is applied to the markup, just as before. But the linked styles, unlike those assigned in a style attribute, won't be picked up by the DOM style property:

```
alert("The font size is " + para.style.fontSize);
```

The DOM style property doesn't retrieve styles declared externally:

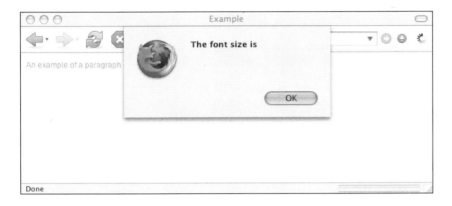

You'll see the same result (or lack thereof) if you add style information between <style> tags in the head of example.html:

```
<style type="text/css">
  p#example {
    color: grey;
    font: 12px 'Arial', sans-serif;
  }
</style>
```

The DOM style property won't pick up that information.

The style object doesn't include stylistic information that has been declared in an external style sheet. It also doesn't include stylistic information that has been declared in the head of a document.

The style object does pick up stylistic information that has been declared inline using the style attribute. But this is of little practical use because styles should be applied separately from the markup.

At this point, you might be thinking that using the DOM to manipulate CSS seems next to useless. However, there is one other situation where the DOM style object correctly reflects stylistic information that you have applied. If you apply styles using the DOM, you will be able to retrieve those styles.

9

Setting styles

Many DOM properties are read-only. That means you can use them to retrieve information, but you can't use them to set or update information. Properties like previousSibling, nextSibling, parentNode, firstChild, and lastChild are invaluable for gathering information about an element's position in the document's node tree, but they can't be used to update information.

The properties of the style object, on the other hand, are read/write. That means you can use an element's style property to retrieve information, and you can also use it to update information. You can do this using the assignment operator: the equals sign:

```
element.style.property = value
```

The value of a style property is always a string. Update the example.html file with some JavaScript that overrides the inline CSS. Set the color property of para to the string "black":

```
<!DOCTYPE html PUBLIC "-//W3C//DTD XHTML 1.1//EN"
"http://www.w3.org/TR/xhtml11/DTD/xhtml11.dtd">
<html xmlns="http://www.w3.org/1999/xhtml" xml:lang="en">
<head>
  <meta http-equiv="content-type" content="text/html; charset=utf-8" />
  <title>Example</title>
  <script type="text/javascript">
window.onload = function() {
  var para = document.getElementById("example");
  para.style.color = "black";
}
  </script>
</head>
<body>
  <p id="example" style="color: grey;
➥ font-family: 'Arial',sans-serif;">
An example of a paragraph
  </p>
</body>
</html>
```

The color property has been changed to "black":

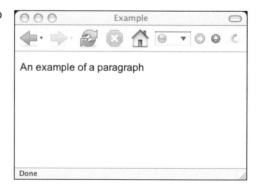

The value must be placed within quotes. You can use either double quotes or single quotes, whichever you prefer:

```
para.style.color = 'black';
```

If you don't use quotes, JavaScript will assume that the value is a variable:

```
para.style.color = black;
```

If you haven't defined a variable called black, the code won't work.

You can set any style property using the assignment operator. You can even use shorthand properties like font:

```
para.style.font = "2em 'Times',serif";
```

This will set the fontSize property to "2em" and the fontFamily property to "'Times',serif":

Setting styles is quite straightforward. I've shown you how. But perhaps the more important question is, "Why?"

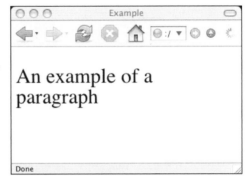

Knowing when to use DOM styling

You've seen how easy it is to set styles using the DOM. But just because you can do something doesn't mean you should. Nine times out of ten, you should be using CSS to declare styles. Just as you should never use the DOM to create important content, you also shouldn't use the DOM to set the majority of styles for a document.

Occasionally however, you can use the DOM to add some small stylistic enhancements to documents where it would be unwieldy to use CSS.

Styling elements in the node tree

CSS can be broadly used in three different ways to apply styles. You can apply styles to all occurrences of a particular element, such as paragraphs:

```
p {
  font-size: 1em;
}
```

You can apply styles to all elements that have a particular class attribute:

```
.fineprint {
  font-size: .8em;
}
```

You can apply styles to an element with a unique id attribute:

```
#intro {
  font-size: 1.2em;
}
```

At the moment, you can't use CSS to apply styles to an element based on its position in the document's node tree. For instance, you can't say, "Apply the following styles to the next sibling of all h1 elements."

The DOM, on the other hand, makes it quite easy to target elements based on their familial relationships with other elements. Using the DOM, you could quite easily find all the h1 elements in a document and then find out what element immediately follows each h1 and apply styles specifically to those elements.

First of all, get all the h1 elements using getElementsByTagName:

```
var headers = document.getElementsByTagName("h1");
```

Loop through all the elements in the node set:

```
for (var i=0; i<headers.length; i++) {
```

You can find the next node in the document using nextSibling:

headers[i].nextSibling

But in this case you actually want to find not just the next node, but specifically the next element node. This is easily done using a function called getNextElement:

```
function getNextElement(node) {
  if(node.nodeType == 1) {
    return node;
  }
  if (node.nextSibling) {
    return getNextElement(node.nextSibling);
  }
  return null;
}
```

Pass this function the nextSibling node of an h1 element as the argument. Assign the result to a variable called elem:

```
var elem = getNextElement(headers[i].nextSibling);
```

Now you can style this element any way you want:

```
elem.style.fontWeight = "bold";
elem.style.fontSize = "1.2em";
```

Wrap the whole thing up in a function called styleHeaderSiblings. Be sure to throw in a test to make sure that the browser understands the DOM methods being used:

```
function styleHeaderSiblings() {
  if (!document.getElementsByTagName) return false;
  var headers = document.getElementsByTagName("h1");
  for (var i=0; i<headers.length; i++) {
    var elem = getNextElement(headers[i].nextSibling);
    elem.style.fontWeight = "bold";
    elem.style.fontSize = "1.2em";
  }
}
function getNextElement(node) {
  if(node.nodeType == 1) {
    return node;
  }
  if (node.nextSibling) {
    return getNextElement(node.nextSibling);
  }
  return null;
}
```

You can call the function using the window.onload event:

```
window.onload = styleHeaderSiblings;
```

Better yet, use the addLoadEvent function so that you can always add more functions to the same event:

```
addLoadEvent(styleHeaderSiblings);
```

Here's the addLoadEvent function, which you can store in an external file:

```
function addLoadEvent(func) {
  var oldonload = window.onload;
  if (typeof window.onload != 'function') {
    window.onload = func;
  } else {
    window.onload = function() {
      oldonload();
      func();
    }
  }
}
```

9

To see the styleHeaderSiblings function in action, write a document that uses level one headings:

```
<!DOCTYPE html PUBLIC "-//W3C//DTD XHTML 1.1//EN"
  "http://www.w3.org/TR/xhtml11/DTD/xhtml11.dtd">
<html xmlns="http://www.w3.org/1999/xhtml" xml:lang="en">
<head>
  <meta http-equiv="content-type" content="text/html; charset=utf-8" />
  <title>Man bites dog</title>
</head>
<body>
  <h1>Hold the front page</h1>
  <p>This first paragraph leads you in.</p>
  <p>Now you get the nitty-gritty of the story.</p>
  <p>The most important information is delivered first.</p>
  <h1>Extra! Extra!</h1>
  <p>Further developments are unfolding.</p>
  <p>You can read all about it here.</p>
</body>
</html>
```

Save this document as story.html:

Create a folder called scripts where you can put your JavaScript files. Then, write a file for the addLoadEvent function and place it in this folder. Call it addLoadEvent.js. Write the styleHeaderSiblings function to a file called styleHeaderSiblings.js and place it in the same folder.

Insert <script> tags into the head of story.html to reference your JavaScript files:

```
<script type="text/javascript" src="scripts/addLoadEvent.js">
</script>
```

```
<script type="text/javascript" src="scripts/styleHeaderSiblings.js">
</script>
```

Load story.html in a web browser to see the results of the DOM-generated styles. The element immediately following every h1 has been styled:

Ideally, this kind of styling should be handled by CSS alone. In reality, that isn't always practical. In this case, you would have to add a class attribute to every element following a level one heading. In a situation where you are regularly editing and updating your content, that can quickly become tiresome. If you are using a Content Management System (CMS) to handle your content, it may not be possible to add classes or other style information to individual parts of the content.

Interestingly, this kind of node targeting is possible in CSS2, the current draft of the CSS specification. Pseudo-classes like :first-child and :last-child are part of the specs. For now, there is limited or no support for these pseudo-classes. In the meantime, you can use the DOM to plug the gaps between current and future CSS support.

Repetitive styling

Let's say you have a list of dates and places. It could be a list of concert dates or an itinerary for a road trip. In any case, there is a direct relationship between each date and place. This is tabular data. The ideal tag for marking up this data is the <table> tag.

> If you're using CSS to lay out your web pages, don't fall into the trap of thinking that all tables are bad. Using tables for layout isn't a good idea. But you should definitely use tables to display tabular data.

Here's how your markup might look:

```
<!DOCTYPE html PUBLIC "-//W3C//DTD XHTML 1.1//EN"
"http://www.w3.org/TR/xhtml11/DTD/xhtml11.dtd">
<html xmlns="http://www.w3.org/1999/xhtml" xml:lang="en">
<head>
  <meta http-equiv="content-type" content="text/html; charset=utf-8" />
  <title>Cities</title>
</head>
<body>
  <table>
    <caption>Itinerary</caption>
    <thead>
    <tr>
      <th>When</th>
      <th>Where</th>
    </tr>
    </thead>
    <tbody>
    <tr>
      <td>June 9th</td>
      <td>Portland, <abbr title="Oregon">OR</abbr></td>
    </tr>
    <tr>
      <td>June 10th</td>
      <td>Seattle, <abbr title="Washington">WA</abbr></td>
    </tr>
    <tr>
      <td>June 12th</td>
      <td>Sacramento, <abbr title="California">CA</abbr></td>
    </tr>
    </tbody>
  </table>
</body>
</html>
```

Save this as `itinerary.html`. If you load this file in a web browser, you will see a perfectly functional, but somewhat dull, table of information:

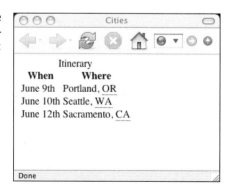

Write a style sheet so that the data is presented in a more readable format:

```css
body {
  font-family: "Helvetica","Arial",sans-serif;
  background-color: #fff;
  color: #000;
}
table {
  margin: auto;
  border: 1px solid #699;
}
caption {
  margin: auto;
  padding: .2em;
  font-size: 1.2em;
  font-weight: bold;
}
th {
  font-weight: normal;
  font-style: italic;
  text-align: left;
  border: 1px dotted #699;
  background-color: #9cc;
  color: #000;
}
th,td {
  width: 10em;
  padding: .5em;
}
```

Save this file as format.css and place it in a folder called styles. Add a link in the head of itinerary.html pointing to this file:

```html
<link rel="stylesheet" type="text/css" media="screen"
➥ href="styles/format.css" />
```

Refresh itinerary.html in a web browser to see the effects of the CSS:

9

A common technique for making table rows more readable is to alternate the background colors. The resulting striped effect helps to separate individual rows. This can be done by applying styles to every second row. In the case of itinerary.html, this could be easily done by assigning a class attribute to each odd or even row. However, this isn't very convenient, especially for larger tables—if a row is added to or removed from the middle of the table, you would have to painstakingly update the class attributes by hand.

Using CSS, there's no easy way of saying, "Apply a style to every second item in this list." JavaScript, on the other hand, is very good at handling repetitive tasks. You can easily loop through a long list using a while or for loop.

You can write a function to stripe your tables by applying styles to every second row:

1. Get all the table elements in the document.

2. For each table, create a variable called odd set to false.

3. Loop through all the rows in the table.

4. If odd is true, apply styles and change odd to false.

5. If odd is false, don't apply styles but change odd to true.

Call the function stripeTables. The function doesn't need to take any arguments, so the parentheses after the function name will be empty. Don't forget to start your function by testing the DOM compliance of the browser:

```
function stripeTables() {
  if (!document.getElementsByTagName) return false;
  var tables = document.getElementsByTagName("table");
  for (var i=0; i<tables.length; i++) {
    var odd = false;
    var rows = tables[i].getElementsByTagName("tr");
    for (var j=0; j<rows.length; j++) {
      if (odd == true) {
        rows[j].style.backgroundColor = "#ffc";
        odd = false;
      } else {
        odd = true;
      }
    }
  }
}
```

Run the function when the page loads. The best way to do this is using the addLoadEvent function again:

```
addLoadEvent(stripeTables);
```

Save the JavaScript to a file called stripeTables.js in a folder called scripts, together with the addLoadEvent.js file.

In the head of itinerary.html, add <script> tags to include both JavaScript files:

```
<script type="text/javascript" src="scripts/addLoadEvent.js">
</script>
<script type="text/javascript" src="scripts/stripeTables.js">
</script>
```

Load itinerary.html in a web browser. Every second row in the table has been styled with a background color:

Incidentally, you could also use the displayAbbreviations function from the previous chapter for this document. Drop the displayAbbreviations.js file into the scripts folder and add one more set of <script> tags to itinerary.html. Refresh the page in a web browser to see the generated definition list:

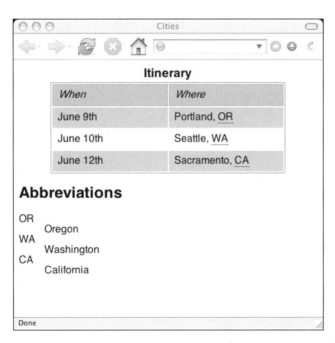

Responding to events

Wherever possible, it's best to use CSS to set styles for a document. That said, you've just seen some situations where CSS could be unwieldy or tedious to deploy. In those situations, the DOM can help.

It's not always easy to know when to use CSS and when to use DOM Scripting to set styles. The biggest grey area concerns the changing of styles based on events.

CSS provides pseudo-classes like :hover that allow you to change the styles of elements based on their state. The DOM also responds to changes of state using event handlers like onmouseover. It's difficult to know when to use :hover and when to use onmouseover.

The simplest solution is to follow the path of least resistance. If you simply want to change the color of your links when they're moused over, then you should definitely use CSS:

```
a:hover {
  color: #c60;
}
```

The :hover pseudo-class is widely supported, at least when it is used for styling links. If you want to style any other elements when they are moused over, browser support isn't quite so widespread.

Take the example of the table in itinerary.html. If you wanted to highlight a row when it is moused over, you could use CSS:

```
tr:hover {
  font-weight: bold;
}
```

In theory, this should bold the text in any table row whenever it is moused over. In practice, this will only work in certain browsers.

In situations like that, the DOM can be used to level the playing field. While support for CSS pseudo-classes remains patchy, the DOM is well supported in most modern browsers. Until CSS support improves, it makes sense to use the DOM to apply styles based on events.

Here's a short function called highlightRows that will bold text whenever a table row is moused over:

```
function highlightRows() {
  if(!document.getElementsByTagName) return false;
  var rows = document.getElementsByTagName("tr");
  for (var i=0; i<rows.length; i++) {
    rows[i].onmouseover = function() {
      this.style.fontWeight = "bold";
    }
    rows[i].onmouseout = function() {
      this.style.fontWeight = "normal";
    }
```

```
    }
}
addLoadEvent(highlightRows);
```

Save it to a file called highlightRows.js in the scripts folder. Add another set of <script> tags to the head of itinerary.html:

```
<script type="text/javascript" src="scripts/highlightRows.js">
</script>
```

Refresh itinerary.html in a web browser. Now hover over one of the rows in the table. The text will turn bold:

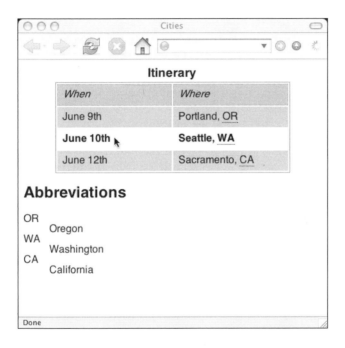

In these kind of situations, you'll need to make the decision whether to use a purely CSS solution or whether to use the DOM to set styles. You'll need to consider factors like:

- What's the simplest solution to this problem?
- Which solution has greater browser support?

To make an informed decision, you'll need to be well versed in both CSS and DOM Scripting. If all you have is a hammer, then everything looks like a nail. If you only feel comfortable using CSS, then you might choose a CSS solution where JavaScript would actually be better. On the other hand, if you only know DOM Scripting, then you may find yourself writing functions to accomplish tasks that are quicker and easier to implement with CSS.

If you want to apply presentation to elements, use CSS. If you want to apply behavior to elements, use the DOM. If you want to apply presentation based on behavior, use your best judgment. There is no "one size fits all" solution.

className

In the examples you've seen so far in this chapter, the DOM has been used to explicitly set stylistic information. This is less than ideal because the behavior layer is doing the work of the presentation layer. If you change your mind about the styles being set, you'll need to dig down into your JavaScript functions and update the relevant statements. It would be better if you could make those kinds of changes in your style sheets.

There's a simple solution. Instead of changing the presentation of an element directly with the DOM, use JavaScript to update the class attribute attached to that element.

Take a look at how the styleHeaderSiblings function is adding stylistic information:

```
function styleHeaderSiblings() {
  if (!document.getElementsByTagName) return false;
  var headers = document.getElementsByTagName("h1");
  for (var i=0; i<headers.length; i++) {
    var elem = getNextElement(headers[i].nextSibling);
    elem.style.fontWeight = "bold";
    elem.style.fontSize = "1.2em";
  }
}
```

If you ever decided that the elements following level one headings should have a CSS font-size value of "1.4em" instead of "1.2em", you would have to update the styleHeaderSiblings function.

It would be better if your style sheet had a declaration for a class named something like "intro":

```
.intro {
  font-weight: bold;
  font-size: 1.2em;
}
```

Now all that the styleHeaderSiblings function needs to do is to apply this class to the element immediately following a level one heading.

You can do this using the setAttribute method.

```
elem.setAttribute("class","intro");
```

An easier solution is to update a property called **className**. This is a read/write property of any element node.

You can use className to get the class of an element.

element.className

You can use the assignment operator to set the class of an element.

element.className = value

This is how the styleHeaderSiblings function looks when you use className instead of setting styles directly with the style property:

```
function styleHeaderSiblings() {
  if (!document.getElementsByTagName) return false;
  var headers = document.getElementsByTagName("h1");
  for (var i=0; i<headers.length; i++) {
    var elem = getNextElement(headers[i].nextSibling);
    elem.className = "intro";
  }
}
```

Now, whenever you want to update the presentation of elements that follow level one headings, you can do so by updating the style declarations for the "intro" class:

```
.intro {
  font-weight: bold;
  font-size: 1.4em;
}
```

There's just one drawback to this technique. If you assign a class using the className property, you will overwrite any classes that are already attached to that element:

```
<h1>Man bites dog</h1>
<p class="disclaimer">This is not a true story</p>
```

If you run the styleHeaderSiblings function on a document containing that piece of markup, the class attribute of the paragraph will be changed from "disclaimer" to "intro". What you really want to do is update the class attribute so that it reads "disclaimer intro". That way the styles for the "disclaimer" and "intro" classes will both be applied.

You can do this by concatenating a space and the name of the new class to the className property:

```
elem.className += " intro";
```

But you really only want to do this when there are existing classes. If there are no existing classes, you can just use the assignment operator with className.

Whenever you want to add a new class to an element, you can run through these steps:

1. Is the value of className null?

2. If so, assign the class value to the className property.

3. If not, concatenate a space and the class value to the className property.

9

You can encapsulate those steps in a function. Call the function addClass. It will need to take two arguments: the element to which you want to add the class and the name of the class you want to add. You can call these arguments element and value:

```
function addClass(element,value) {
  if (!element.className) {
    element.className = value;
  } else {
    newClassName = element.className;
    newClassName+= " ";
    newClassName+= value;
    element.className = newClassName;
  }
}
```

Call the addClass function from the styleHeaderSiblings function:

```
function styleHeaderSiblings() {
  if (!document.getElementsByTagName) return false;
  var headers = document.getElementsByTagName("h1");
  for (var i=0; i<headers.length; i++) {
    var elem = getNextElement(headers[i].nextSibling);
    addClass(elem,"intro");
  }
}
```

You could also update the stripeTables function. Right now, the background color of every second row in every table is being changed directly with JavaScript:

```
function stripeTables() {
  if (!document.getElementsByTagName) return false;
  var tables = document.getElementsByTagName("table");
  for (var i=0; i<tables.length; i++) {
    var odd = false;
    var rows = tables[i].getElementsByTagName("tr");
    for (var j=0; j<rows.length; j++) {
      if (odd == true) {
        rows[j].style.backgroundColor = "#ffc";
        odd = false;
      } else {
        odd = true;
      }
    }
  }
}
```

Update format.css with a new class named "odd":

```
.odd {
  background-color: #ffc;
}
```

Now use the addClass function from within stripeTables:

```
function stripeTables() {
  if (!document.getElementsByTagName) return false;
  var tables = document.getElementsByTagName("table");
  for (var i=0; i<tables.length; i++) {
    var odd = false;
    var rows = tables[i].getElementsByTagName("tr");
    for (var j=0; j<rows.length; j++) {
      if (odd == true) {
        addClass(rows[j],"odd");
        odd = false;
      } else {
        odd = true;
      }
    }
  }
}
```

The final result will be exactly the same as before. The difference is that now presentational information is being set using CSS rather than being set by the DOM. The JavaScript functions are updating the className property and the style property is left untouched. This ensures better separation between presentation and behavior.

Abstracting a function

All of your functions are working fine and you can leave them as they are. However, you can make some small changes that will make your functions easier to reuse in the future. The process of taking something very specific and turning it into something more general is called **abstraction**.

If you look at the styleHeaderSiblings function, you'll see that it is very specific to h1 elements. The className value of "intro" is also hard-coded into the function:

```
function styleHeaderSiblings() {
  if (!document.getElementsByTagName) return false;
  var headers = document.getElementsByTagName("h1");
  for (var i=0; i<headers.length; i++) {
    var elem = getNextElement(headers[i].nextSibling);
    addClass(elem,"intro");
  }
}
```

If you wanted to turn this into a more generic function, you could make those values into arguments. Call the new function styleElementSiblings and give it two arguments, tag and theclass:

```
function styleElementSiblings(tag,theclass)
```

9

Now, replace the string "h1" with the argument tag and replace the string "intro" with the argument theclass. You might also want to change the name of the variable headers to something more descriptive, like elems:

```
function styleElementSiblings(tag,theclass) {
  if (!document.getElementsByTagName) return false;
  var elems = document.getElementsByTagName(tag);
  for (var i=0; i<elems.length; i++) {
    var elem = getNextElement(elems[i].nextSibling);
    addClass(elem,theclass);
  }
}
```

You can achieve the same effect as before by passing this function the values "h1" and "intro":

```
styleElementSiblings("h1","intro");
```

Whenever you spot a chance to abstract a function like this, it's usually a good idea to do so. You may find yourself needing to accomplish a similar effect to styleHeaderSiblings, but on a different element or with a different class. That's when a generic function like styleElementSiblings will come in useful.

What's next?

In this chapter, you've seen a whole new side to the Document Object Model. You have previously been introduced to methods and properties that belonged either to the DOM Core or to HTML-DOM. This chapter introduced CSS-DOM, which involves getting and setting properties of the style object. The style object is itself a property of every element node in a document.

The biggest limitation to using the style property is that it doesn't pick up styles that have been set in an external style sheet. But you can still use style to alter the presentation of elements. This can be useful in situations where it would be too unwieldy or unpredictable to use CSS. Wherever possible, it's best to update the className property rather than updating properties of the style object directly.

You've seen a few short examples of CSS-DOM in action:

- Styling an element based on its position in the node tree (styleHeaderSiblings)
- Styling elements by looping through a node set (stripeTables)
- Styling an element in response to an event (highlightRows)

These are situations where JavaScript takes over from CSS. This is either because CSS can't target elements in the same way, or because CSS support for that level of targeting isn't yet widely supported. In the future, it may be possible to discard a lot of this kind of DOM Scripting in favor of advanced CSS techniques.

There's one area where CSS is unlikely to ever be in competition with the DOM. JavaScript can repeat actions at regular intervals. By making incremental changes to style information over time, you can create effects that would be impossible using just CSS.

In the next chapter, you're going to see an example of that. You will write a function that will update an element's position over time. Simply put, you're going to create animation.

9

10 ANIMATED SLIDESHOW

What this chapter covers:

- Defining animation
- Enhancing with animation
- Making movement smoother

In this chapter, you'll see one of the most dynamic applications of CSS-DOM: the ability to animate elements.

What is animation?

In the last chapter, I introduced the DOM's ability to update the styles attached to a document. Using JavaScript to add presentational information can save you time and effort but, for the most part, CSS remains the best tool for the job.

There's one area, however, where CSS can't help. If you want to change an element's style information over time, you'll need to use JavaScript. JavaScript allows you to execute functions at set intervals. This means that you can alter an element's style with the passage of time.

Animation is the perfect example of this kind of change. In a nutshell, animation involves changing an element's position over time.

Position

An element's position in the browser window is presentational information. As such, it is usually added using CSS. Here's an example of some CSS that set an element's position on the page:

```
element {
  position: absolute;
  top: 50px;
  left: 100px;
}
```

That will position the element 100 pixels from the left of the browser window and 50 pixels from the top. Here's the DOM equivalent of the same information:

```
element.style.position = "absolute";
element.style.left = "100px";
element.style.top = "50px";
```

Valid values for the position property are "static", "fixed", "relative", and "absolute". Elements have a position value of "static" by default, which simply means that they appear one after the other in the same sequence as they occur in the markup. The "relative" value is similar. The difference is that relatively positioned elements can be taken out of the regular flow of the document by applying the float property.

By applying a value of "absolute" to an element's position, you can place the element wherever you want in relation to its container. The container is usually the document itself. It doesn't matter where the element appears in the original markup, because its position will be determined by properties like top, left, right, and bottom. You can set any of those properties using pixels or percentages.

Setting an element's top property will place the element a specified distance from the top of the document. Alternatively, an element's bottom property will place it a specified distance from the bottom of the document. Likewise, left and right can be used to place the element a specified distance from the left and right edges of the document respectively. It's a good idea to use either top or bottom, but not both. Likewise with left and right.

Positioning an element in the document is relatively straightforward. Say you had an element like this:

```
<p id="message">Whee!</p>
```

You could set that element's position in JavaScript with a function like this:

```
function positionMessage() {
  if (!document.getElementById) return false;
  if (!document.getElementById("message")) return false;
  var elem = document.getElementById("message");
  elem.style.position = "absolute";
  elem.style.left = "50px";
  elem.style.top = "100px";
}
```

Calling the positionMessage function when the page loads will position the paragraph 50 pixels from the left and 100 pixels from the top of the browser window:

```
window.onload = positionMessage;
```

Better yet, use the addLoadEvent function:

```
function addLoadEvent(func) {
  var oldonload = window.onload;
  if (typeof window.onload != 'function') {
    window.onload = func;
  } else {
    window.onload = function() {
      oldonload();
      func();
    }
  }
}
addLoadEvent(positionMessage);
```

10

Here, the element has been positioned absolutely:

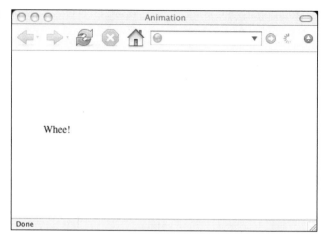

Updating an element's position is also quite easy. You just need to run a function that updates a style property like top or left:

```
function moveMessage() {
    if (!document.getElementById) return false;
    if (!document.getElementById("message")) return false;
    var elem = document.getElementById("message");
    elem.style.left = "200px";
}
```

But how do you activate that function? If you execute moveMessage when the page loads, the element's position will be updated instantaneously. The original positioning, as specified by positionMessage, will be overridden instantly:

```
addLoadEvent(positionMessage);
addLoadEvent(moveMessage);
```

Now the element's position has been changed:

The change in position is immediate. This isn't true animation. Animation involves changing an element's position over time.

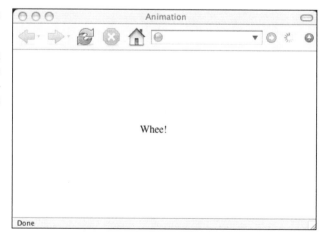

Time

The problem in this situation is that JavaScript is too efficient. Functions are executed one after another without any noticeable pause. To create animation, you need to create delays, which is what we will look at next.

setTimeout

The JavaScript function **setTimeout** allows you to execute a function after a specified amount of time has elapsed. It takes two arguments. The first argument is a string containing the function you want to execute. The second argument is the number of milliseconds that will elapse before the first argument is executed:

        setTimeout("function",interval)

It's a good idea to always assign a variable to this function:

        variable = setTimeout("function",interval)

You'll need to do this if you want to cancel the action that has been queued up. You can cancel a pending action using a function called clearTimeout. This function takes one argument, which is a variable that has been assigned to a setTimeout function:

        clearTimeout(variable)

I'm going to update the positionMessage function so that it calls moveMessage after five seconds (5,000 milliseconds):

```
function positionMessage() {
  if (!document.getElementById) return false;
  if (!document.getElementById("message")) return false;
  var elem = document.getElementById("message");
  elem.style.position = "absolute";
  elem.style.left = "50px";
  elem.style.top = "100px";
  movement = setTimeout("moveMessage()",5000);
}
```

The positionMessage function is called when the page loads:

        addLoadEvent(positionMessage);

At first, the message appears at its specified coordinates. After five seconds, the message jumps 150 pixels to the right.

If I wanted to cancel that action any time before the five seconds elapse, I could do so with this statement:

        clearTimeout(movement);

10

The movement variable refers to the setTimeout function defined in positionMessage. It's a global variable: it wasn't declared with the var keyword. This means the action can be cancelled outside of the positionMessage function.

Increments

Moving an element by 150 pixels after an interval of five seconds is a sort of animation, albeit a very primitive one. Effective animation uses incremental movement. Moving from the starting position to the final location should happen in a series of steps rather than one quick jump.

I'm going to update the moveMessage function so that movement occurs incrementally. Here's the logic behind the new function:

1. Get the element's current position.

2. If the element has reached its final destination, leave the function.

3. Otherwise, move the element closer to its destination.

4. Repeat from step 1 after a pause.

The first step is getting the element's current position. I can do this by querying properties of the element's style property. I want to find the left and top properties. I'm going to assign them to the variables xpos and ypos, respectively:

```
var xpos = elem.style.left;
var ypos = elem.style.top;
```

When the moveMessage function is called after the positionMessage function, xpos will have a value of "50px". The ypos variable will have a value of "100px". These values are strings, which presents me with a bit of a problem. The next step in the function involves arithmetical comparison operators. I need to work with numbers, not strings.

parseInt

The JavaScript function **parseInt** can extract numeric information from a string. If you pass it a string that begins with a number, it will return the number:

parseInt(string)

Here's an example:

```
parseInt("39 steps");
```

That will return the number 39.

The parseInt function will return whole numbers (integers). If you need to extract numbers with decimal places (floating-point numbers), there is a corresponding parseFloat function:

parseFloat(string)

I'll be dealing with integers in the moveMessage function so I'm going to use parseInt:

```
var xpos = parseInt(elem.style.left);
var ypos = parseInt(elem.style.top);
```

The parseInt function converts the string "50px" to the number 50. The string "100px" becomes the number 100. Now the xpos and ypos variables contain those numbers.

The next few steps in the moveMessage function require the use of lots of comparison operators.

The first comparison I want to make is to run a test for equality. I want to find out if xpos is equal to the final left position and if ypos is equal to the final top position. If they are, I'm going to exit the function. I can do this test by using the comparison operator, which consists of two equals signs:

> Remember, a single equals sign is used for assignment, not comparison.

```
if (xpos == 200 && ypos == 100) {
   return true;
}
```

Everything after this line will only be executed if the message element has not reached its final position.

I'm going to update the xpos and ypos numbers based on their relationship to the final position. I want to bring them both closer to the final coordinates.

If the value of xpos is less than the final left position, increase it by one:

```
if (xpos < 200) {
   xpos++;
}
```

If it's greater than the final left position, decrease it:

```
if (xpos > 200) {
   xpos--;
}
```

The same applies for the relationship between the ypos variable and the final top position:

```
if (ypos < 100) {
   ypos++;
}
if (ypos > 100) {
   ypos--;
}
```

10

You can see why I need xpos and ypos to be numbers rather than strings. I'm using the "less than" and "greater than" operators to compare numerical values and update the variables accordingly.

Now I want to apply the xpos and ypos variables to the style property of the element. I do this by adding the string "px" to their values and applying them to the left and top properties:

```
elem.style.left = xpos + "px";
elem.style.top = ypos + "px";
```

Finally, I want to repeat the whole function afresh after a slight pause (calling the same function from within itself like this is called **recursion**). I'll make the pause one hundredth of a second, which is ten milliseconds:

```
movement = setTimeout("moveMessage()",10);
```

The finished moveMessage function looks like this:

```
function moveMessage() {
  if (!document.getElementById) return false;
  if (!document.getElementById("message")) return false;
  var elem = document.getElementById("message");
  var xpos = parseInt(elem.style.left);
  var ypos = parseInt(elem.style.top);
  if (xpos == 200 && ypos == 100) {
    return true;
  }
  if (xpos < 200) {
    xpos++;
  }
  if (xpos > 200) {
    xpos--;
  }
  if (ypos < 100) {
    ypos++;
  }
  if (ypos > 100) {
    ypos--;
  }
  elem.style.left = xpos + "px";
  elem.style.top = ypos + "px";
  movement = setTimeout("moveMessage()",10);
}
```

The message moves across the screen, one pixel at a time. Once the top property is "100px" and the left property is "200px", the function stops. That's animation. It's pretty pointless, but it's animation nonetheless. We will be applying the same principles to something much more useful later on.

Abstraction

As it stands, the moveMessage function accomplishes a very specific task. It moves a specific element to a specific place, pausing for a specific amount of time between movements. All of that information is hardcoded into the function:

```
function moveMessage() {
  if (!document.getElementById) return false;
  if (!document.getElementById("message"))
return false;
  var elem = document.getElementById("message");
  var xpos = parseInt(elem.style.left);
  var ypos = parseInt(elem.style.top);
  if (xpos == 200 && ypos == 100) {
    return true;
  }
  if (xpos < 200) {
    xpos++;
  }
  if (xpos > 200) {
    xpos--;
  }
  if (ypos < 100) {
    ypos++;
  }
  if (ypos > 100) {
    ypos--;
  }
  elem.style.left = xpos + "px";
  elem.style.top = ypos + "px";
  movement = setTimeout("moveMessage()",10);
}
```

If all of those things were variables, the function would be a lot more flexible. By abstracting the moveMessage function, you can create something more portable and reusable.

Call your new function moveElement. Unlike moveMessage, this function will take a number of arguments. These are the things that you can vary each time you call the function:

1. The ID of the element you want to move

2. The left position to which you want to move the element

3. The top position to which you want to move the element

4. How long to wait between each movement

These arguments should all have descriptive names:

1. elementID

2. final_x

3. final_y

4. interval

10

Begin the moveElement function with these arguments:

```
function moveElement(elementID,final_x,final_y,interval) {
```

Substitute these for the values that were previously hardcoded into moveMessage. The moveMessage function began with these lines:

```
if (!document.getElementById) return false;
if (!document.getElementById("message")) return false;
var elem = document.getElementById("message");
```

Replace all the instances of getElementById("message") with getElementById(elementID):

```
if (!document.getElementById) return false;
if (!document.getElementById(elementID)) return false;
var elem = document.getElementById(elementID);
```

The variable elem now refers to whichever element you want to move.

The next step of the function remains the same. The left and top properties of the element are converted to numbers and assigned to the variables xpos and ypos respectively:

```
var xpos = parseInt(elem.style.left);
var ypos = parseInt(elem.style.top);
```

Next, check to see if the element has reached its final position. In moveMessage, these coordinates were the values 200 (for the left position) and 100 (for the top position):

```
if (xpos == 200 && ypos == 100) {
  return true;
}
```

In moveElement, these coordinates are provided by the arguments final_x and final_y:

```
if (xpos == final_x && ypos == final_y) {
  return true;
}
```

Update the values of the xpos and ypos variables. If xpos is less than the final left position, increase its value by one.

The final left position used to be hardcoded as 200:

```
if (xpos < 200) {
  xpos++;
}
```

Now the final left position is contained in the final_x argument:

```
if (xpos < final_x) {
  xpos++;
}
```

Likewise, if the value of xpos is greater than the final left position, decrease the value of xpos by one:

```
if (xpos > final_x) {
  xpos--;
}
```

Do the same for ypos. If its value is less than final_y, increase it by one. If it is greater than final_y, decrease it by one:

```
if (ypos < final_y) {
  ypos++;
}
if (ypos > final_y) {
  ypos--;
}
```

The next step remains the same. Update the left and top style properties of the element elem. Assign the values of xpos and ypos with the string "px" attached:

```
elem.style.left = xpos + "px";
elem.style.top = ypos + "px";
```

Finally, you want to call the function again after a suitable interval. In moveMessage, this was quite straightforward. The moveMessage function is called after ten milliseconds:

```
movement = setTimeout("moveMessage()",10);
```

In moveElement, it gets a little trickier. As well as calling the function again, you need to pass it the same arguments: elementID, final_x, final_y, and interval. The whole thing needs to be contained as a string:

```
"moveElement('"+elementID+"','"+final_x+","+final_y+","+interval+")"
```

That's a lot of concatenating! Rather than inserting that long string directly into the setTimeout function, assign the string to a variable called repeat.

```
var repeat =
➡ "moveElement('"+elementID+"','"+final_x+","+final_y+","+interval+")";
```

Now you can simply insert repeat as the first argument of the setTimeout function. The second argument is the length of the pause before the first argument is called. This used to be hardcoded as ten milliseconds. Now it's whatever value is contained by the variable interval:

```
movement = setTimeout(repeat,interval);
```

Close the function with a curly brace:

```
}
```

The finished moveElement function looks like this:

```
function moveElement(elementID,final_x,final_y,interval) {
  if (!document.getElementById) return false;
  if (!document.getElementById(elementID)) return false;
  var elem = document.getElementById(elementID);
  var xpos = parseInt(elem.style.left);
  var ypos = parseInt(elem.style.top);
  if (xpos == final_x && ypos == final_y) {
    return true;
  }
  if (xpos < final_x) {
    xpos++;
  }
  if (xpos > final_x) {
    xpos--;
  }
  if (ypos < final_y) {
    ypos++;
  }
  if (ypos > final_y) {
    ypos--;
  }
  elem.style.left = xpos + "px";
  elem.style.top = ypos + "px";
  var repeat =
➨ "moveElement('"+elementID+"','"+final_x+"','"+final_y+"','"+interval+")";
  movement = setTimeout(repeat,interval);
}
```

Save the moveElement function to a file called moveElement.js. Place this file in a folder called scripts, along with that old workhorse, addLoadEvent.js.

Let's take this function for a test drive.

Start by re-creating the previous example. Create a document called message.html, which contains a paragraph identified as "message":

```
<!DOCTYPE html PUBLIC "-//W3C//DTD XHTML 1.1//EN"
"http://www.w3.org/TR/xhtml11/DTD/xhtml11.dtd">
<html xmlns="http://www.w3.org/1999/xhtml" xml:lang="en">
<head>
  <meta http-equiv="content-type" content="text/html; charset=utf-8" />
  <title>Message</title>
</head>
<body>
  <p id="message">Whee!</p>
</body>
</html>
```

Before you can animate the message, you need to position it. Write another JavaScript file called positionMessage.js. At the end of the positionMessage function, call the moveElement function:

```
function positionMessage() {
  if (!document.getElementById) return false;
  if (!document.getElementById("message")) return false;
  var elem = document.getElementById("message");
  elem.style.position = "absolute";
  elem.style.left = "50px";
  elem.style.top = "100px";
  moveElement("message",200,100,10);
}
addLoadEvent(positionMessage);
```

You are passing the string "message" as the value of the elementID argument. The final_x argument is 200. The final_y argument is 100. The value of interval is 10.

Now you have three files in your scripts folder: addLoadEvent.js, positionMessage.js, and moveElement.js. Reference those files from message.html using <script> tags:

```
<!DOCTYPE html PUBLIC "-//W3C//DTD XHTML 1.1//EN"
"http://www.w3.org/TR/xhtml11/DTD/xhtml11.dtd">
<html xmlns="http://www.w3.org/1999/xhtml" xml:lang="en">
<head>
  <meta http-equiv="content-type" content="text/html; charset=utf-8" />
  <title>Message</title>
  <script type="text/javascript" src="scripts/addLoadEvent.js">
  </script>
  <script type="text/javascript" src="scripts/positionMessage.js">
  </script>
  <script type="text/javascript" src="scripts/moveElement.js">
  </script>
</head>
<body>
  <p id="message">Whee!</p>
</body>
</html>
```

Load message.html in a web browser to see the animation in action. The element moves horizontally across the screen:

10

So far, so good. The moveElement function is working exactly like the moveMessage function. You abstracted the function so that you could send it any arguments you like. By altering the values of final_x and final_y, you can change the direction of the animation. Altering the value of interval changes the speed of the animation:

```
function moveElement(elementID,final_x,final_y,interval)
```

Update the last line of the positionMessage function in positionMessage.js so that these three values are changed:

```
function positionMessage() {
  if (!document.getElementById) return false;
  if (!document.getElementById("message")) return false;
  var elem = document.getElementById("message");
  elem.style.position = "absolute";
  elem.style.left = "50px";
  elem.style.top = "100px";
  moveElement("message",125,25,20);
}
addLoadEvent(positionMessage);
```

Refresh message.html in a web browser to see the change. The element now moves diagonally and more slowly:

The other argument that you can change in moveElement is the value of elementID:

```
function moveElement(elementID,final_x,final_y,interval)
```

Add a new element to message.html. Give it an id attribute of "message2":

```
<!DOCTYPE html PUBLIC "-//W3C//DTD XHTML 1.1//EN"
"http://www.w3.org/TR/xhtml11/DTD/xhtml11.dtd">
<html xmlns="http://www.w3.org/1999/xhtml" xml:lang="en">
<head>
```

```
      <meta http-equiv="content-type" content="text/html; charset=utf-8" />
      <title>Message</title>
      <script type="text/javascript" src="scripts/addLoadEvent.js">
      </script>
      <script type="text/javascript" src="scripts/positionMessage.js">
      </script>
      <script type="text/javascript" src="scripts/moveElement.js"></script>
  </head>
  <body>
    <p id="message">Whee!</p>
    <p id="message2">Whoa!</p>
  </body>
  </html>
```

Now update `positionMessage.js`. Set the initial position of "message2" and call the
`moveElement` function again, this time passing it "message2" as the first argument:

```
      function positionMessage() {
        if (!document.getElementById) return false;
        if (!document.getElementById("message")) return false;
        var elem = document.getElementById("message");
        elem.style.position = "absolute";
        elem.style.left = "50px";
        elem.style.top = "100px";
        moveElement("message",125,25,20);
        if (!document.getElementById("message2")) return false;
        var elem = document.getElementById("message2");
        elem.style.position = "absolute";
        elem.style.left = "50px";
        elem.style.top = "50px";
        moveElement("message2",125,75,20);
      }
      addLoadEvent(positionMessage);
```

10

Reload `message.html` to see
the new animation. Both
elements move in different
directions at the same time.

The `moveElement` function is
doing all the work in both
cases. By simply changing
the arguments that you send
to the function, you can
reuse it as often as you like.
This is the great advantage
of using arguments instead
of hardcoding values.

221

Practical animation

With moveElement, you have a reusable function that you can use to move page elements in any direction. From a programming point of view, that's quite impressive. From a practical standpoint, it seems fairly pointless.

Arbitrarily animating elements in a web page is the ideal way to annoy your visitors. It's also frowned upon from an accessibility point of view. Checkpoint 7.2 of the W3C's Web Content Accessibility Guidelines states, "Until user agents allow users to freeze moving content, avoid movement in pages. [Priority 2] When a page includes moving content, provide a mechanism within a script or applet to allow users to freeze motion or updates."

The key issue here is one of user control. Animating a page element based on an action initiated by the user could potentially enhance a web page. I'd like to show one example of this kind of enhancement.

The situation

I have a web page that contains a list of links. When the user hovers over one of these links, I want to provide some kind of sneak preview of where the link will lead. I'd like to show an image.

The document is called list.html. Here's the markup:

```
<!DOCTYPE html PUBLIC "-//W3C//DTD XHTML 1.1//EN"
"http://www.w3.org/TR/xhtml11/DTD/xhtml11.dtd">
<html xmlns="http://www.w3.org/1999/xhtml" xml:lang="en">
<head>
  <meta http-equiv="content-type" content="text/html; charset=utf-8" />
  <title>Web Design</title>
</head>
<body>
  <h1>Web Design</h1>
  <p>These are the things you should know.</p>
  <ol id="linklist">
    <li>
      <a href="structure.html">Structure</a>
    </li>
    <li>
      <a href="presentation.html">Presentation</a>
    </li>
    <li>
      <a href="behavior.html">Behavior</a>
    </li>
  </ol>
</body>
</html>
```

Each link leads to a page covering a particular aspect of web design. The text within each link succinctly describes the content of the linked page:

As it stands, this document is perfectly fine. That said, showing a visual clue about the destination documents would be a nice touch.

In some ways, this situation is similar to that of the JavaScript image gallery. Both contain lists of links. In both cases, I want to show an image. The difference is that here, I want to show the image when an onmouseover event handler is triggered, instead of an onclick.

I could adapt the image gallery script. All I'd need to do is change the event handler for each link from onclick to onmouseover. That would work, but it wouldn't be very smooth. The first time that the user hovers over a link, the new image would be loaded. Even on a fast connection, this will take a little time. I want a more immediate response.

The solution

If I use a different image for the visual preview of each link, there will be delays in swapping out the images. Besides, simply swapping out the images isn't the effect I'm looking for. I want something with a bit more "pizzazz."

This is what I'm going to do:

- Make a composite image of all the previews
- Hide most of this image
- When the user hovers over a link, display just a part of the image

I've made a composite image of the three previews plus one default view:

Choose a topic

The image is called topics.gif. It is 400 pixels wide and 100 pixels tall.

I'm going to insert the topics.gif image into list.html, giving it an id of "preview":

```
<!DOCTYPE html PUBLIC "-//W3C//DTD XHTML 1.1//EN"
"http://www.w3.org/TR/xhtml11/DTD/xhtml11.dtd">
<html xmlns="http://www.w3.org/1999/xhtml" xml:lang="en">
<head>
  <meta http-equiv="content-type" content="text/html; charset=utf-8" />
  <title>Web Design</title>
</head>
<body>
  <h1>Web Design</h1>
  <p>These are the things you should know.</p>
  <ol id="linklist">
    <li>
      <a href="structure.html">Structure</a>
    </li>
    <li>
      <a href="presentation.html">Presentation</a>
    </li>
    <li>
      <a href="behavior.html">Behavior</a>
    </li>
  </ol>
  <img src="topics.gif" alt="building blocks of web design"
➥ id="preview" />
</body>
</html>
```

Here's the web page with the list of links and the composite image:

Right now, the entire image is visible. I only want a 100 by 100 pixel portion to be visible at any one time. I can't do that with JavaScript, but I can do it with CSS.

CSS

The CSS overflow property dictates how content within an element should be displayed when the content is larger than its container element. When an element contains content that is larger than itself, there is an overflow. In that situation, you can clip the content so that only a portion of it is visible. You can also specify whether or not the web browser should display scroll bars, allowing the user to see the rest of the content.

There are four possible values for the overflow property: "visible", "hidden", "scroll", and "auto".

- If the overflow of an element is set to "visible", then no clipping occurs. The content overflows and is rendered outside the element.
- A value of "hidden" will cause the excess content to be clipped. Only a portion of the content will be visible.
- The "scroll" value is similar to "hidden". The content will be clipped but the web browser will display scroll bars so that the rest of the content can be viewed.
- A value of "auto" is just like "scroll" except that the scroll bars will only be displayed if the content overflows its container element. If there is no overflow, no scroll bars appear.

Of these four values, "hidden" sounds like the most promising for my purposes. I want to display just a 100 by 100 pixel portion of an image that is 400 by 100 pixels in size.

First, I'm going to wrap the image in a container element. I'll put it in a div element with an id of "slideshow":

```
<div id="slideshow">
 <img src="topics.gif" alt="building blocks of web design"
➥ id="preview" />
</div>
```

Now, I'll create a style sheet called layout.css. I'll put this file in a folder called styles.

In layout.css, I can set the size of the "slideshow" div:

```
#slideshow {
  width: 100px;
  height: 100px;
  position: relative;
}
```

10

By applying an overflow value of "hidden", I can ensure that the content within the div will be clipped:

```css
#slideshow {
  width: 100px;
  height: 100px;
  position: relative;
  overflow: hidden;
}
```

I'm attaching the layout.css style sheet to list.html using the CSS @import command. This is contained within <style> tags in the head of the document:

```html
<!DOCTYPE html PUBLIC "-//W3C//DTD XHTML 1.1//EN"
"http://www.w3.org/TR/xhtml11/DTD/xhtml11.dtd">
<html xmlns="http://www.w3.org/1999/xhtml" xml:lang="en">
<head>
  <meta http-equiv="content-type" content="text/html; charset=utf-8" />
  <title>Web Design</title>
  <style type="text/css" media="screen">
    @import url("styles/layout.css");
  </style>
</head>
<body>
  <h1>Web Design</h1>
  <p>These are the things you should know.</p>
  <ol id="linklist">
    <li>
      <a href="structure.html">Structure</a>
    </li>
    <li>
      <a href="presentation.html">Presentation</a>
    </li>
    <li>
      <a href="behavior.html">Behavior</a>
    </li>
  </ol>
  <div id="slideshow">
    <img src="topics.gif" alt="building blocks of web design"
➥ id="preview" />
  </div>
</body>
</html>
```

Load list.html in a web browser to see the difference. The image has been clipped:

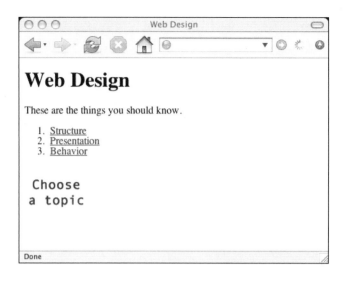

Now only a portion of `topics.gif` is visible. Currently, only the first 100 pixels are visible.

The next part of my plan revolves around the actions of the user. I want to display a different portion of `topics.gif` in the "slideshow" div depending on which link the user hovers their mouse over. This is a behavioral change: definitely a job for JavaScript and the Document Object Model.

JavaScript

My plan is to use the `moveElement` function to move the `topics.gif` image around. I'll move the image to the left or to the right, depending on which link the user is currently hovering over.

I need to attach that behavior (calling the `moveElement` function) to the onmouseover event of each link in the link list.

Here's a function called `prepareSlideshow`, which does just that:

```
function prepareSlideshow() {
// Make sure the browser understands the DOM methods
  if (!document.getElementsByTagName) return false;
  if (!document.getElementById) return false;
// Make sure the elements exist
  if (!document.getElementById("linklist")) return false;
  if (!document.getElementById("preview")) return false;
// Apply styles to the preview image
  var preview = document.getElementById("preview");
  preview.style.position = "absolute";
  preview.style.left = "0px";
  preview.style.top = "0px";
```

```
// Get all the links in the list
  var list = document.getElementById("linklist");
  var links = list.getElementsByTagName("a");
// Attach the animation behavior to the mouseover event
  links[0].onmouseover = function() {
    moveElement("preview",-100,0,10);
  }
  links[1].onmouseover = function() {
    moveElement("preview",-200,0,10);
  }
  links[2].onmouseover = function() {
    moveElement("preview",-300,0,10);
  }
}
```

First of all, the prepareSlideshow function checks for browser compatibility with the DOM methods that will be used:

```
if (!document.getElementsByTagName) return false;
if (!document.getElementById) return false;
```

Next, there's a check to make sure that the "linklist" and "preview" elements exist. Remember, "preview" is the id value of the topics.gif image:

```
if (!document.getElementById("linklist")) return false;
if (!document.getElementById("preview")) return false;
```

After that, a default position is given to the "preview" image. I'm setting the left property to "0px" and the top property to "0px":

```
var preview = document.getElementById("preview");
preview.style.position = "absolute";
preview.style.left = "0px";
preview.style.top = "0px";
```

This doesn't mean that the topics.gif image will appear in the top left corner of the screen. Instead, it will appear in the top left corner of its container element, the "slideshow" div. That's because the CSS position value of the div is "relative". Any absolutely positioned elements contained by a relatively positioned element will be placed in relation to that container element. In other words, the "preview" image will appear zero pixels to the left and zero pixels from the top of the "slideshow" element.

Finally, I'm attaching the onmouseover behaviors to the links in the list. The variable links contains a node set of all the a elements contained within the "linklist" element. The first link is links[0], the second link is links[1], and the third link is links[2]:

```
var list = document.getElementById("linklist");
var links = list.getElementsByTagName("a");
```

When the user hovers over the first link, the moveElement function is called. The elementID argument has a value of "preview". The final_x argument has a value of -100. The final_y argument has a value of 0. The interval argument is ten milliseconds:

```
links[0].onmouseover = function() {
  moveElement("preview",-100,0,10);
}
```

The same behavior applies for the second link, except that the final_x argument is -200:

```
links[1].onmouseover = function() {
  moveElement("preview",-200,0,10);
}
```

The third link will move the "preview" element -300 pixels to the left:

```
links[2].onmouseover = function() {
  moveElement("preview",-300,0,10);
}
```

The prepareSlideshow function is called using the addLoadEvent function. The behaviors are attached when the page loads:

```
addLoadEvent(prepareSlideshow);
```

Save the prepareSlideshow function to a file called prepareSlideshow.js in a folder called scripts. Place the moveElement.js and addLoadEvent.js files in the same folder.

I'm going to reference all three scripts from list.html by adding <script> tags to the head of the document:

```
<!DOCTYPE html PUBLIC "-//W3C//DTD XHTML 1.1//EN"
"http://www.w3.org/TR/xhtml11/DTD/xhtml11.dtd">
<html xmlns="http://www.w3.org/1999/xhtml" xml:lang="en">
<head>
  <meta http-equiv="content-type" content="text/html; charset=utf-8" />
  <title>Web Design</title>
  <style type="text/css" media="screen">
    @import url("styles/layout.css");
  </style>
  <script type="text/javascript" src="scripts/addLoadEvent.js">
  </script>
  <script type="text/javascript" src="scripts/moveElement.js">
  </script>
  <script type="text/javascript" src="scripts/prepareSlideshow.js">
  </script>
</head>
<body>
  <h1>Web Design</h1>
  <p>These are the things you should know.</p>
  <ol id="linklist">
```

10

229

```
      <li>
        <a href="structure.html">Structure</a>
      </li>
      <li>
        <a href="presentation.html">Presentation</a>
      </li>
      <li>
        <a href="behavior.html">Behavior</a>
      </li>
    </ol>
    <div id="slideshow">
      <img src="topics.gif" alt="building blocks of web design"
➥ id="preview" />
    </div>
  </body>
</html>
```

Load list.html in a web browser. Hover over one of the links in the list to see the slideshow in action:

Depending on which link in the list you hover over, a different portion of the topics.gif image will slide into view.

But something's not quite right. If you move quickly from link to the link, the animation becomes confused. There's something wrong with the moveElement function.

A question of scope

The animation problem is being caused by a global variable.

When I abstracted the moveMessage function and turned it into the moveElement function, I left the variable movement as it was:

```
function moveElement(elementID,final_x,final_y,interval) {
  if (!document.getElementById) return false;
  if (!document.getElementById(elementID)) return false;
  var elem = document.getElementById(elementID);
  var xpos = parseInt(elem.style.left);
  var ypos = parseInt(elem.style.top);
  if (xpos == final_x && ypos == final_y) {
    return true;
  }
  if (xpos < final_x) {
    xpos++;
  }
  if (xpos > final_x) {
    xpos--;
  }
  if (ypos < final_y) {
    ypos++;
  }
  if (ypos > final_y) {
    ypos--;
  }
  elem.style.left = xpos + "px";
  elem.style.top = ypos + "px";
  var repeat =
➥ "moveElement('"+elementID+"',"+final_x+","+final_y+","+interval+")";
  movement = setTimeout(repeat,interval);
}
```

This is causing a problem now that the moveElement function is being called whenever the user hovers over a link. Regardless of whether or not the previous call to the function has finished moving the image, the function is being asked to move the same element somewhere else. In other words, the moveElement function is attempting to move the same element to two different places at once and the movement variable has become the rope in a tug of war. As the user quickly moves from link to link, there is a backlog of events building up in the setTimeout queue.

I can flush out this backlog by using clearTimeout:

```
clearTimeout(movement);
```

But if this statement is executed before movement has been set, I'll get an error.

10

I can't use a local variable:

```
var movement = setTimeout(repeat,interval);
```

If I do that, then the clearTimeout statement won't work; the movement variable will no longer exist.

I can't use a global variable. I can't use a local variable. I need something in between. I need a variable that applies just to the element being moved.

Element-specific variables do exist. In fact, you've been using them all the time. What I've just described is a property.

Until now, you've used properties provided by the DOM:

```
element.firstChild
element.style
etc.
```

You can also assign your own properties:

```
element.property = value
```

If you wanted, you could create a property called foo with a value of "bar":

```
element.foo = "bar";
```

It's just like creating a variable. The difference is that the variable belongs just to that element.

I'm going to change movement from being a global variable to a property of the element being moved, elem. That way, I can test for its existence and, if it exists, use clearTimeout:

```
function moveElement(elementID,final_x,final_y,interval) {
  if (!document.getElementById) return false;
  if (!document.getElementById(elementID)) return false;
  var elem = document.getElementById(elementID);
  if (elem.movement) {
    clearTimeout(elem.movement);
  }
  var xpos = parseInt(elem.style.left);
  var ypos = parseInt(elem.style.top);

  if (xpos == final_x && ypos == final_y) {
    return true;
  }
  if (xpos < final_x) {
    xpos++;
  }
  if (xpos > final_x) {
    xpos--;
  }
  if (ypos < final_y) {
    ypos++;
```

```
    }
    if (ypos > final_y) {
      ypos--;
    }
    elem.style.left = xpos + "px";
    elem.style.top = ypos + "px";
    var repeat =
➡ "moveElement('"+elementID+"',"+final_x+","+final_y+","+interval+")";
    elem.movement = setTimeout(repeat,interval);
  }
```

Whichever element is currently being moved by the moveElement function is assigned a property called movement. If the element already has this property at the start of the function, it is reset using clearTimeout. That means, even if the same element is being told to move in different directions, there is only ever one setTimeout statement.

Reload list.html. Moving quickly from link to link no longer creates a problem. There is no backlog of events being queued up. The animation changes direction as you move up and down the list of links.

Still, the animation is a bit lackluster.

Refining the animation

The moveElement function moves an element one pixel at a time until it reaches the co-ordinates specified by the final_x and final_y arguments. The movement is smooth, but it's also kind of boring.

I'm going to spice up the animation a bit.

Take a look at this simple bit of code in moveElement.js:

```
    if (xpos < final_x) {
      xpos++;
    }
```

The variable xpos is the element's current left position. The variable final_x is the element's final left position. This piece of code states, "If the variable xpos is less than the variable final_x, increase the value of xpos by one."

No matter how far away the element is from its final position, it will always move toward it one pixel at a time. I'm going to change that. If the element is far away from its final position, I want it to move a large distance. If the element is near to its final position, I want it to move a short distance.

First of all, I need to figure out how far the element is from its final destination. If xpos is less than final_x, I want to know by how much. I can find out by subtracting xpos, the current left position, from final_x, the desired left position:

```
    var dist = final_x - xpos;
```

That's the distance that the element needs to travel. I'm going to move the element one-tenth of this distance. I've chosen one-tenth as a nice round fraction. You can try other values if you like:

```
var dist = (final_x - xpos)/10;
xpos = xpos + dist;
```

This will move the element one-tenth of the distance it needs to go.

If xpos is 500 pixels away from final_x, the variable dist will have a value of 50. The value of xpos is increased by 50.

If xpos is 100 pixels less than final_x, xpos is increased by 10.

A problem occurs when the distance between xpos and final_x is less than 10. When that value is divided by 10, the result will be less than one. You can't move an element by less than one pixel.

Using the ceil property of the Math object, you can round up the value of the variable dist.

The ceil property has the following syntax:

```
Math.ceil(number)
```

This will round up any floating-point number to the nearest integer. There is a corresponding floor property that will round any floating-point number down to the nearest integer. The round property will round any floating-point number to whichever whole number is closest:

```
Math.floor(number)
Math.round(number)
```

For the moveElement function, I'm going to round upward. If I used floor or round, the element might never reach its final destination:

```
var dist = Match.ceil((final_x - xpos)/10);
xpos = xpos + dist;
```

This covers the situation when xpos is less than final_x:

```
if (xpos < final_x) {
  var dist = Math.ceil((final_x - xpos)/10);
  xpos = xpos + dist;
}
```

If xpos is greater than final_x, then the distance to travel is calculated by subtracting final_x from xpos. This value is divided by 10 and rounded up to the nearest whole number to give the variable dist. This is then subtracted from xpos to bring the element closer to its final destination:

```
if (xpos > final_x) {
  var dist = Math.ceil((xpos - final_x)/10);
  xpos = xpos - dist;
}
```

The same logic applies for ypos and final_y:

```
if (ypos < final_y) {
  var dist = Math.ceil((final_y - ypos)/10);
  ypos = ypos + dist;
}
if (ypos > final_y) {
  var dist = Math.ceil((ypos - final_y)/10);
  ypos = ypos - dist;
}
```

The updated moveElement function looks like this:

```
function moveElement(elementID,final_x,final_y,interval) {
  if (!document.getElementById) return false;
  if (!document.getElementById(elementID)) return false;
  var elem = document.getElementById(elementID);
  if (elem.movement) {
    clearTimeout(elem.movement);
  }
  var xpos = parseInt(elem.style.left);
  var ypos = parseInt(elem.style.top);
  if (xpos == final_x && ypos == final_y) {
    return true;
  }
  if (xpos < final_x) {
    var dist = Math.ceil((final_x - xpos)/10);
    xpos = xpos + dist;
  }
  if (xpos > final_x) {
    var dist = Math.ceil((xpos - final_x)/10);
    xpos = xpos - dist;
  }
  if (ypos < final_y) {
    var dist = Math.ceil((final_y - ypos)/10);
    ypos = ypos + dist;
  }
  if (ypos > final_y) {
    var dist = Math.ceil((ypos - final_y)/10);
    ypos = ypos - dist;
  }
  elem.style.left = xpos + "px";
  elem.style.top = ypos + "px";
  var repeat =
➥ "moveElement('"+elementID+"',"+final_x+","+final_y+","+interval+")";
  elem.movement = setTimeout(repeat,interval);
}
```

10

Save these changes to moveElement.js. Reload list.html to see the difference:

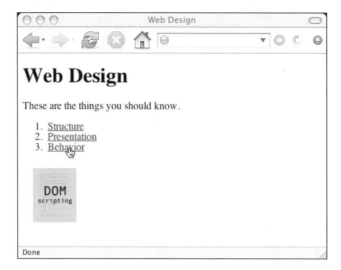

The animation now feels much smoother and snappier. When you first hover over a link, the image jumps quite a distance. As the image approaches its final destination, it "eases" into place.

The markup, the CSS, and the JavaScript all come together to create this slideshow effect. Everything is working fine, but there's always room for some small tweaks.

Final touches

The moveElement function is working really well now. There's just one thing that bothers me. There is an assumption being made near the start of the function:

```
var xpos = parseInt(elem.style.left);
var ypos = parseInt(elem.style.top);
```

I'm assuming that the element elem has a left style property and a top style property. I should really check to make sure that this is the case.

If the left or top properties haven't been set, I have a couple of options. I could simply exit the function there and then:

```
if (!elem.style.left || !elem.style.top) {
  return false;
}
```

If JavaScript can't read those properties, then the function stops without throwing up an error message.

Another solution is to apply default left and top properties in the moveElement function. If either property hasn't been set, I can give them a default value of "0px":

```
if (!elem.style.left) {
  elem.style.left = "0px";
}
if (!elem.style.top) {
  elem.style.top = "0px";
}
```

The moveElement function now looks like this:

```
function moveElement(elementID,final_x,final_y,interval) {
  if (!document.getElementById) return false;
  if (!document.getElementById(elementID)) return false;
  var elem = document.getElementById(elementID);
  if (elem.movement) {
    clearTimeout(elem.movement);
  }
  if (!elem.style.left) {
    elem.style.left = "0px";
  }
  if (!elem.style.top) {
    elem.style.top = "0px";
  }
  var xpos = parseInt(elem.style.left);
  var ypos = parseInt(elem.style.top);
  if (xpos == final_x && ypos == final_y) {
    return true;
  }
  if (xpos < final_x) {
    var dist = Math.ceil((final_x - xpos)/10);
    xpos = xpos + dist;
  }
  if (xpos > final_x) {
    var dist = Math.ceil((xpos - final_x)/10);
    xpos = xpos - dist;
  }
  if (ypos < final_y) {
    var dist = Math.ceil((final_y - ypos)/10);
    ypos = ypos + dist;
  }
  if (ypos > final_y) {
    var dist = Math.ceil((ypos - final_y)/10);
    ypos = ypos - dist;
  }
  elem.style.left = xpos + "px";
  elem.style.top = ypos + "px";
  var repeat =
➥ "moveElement('"+elementID+"',"+final_x+","+final_y+","+interval+")";
  elem.movement = setTimeout(repeat,interval);
}
```

10

With that safety check in place, I no longer need to explicitly set the position of the "preview" element. Right now I'm doing that in the prepareSlideshow function. I can remove these lines:

```
preview.style.left = "0px";
preview.style.top = "0px";
```

While I'm at it, I'm going to overhaul the prepareSlideshow function.

Generating markup

The list.html document contains some markup that exists just for the JavaScript slideshow:

```
<div id="slideshow">
  <img src="topics.gif" alt="building blocks of web design"
➡ id="preview" />
</div>
```

If the user doesn't have JavaScript enabled, this content is somewhat superfluous. The div and the img element are there purely for the slideshow effect. Instead of hardcoding these elements into the document, it makes sense to use JavaScript to generate them. I'm going to do that in prepareSlideshow.js.

First of all, create the div element:

```
var slideshow = document.createElement("div");
slideshow.setAttribute("id","slideshow");
```

Then, create the img element:

```
var preview = document.createElement("img");
preview.setAttribute("src","topics.gif");
preview.setAttribute("alt","building blocks of web design");
preview.setAttribute("id","preview");
```

Place the img inside the div:

```
slideshow.appendChild(preview);
```

Finally, I want these newly created elements to appear right after the list of links. I'm going to do this using the insertAfter function from Chapter 7:

```
var list = document.getElementById("linklist");
insertAfter(list,slideshow);
```

The finished prepareSlideshow function looks like this:

```
function prepareSlideshow() {
// Make sure the browser understands the DOM methods
  if (!document.getElementsByTagName) return false;
```

```
  if (!document.getElementById) return false;
// Make sure the elements exist
  if (!document.getElementById("linklist")) return false;
  var slideshow = document.createElement("div");
  slideshow.setAttribute("id","slideshow");
  var preview = document.createElement("img");
  preview.setAttribute("src","topics.gif");
  preview.setAttribute("alt","building blocks of web design");
  preview.setAttribute("id","preview");
  slideshow.appendChild(preview);
  var list = document.getElementById("linklist");
  insertAfter(list,slideshow);
// Get all the links in the list
  var links = list.getElementsByTagName("a");
// Attach the animation behavior to the mouseover event
  links[0].onmouseover = function() {
    moveElement("preview",-100,0,10);
  }
  links[1].onmouseover = function() {
    moveElement("preview",-200,0,10);
  }
  links[2].onmouseover = function() {
    moveElement("preview",-300,0,10);
  }
}
addLoadEvent(prepareSlideshow);
```

Now I need to make some changes to list.html. I can remove the markup with the "slideshow" div and the "preview" image. I also need to include one more set of <script> tags to reference the insertAfter.js file:

```
<!DOCTYPE html PUBLIC "-//W3C//DTD XHTML 1.1//EN"
"http://www.w3.org/TR/xhtml11/DTD/xhtml11.dtd">
<html xmlns="http://www.w3.org/1999/xhtml" xml:lang="en">
<head>
  <meta http-equiv="content-type" content="text/html; charset=utf-8" />
  <title>Web Design</title>
  <style type="text/css" media="screen">
    @import url(styles/layout.css);
  </style>
  <script type="text/javascript" src="scripts/addLoadEvent.js">
  </script>
  <script type="text/javascript" src="scripts/insertAfter.js">
  </script>
  <script type="text/javascript" src="scripts/moveElement.js">
  </script>
  <script type="text/javascript" src="scripts/prepareSlideshow.js">
  </script>
</head>
```

10

```
<body>
  <h1>Web Design</h1>
  <p>These are the things you should know.</p>
  <ol id="linklist">
    <li>
      <a href="structure.html">Structure</a>
    </li>
    <li>
      <a href="presentation.html">Presentation</a>
    </li>
    <li>
      <a href="behavior.html">Behavior</a>
    </li>
  </ol>
</body>
</html>
```

Write the insertAfter function to a file called insertAfter.js and place it in the scripts folder:

```
function insertAfter(newElement,targetElement) {
  var parent = targetElement.parentNode;
  if (parent.lastChild == targetElement) {
    parent.appendChild(newElement);
  } else {
    parent.insertBefore(newElement,targetElement.nextSibling);
  }
}
```

The other file I need to update is the style sheet, layout.css. I removed this line from prepareSlideshow.js:

```
preview.style.position = "absolute";
```

I can place that declaration in the style sheet, where it belongs:

```
#slideshow {
  width: 100px;
  height: 100px;
  position: relative;
  overflow: hidden;
}
#preview {
  position: absolute;
}
```

Now refresh list.html in a web browser. You will see no difference in functionality. Everything is behaving just as before. The difference is that now there is better separation of structural, presentational, and behavioral elements. If you view the same page with JavaScript disabled, the slideshow image simply doesn't appear.

Functionally, the JavaScript slideshow is working very well. With JavaScript enabled, the slideshow adds some nice visual feedback, responding to the user's actions. With JavaScript disabled, the functionality degrades gracefully.

If you wanted to visually associate the list of links more closely with the slideshow, you could do that by editing `layout.css`. You could float the two elements side by side. You could also place a border around the slideshow if you wanted it to stand out more.

What's next?

This chapter began with a definition of animation: changing an element's position over time. Using a combination of CSS-DOM and JavaScript's setTimeout function, it's quite easy to create a simple animation.

The difficulty with animation isn't technical, it's practical. You can create a lot of cool effects with animation, but there aren't many situations where it's useful or helpful to the user to move elements around. The JavaScript slideshow that you've created is a notable exception. It took some work to get it to work smoothly and degrade gracefully, but the final result is worth it.

You now have a reusable function that you can use whenever you want to create a slideshow or some other practical use of animation.

The JavaScript slideshow is one more example of using JavaScript and the Document Object Model to enhance your web pages. Until now, you've seen DOM scripting enhancements in isolation. In the next chapter, I'm going to apply all the concepts and techniques that you've been learning.

It's time to put it all together.

10

11 PUTTING IT ALL TOGETHER

What this chapter covers:

- Structuring the content
- Designing the site
- Applying styles
- Enhancing the site with JavaScript and the DOM

You've seen a lot of examples of the Document Object Model in action. I've shown those theoretical examples in isolation. Now it's time to put them all together in a real-world situation. In this chapter, you're going to build a website from scratch, complete with JavaScript enhancements.

The brief

You are one lucky web designer. You have been chosen to design the website for what is quite possibly the coolest band on the planet: Jay Skript and the Domsters!

All right, so there's no such band. But play along with me here. For the purposes of this chapter, pretend not only that the band exists, but that you have indeed been asked to design their website.

The website, like the band, needs to look cool. If you can add some nifty interactive features, that will go down well. However, the site also needs to be accessible and search engine friendly.

The purpose of the site is to provide information about the band. Whatever design decisions you make, that must remain the top priority.

That's your task.

Raw materials

The client has provided you with the building blocks for the website. There's some introductory text about the band, a list of tour dates, and some pictures. This won't be a large website. It's basically a brochure site, which makes it even more important that it conveys the right feeling.

Site structure

Based on the content provided by the client, you can create a site map fairly easily. The structure isn't very complicated. You can store all the pages in one folder.

In preparation for building the site, create a folder called images to hold the image files you will use. Create another folder called styles where you can put your CSS. Lastly, create a folder called scripts to hold your JavaScript files.

Your directory structure now looks like this:

- /images
- /styles
- /scripts

You need one page to provide all the background information about the band. You can put the photos together in an image gallery on another page. The tour dates will also get their own page. You'll need to create a contact page where visitors can get in touch with the band. Finally, an introductory home page will set the scene and give a brief description of what awaits the visitor within the site.

That gives you this list of pages to work with, as shown in Figure 11-1:

- Home
- About
- Photos
- Live
- Contact

You will turn that list into these files:

- index.html
- about.html
- photos.html
- live.html
- contact.html

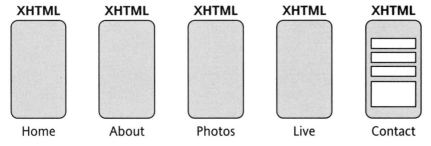

Figure 11-1. A site map for a very simple site

The content on each page will be different, but each page will use the same basic structure. It's time to create a template for these pages.

Page structure

Each page of the site will be divided into a number of sections.

1. The header will contain the branding for the site. This is where the logo will go.

2. The navigation will have a list of links to all the pages.

3. The content will contain the meat and bones of each page.

Seeing as you're dividing up the page, it makes sense to use the <div> tag. These divs will have the ids "header", "navigation", and "content".

You can create a template like this in fairly short order:

```
<!DOCTYPE html PUBLIC "-//W3C//DTD XHTML 1.1//EN"
"http://www.w3.org/TR/xhtml11/DTD/xhtml11.dtd">
<html xmlns="http://www.w3.org/1999/xhtml" xml:lang="en">
<head>
  <meta http-equiv="content-type" content="text/html; charset=utf-8" />
  <title>Jay Skript And The Domsters</title>
</head>
<body>
  <div id="header">
  </div>
  <div id="navigation">
    <ul>
      <li><a href="index.html">Home</a></li>
      <li><a href="about.html">About</a></li>
      <li><a href="photos.html">Photos</a></li>
      <li><a href="live.html">Live</a></li>
      <li><a href="contact.html">Contact</a></li>
    </ul>
  </div>
  <div id="content">
  </div>
</body>
</html>
```

Save this as template.html. Now that you have a structure in place, you can begin to insert the content on a page-by-page basis.

Before doing that, let's see how the final design is going to look.

Design

You know what structural elements need to be included in every page of the site. Armed with this knowledge, and the raw materials provided by the client, you can get to work on the visual design. It's time to fire up Photoshop, Fireworks, or any other graphic design tools of your choice.

Of course, I can't predict what kind of design you would create. But in the words of the best celebrity chefs, "Here's one I made earlier."

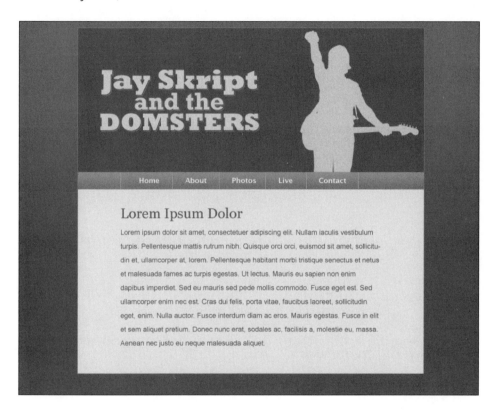

With the visual design finalized, you can slice up your mock-up for graphical elements. Save a portion of the tiling background image as background.gif. The band name becomes logo.gif. A portion of the tiling gradient in the navigation bar becomes navbar.gif. Save the silhouetted figure as guitarist.gif. Put all these files in the images folder.

11

CSS

You have a basic XHTML template. You know how you want the website to look. By applying Cascading Style Sheets to the template, you can reproduce your design for the Web.

You could write all your CSS in one file. But this can make it much trickier to edit afterward. You'll probably find it easier to make changes later if you split your CSS up now.

You can divide up your CSS however you like. I recommend having one file for the overall layout, another that deals purely with color, and a third for handling typography:

- layout.css
- color.css
- typography.css

Each one of these files can be imported from a basic style sheet:

```
@import url(layout.css);
@import url(color.css);
@import url(typography.css);
```

Save this three-line file as basic.css in the styles folder. If you ever need to add a new style sheet or remove an existing one, you only need to edit basic.css.

You can call this basic style sheet from your template with a <link> tag in the head of the document. While you're at it, add an <img> tag inside the "header" div, pointing to the logo. You can also add some dummy "lorem ipsum" text:

```
<!DOCTYPE html PUBLIC "-//W3C//DTD XHTML 1.1//EN"
"http://www.w3.org/TR/xhtml11/DTD/xhtml11.dtd">
<html xmlns="http://www.w3.org/1999/xhtml" xml:lang="en">
<head>
  <meta http-equiv="content-type" content="text/html; charset=utf-8" />
  <title>Jay Skript And The Domsters</title>
  <link rel="stylesheet" type="text/css" media="screen"
➥ href="styles/basic.css" />
</head>
<body>
  <div id="header">
    <img src="images/logo.gif" alt="Jay Skript and the Domsters" />
  </div>
  <div id="navigation">
    <ul>
      <li><a href="index.html">Home</a></li>
      <li><a href="about.html">About</a></li>
      <li><a href="photos.html">Photos</a></li>
      <li><a href="live.html">Live</a></li>
      <li><a href="contact.html">Contact</a></li>
    </ul>
```

```
    </div>
    <div id="content">
      <h1>Lorem Ipsum Dolor</h1>
      <p>Lorem ipsum dolor sit amet, consectetuer adipiscing elit.
Nullam iaculis vestibulum turpis. Pellentesque mattis rutrum
nibh. Quisque orci orci, euismod sit amet, sollicitudin et,
ullamcorper at, lorem.
Pellentesque habitant morbi tristique senectus et netus
et malesuada fames ac turpis egestas.
Ut lectus. Mauris eu sapien non enim dapibus imperdiet.
Sed eu mauris sed pede mollis commodo.
Fusce eget est. Sed ullamcorper enim nec est.
Cras dui felis, porta vitae, faucibus laoreet, sollicitudin eget,
enim. Nulla auctor. Fusce interdum diam ac eros.
Mauris egestas. Fusce in elit et sem aliquet pretium.
Donec nunc erat, sodales ac, facilisis a, molestie eu, massa.
Aenean nec justo eu neque malesuada aliquet.</p>
    </div>
  </body>
</html>
```

Here's the basic template without any style sheets:

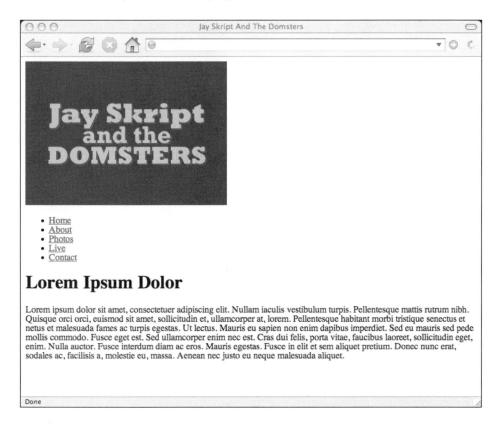

Color

The color.css style sheet is the most straightforward. Make sure that wherever you apply a color to an element, you also specify a background color. Otherwise, there's a danger that you might accidentally make some of your text invisible:

```css
body {
  color: #fb5;
  background-color: #334;
}
a:link {
  color: #445;
  background-color: #eb6;
}
a:visited {
  color: #345;
  background-color: #eb6;
}
a:hover {
  color: #667;
  background-color: #fb5;
}
a:active {
  color: #778;
  background-color: #ec8;
}
#header {
  color: #ec8;
  background-color: #334;
  border-color: #667;
}
#navigation {
  color: #455;
  background-color: #789;
  border-color: #667;
}
#content {
  color: #223;
  background-color: #edc;
  border-color: #667;
}
#navigation ul {
  border-color: #99a;
}
#navigation a:link,#navigation a:visited {
  color: #eef;
  background-color: transparent;
  border-color: #99a;
}
```

```
#navigation a:hover {
  color: #445;
  background-color: #eb6;
}
#navigation a:active {
  color: #667;
  background-color: #ec8;
}
```

Now the template looks more colorful:

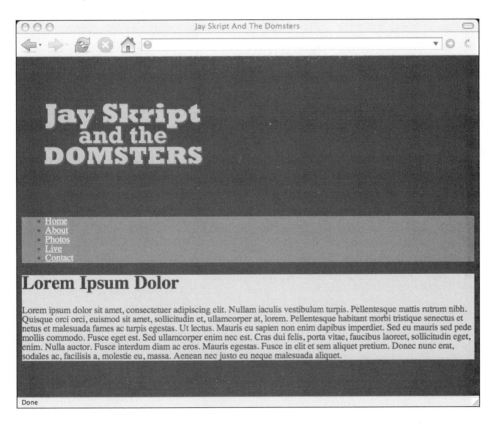

Layout

The basic layout of each page is relatively straightforward. All the content is contained in one column.

Some floating is required to make the items in the navigation list appear horizontally. Apart from that, layout.css is mercifully simple.

The style sheet begins by using the wildcard selector to set the margins and paddings of every element to zero. This removes the default margins and paddings, which can vary from browser to browser. Resetting these values levels the playing field:

```css
* {
  padding: 0;
  margin: 0;
}
body {
  margin: 1em 10%;
  background-image: url(../images/background.gif);
  background-attachment: fixed;
  background-position: top left;
  background-repeat: repeat-x;
  max-width: 80em;
}
#header {
  background-image: url(../images/guitarist.gif);
  background-repeat: no-repeat;
  background-position: bottom right;
  border-width: .1em;
  border-style: solid;
  border-bottom-width: 0;
}
#navigation {
  background-image: url(../images/navbar.gif);
  background-position: bottom left;
  background-repeat: repeat-x;
  border-width: .1em;
  border-style: solid;
  border-bottom-width: 0;
  border-top-width: 0;
  padding-left: 10%;
}
#navigation ul {
  width: 100%;
  overflow: hidden;
  border-left-width: .1em;
  border-left-style: solid;
}
#navigation li {
  display: inline;
}
#navigation li a {
  display: block;
  float: left;
  padding: .5em 2em;
  border-right: .1em solid;
}
```

```
#content {
  border-width: .1em;
  border-style: solid;
  border-top-width: 0;
  padding: 2em 10%;
  line-height: 1.8em;
}
```

Color and layout have now been applied with CSS:

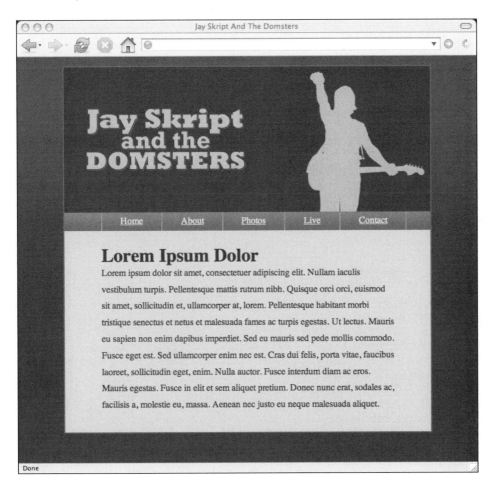

11

Typography

It isn't always easy to decide where to put certain style declarations. Defining fonts and sizes clearly belongs in the typography.css file. But what about margins and padding? It's hard to say whether they're part of the layout or if they should be considered typographical information. Here, the padding information is in layout.css. Margins are applied in typography.css:

```css
body {
  font-size: 76%;
  font-family: "Helvetica","Arial",sans-serif;
}
body * {
  font-size: 1em;
}
a {
  font-weight: bold;
  text-decoration: none;
}
#navigation {
  font-family: "Lucida Grande","Helvetica","Arial",sans-serif;
}
#navigation a {
  text-decoration: none;
  font-weight: bold;
}
#content {
  line-height: 1.8em;
}
#content p {
  margin: 1em 0;
}
h1 {
  font-family: "Georgia","Times New Roman",sans-serif;
  font: 2.4em normal;
}
h2 {
  font-family: "Georgia","Times New Roman",sans-serif;
  font: 1.8em normal;
  margin-top: 1em;
}
h3 {
  font-family: "Georgia","Times New Roman",sans-serif;
  font: 1.4em normal;
  margin-top: 1em;
}
```

Here's the template with color, layout, and typography styles applied:

Each of these files, color.css, layout.css, and typography.css, reside in the styles folder along with the basic.css style sheet.

Markup

Your template looks just like you want it. Your style sheets are working well. Now you can start to build the pages of the site.

Begin with the home page, index.html. It contains a single introductory paragraph within the "content" div:

```
<p id="intro">
Welcome to the official website of Jay Skript and the Domsters.
Here, you can <a href="about.html">learn more about the band</a>,
view <a href="photos.html">photos of the band</a>,
find out about <a href="live.html">tour dates</a>
and <a href="contact.html">get in touch with the band</a>.
</p>
```

Here's the home page:

This paragraph has been marked up with an id of "intro". You could use this to style the introduction in a special way. You can also use it as a hook for some DOM Scripting.

JavaScript

Before you start adding enhancements with the DOM, you should think about how you are going to manage your JavaScript files.

While there are some scripts that you will only need to call for one page, others will be used over and over. Put all of these reusable scripts together in a file called global.js.

You will definitely be using the addLoadEvent function. You will need this whenever you write a function that should be executed when the document is fully loaded:

```
function addLoadEvent(func) {
  var oldonload = window.onload;
  if (typeof window.onload != 'function') {
    window.onload = func;
  } else {
    window.onload = function() {
```

```
        oldonload();
        func();
      }
    }
  }
}
```

The insertAfter function will also come in handy. It's a useful corollary to the insertBefore method:

```
function insertAfter(newElement,targetElement) {
  var parent = targetElement.parentNode;
  if (parent.lastChild == targetElement) {
    parent.appendChild(newElement);
  } else {
    parent.insertBefore(newElement,targetElement.nextSibling);
  }
}
```

You may also need the addClass function you wrote in Chapter 9:

```
function addClass(element,value) {
  if (!element.className) {
    element.className = value;
  } else {
    newClassName = element.className;
    newClassName+= " ";
    newClassName+= value;
    element.className = newClassName;
  }
}
```

Save global.js in the scripts folder. Call this file by adding a <script> tag to the head of every page:

```
<script type="text/javascript" src="scripts/global.js"></script>
```

There's one more script to add to the global.js file.

Page highlighting

When you are creating each page from your existing template, you will be inserting markup into the "content" div. This is the part of the document that changes from page to page.

Ideally, you should also be updating the "navigation" div. If the current page is index.html, then there's no reason for a link to index.html in the navigation list.

In practice, it isn't always possible to edit the navigation on a page-by-page basis. Quite often, the fragment of markup containing the navigation will be dropped into each page using a server-side include.

11

Let's assume that that's the case with this website. There could be a server-side include containing this chunk of markup:

```
<body>
  <div id="header">
    <img src="images/logo.gif" alt="Jay Skript and the Domsters" />
  </div>
  <div id="navigation">
    <ul>
      <li><a href="index.html">Home</a></li>
      <li><a href="about.html">About</a></li>
      <li><a href="photos.html">Photos</a></li>
      <li><a href="live.html">Live</a></li>
      <li><a href="contact.html">Contact</a></li>
    </ul>
  </div>
```

This could be included using Apache Server Side Includes, PHP, ASP, or a number of other server-side languages.

The advantage of this technique is that reusable chunks of markup are centralized. If you ever need to update the header or the navigation, you can do so in one file. The disadvantage is that it becomes harder to customize these chunks for each page.

At the very least, the current page should be highlighted in some way. The visitor should have some kind of "you are here" message.

Update the color.css file to include styles for a class called here:

```
#navigation a.here:link,
#navigation a.here:visited,
#navigation a.here:hover,
#navigation a.here:active {
  color: #eef;
  background-color: #799;
}
```

To apply those colors, you will want to add the here class to the navigation link pointing to the current page:

```
<a href="index.html" class="here">Home</a></li>
```

If you're using a server-side include, this might not be so easy. Ideally, the server-side technology will be robust enough to create the right markup for each page. This isn't always the case, though.

JavaScript rides to the rescue.

In this case, JavaScript is a last resort. It would be much better if the here class were added directly in the markup. Only use the JavaScript solution when the markup is beyond your control.

Write a function called highlightPage to do the following:

1. Get all the links in the navigation list.

2. Loop through these links.

3. If you find a link that matches the current URL, add the here class.

As usual, begin the function with a test for the DOM methods you will be using. You should also test that the "navigation" div exists:

```
function highlightPage() {
    if (!document.getElementsByTagName) return false;
    if (!document.getElementById) return false;
    if (!document.getElementById("navigation")) return false;
    var nav = document.getElementById("navigation");
```

Grab all the navigation links and start looping through them.

```
var links = nav.getElementsByTagName("a");
for (var i=0; i<links.length; i++) {
```

Next, you're going to compare the URL of the link with the URL of the current page. You can get the URL of the link using getAttribute("href"). You can get the URL of the current page using window.location.href:

```
var linkurl = links[i].getAttribute("href");
var currenturl = window.location.href;
```

JavaScript provides a number of methods for comparing strings. The indexOf method finds the position of a substring within a string:

string.indexOf(substring)

This method returns the first occurrence of the substring. In this case, you simply want to find out if one string is within another: "Is the link URL within the current URL":

```
currenturl.indexOf(linkurl)
```

If a match is not found, the indexOf method will return a value of -1. If any other value is returned, there was a positive match. If the indexOf method does not return a value of -1, you want to proceed with the final step of the function:

```
if (currenturl.indexOf(linkurl) != -1) {
```

This link must be a link to the current page. Add the here class to the link:

```
links[i].className = "here";
```

11

All that remains is to close the if statement, close the for loop, and close the function. Do this with closing curly braces. Then call highlightPage using the addLoadEvent function:

```
function highlightPage() {
  if (!document.getElementsByTagName) return false;
  if (!document.getElementById) return false;
  if (!document.getElementById("navigation")) return false;
  var nav = document.getElementById("navigation");
  var links = nav.getElementsByTagName("a");
  for (var i=0; i<links.length; i++) {
    var linkurl = links[i].getAttribute("href");
    var currenturl = window.location.href;
    if (currenturl.indexOf(linkurl) != -1) {
      links[i].className = "here";
    }
  }
}
addLoadEvent(highlightPage);
```

Save this function in global.js. If you reload index.html, you will see that the "Home" link is now highlighted.

Here's the home page with the current page highlighted in the navigation:

You can expand the highlightPage function to kill two birds with one stone.

If you can give a unique id attribute to the body element of each page, you will be able to add styles specifically for that page. You can add a unique id to each page by grabbing the text from the current link: the one that now has the class here. Convert this string to low-ercase using JavaScript's toLowerCase method:

```
var linktext = links[i].lastChild.nodeValue.toLowerCase();
```

This takes the value of the last child of the current link, which is the link text, and converts it to lowercase. If the text within the link is "Home", then the linktext variable will be "home". Apply this variable as the id attribute of the body element:

```
document.body.setAttribute("id",linktext);
```

This is the equivalent of writing id="home" in the <body> tag.

The highlightPage function now looks like this:

```
function highlightPage() {
  if (!document.getElementsByTagName) return false;
  if (!document.getElementById) return false;
  if (!document.getElementById("navigation")) return false;
  var nav = document.getElementById("navigation");
  var links = nav.getElementsByTagName("a");
  for (var i=0; i<links.length; i++) {
    var linkurl = links[i].getAttribute("href");
    var currenturl = document.location.href;
    if (currenturl.indexOf(linkurl) != -1) {
      links[i].className = "here";
      var linktext = links[i].lastChild.nodeValue.toLowerCase();
      document.body.setAttribute("id",linktext);
    }
  }
}
addLoadEvent(highlightPage);
```

The index.html file now has an id of "home" on the body element. The about.html file has an id of "about". The photos.html file has an id of "live", and so on.

These newly inserted identifiers act as hooks in your CSS. You can specify a different back-ground image for the "header" div of each individual page.

Create an image for each page, 250 pixels by 250 pixels. Again, I made some earlier: lineup.gif, basshead.gif, bassist.gif, and drummer.gif. Put these files in the images folder.

Whatever images you decide to make, you can now update the `layout.css` file with background-image declarations:

```
#about #header {
  background-image: url(../images/lineup.gif);
}
#photos #header {
  background-image: url(../images/basshead.gif);
}
#live #header {
  background-image: url(../images/bassist.gif);
}
#contact #header {
  background-image: url(../images/drummer.gif);
}
```

Now each page will show its own unique image in the header.

JavaScript slideshow

The home page needs something special. It's the first page that most visitors to the site will see, so it's the ideal place to add some sizzle. The JavaScript slideshow that you built in the last chapter is perfect for this.

The "intro" paragraph has links to all the other pages on the site. When a visitor hovers over one of those links, it would be good to give them a glimpse of what awaits them. You could show smaller versions of the images from the headers of each page.

Shrink all the header images down to 150 by 150 pixels and combine them into one 750 pixel long image called `slideshow.gif`. Place this image in the images folder.

The montage image looks like this:

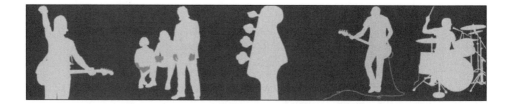

Create a JavaScript file called `home.js` in the scripts folder. This is where you will write the functions for the slideshow. The slideshow will only appear on the home page, so this file will only be called by `index.html`.

For the slideshow to work, you'll need the moveElement function that you wrote in Chapter 10:

```
function moveElement(elementID,final_x,final_y,interval) {
  if (!document.getElementById) return false;
```

```
  if (!document.getElementById(elementID)) return false;
  var elem = document.getElementById(elementID);
  if (elem.movement) {
    clearTimeout(elem.movement);
  }
  if (!elem.style.left) {
    elem.style.left = "0px";
  }
  if (!elem.style.top) {
    elem.style.top = "0px";
  }
  var xpos = parseInt(elem.style.left);
  var ypos = parseInt(elem.style.top);
  if (xpos == final_x && ypos == final_y) {
    return true;
  }
  if (xpos < final_x) {
    var dist = Math.ceil((final_x - xpos)/10);
    xpos = xpos + dist;
  }
  if (xpos > final_x) {
    var dist = Math.ceil((xpos - final_x)/10);
    xpos = xpos - dist;
  }
  if (ypos < final_y) {
    var dist = Math.ceil((final_y - ypos)/10);
    ypos = ypos + dist;
  }
  if (ypos > final_y) {
    var dist = Math.ceil((ypos - final_y)/10);
    ypos = ypos - dist;
  }
  elem.style.left = xpos + "px";
  elem.style.top = ypos + "px";
  var repeat =
➡ "moveElement('"+elementID+"',"+final_x+","+final_y+","+interval+")";
  elem.movement = setTimeout(repeat,interval);
}
```

Now you need to create the slideshow elements and prepare the links. In this case, the slideshow will be placed right after the "intro" paragraph:

```
function prepareSlideshow() {
  if (!document.getElementsByTagName) return false;
  if (!document.getElementById) return false;
  if (!document.getElementById("intro")) return false;
  var intro = document.getElementById("intro");
  var slideshow = document.createElement("div");
  slideshow.setAttribute("id","slideshow");
```

```
var preview = document.createElement("img");
preview.setAttribute("src","images/slideshow.gif");
preview.setAttribute("alt","a glimpse of what awaits you");
preview.setAttribute("id","preview");
slideshow.appendChild(preview);
insertAfter(slideshow,intro);
```

Now loop through all the links in the "intro" paragraph. Move the preview element based on which link is being moused over. For instance, if the href value of the link contains the string "about.html", then move the preview element to -150 pixels. If the href value contains the string "photos.html", move the preview element to -300 pixels, and so on.

To make the animation snappy, pass the moveElement function an interval value of just five milliseconds:

```
var links = intro.getElementsByTagName("a");
for (var i=0; i<links.length; i++) {
  links[i].onmouseover = function() {
    var destination = this.getAttribute("href");
    if (destination.indexOf("index.html") != -1) {
      moveElement("preview",0,0,5);
    }
    if (destination.indexOf("about.html") != -1) {
      moveElement("preview",-150,0,5);
    }
    if (destination.indexOf("photos.html") != -1) {
      moveElement("preview",-300,0,5);
    }
    if (destination.indexOf("live.html") != -1) {
      moveElement("preview",-450,0,5);
    }
    if (destination.indexOf("contact.html") != -1) {
      moveElement("preview",-600,0,5);
    }
  }
}
```

Call the function using addLoadEvent:

```
addLoadEvent(prepareSlideshow);
```

Save all this in home.js. You'll need to call that JavaScript file by adding a <script> tag to the head of index.html:

```
<script type="text/javascript" src="scripts/home.js"></script>
```

You'll also need to update your styles. Add these lines to layout.css:

```
#slideshow {
  width: 150px;
  height: 150px;
  position: relative;
  overflow: hidden;
}
```

Refresh index.html in a web browser to see the slideshow in action.

It looks pretty good. You can make it look even better by placing the animation in a window frame.

Create an image, 150 by 150 pixels, that is mostly transparent, but with some rounded corners the same color as the background of the "content" div. Call it frame.gif and put it in the images folder.

Add these lines to the prepareSlideshow function in home.js. Put them right after the creation of the slideshow element:

```
var frame = document.createElement("img");
frame.setAttribute("src","images/frame.gif");
frame.setAttribute("alt","");
frame.setAttribute("id","frame");
slideshow.appendChild(frame);
```

To make sure that this container appears above the animation, add these lines to layout.css:

```
#frame {
  position: absolute;
  top: 0;
  left: 0;
  z-index: 99;
}
```

Refresh index.html to see the slideshow, complete with window frame.

Right now, the slideshow animates whenever a visitor hovers over a link in the "intro" paragraph. If you want, the animation could also happen when a link in the "navigation" div is moused over.

Change this line:

```
var links = intro.getElementsByTagName("a");
```

to this:

```
var links = document.getElementsByTagName("a");
```

11

The finished prepareSlideshow function now looks like this:

```
function prepareSlideshow() {
  if (!document.getElementsByTagName) return false;
  if (!document.getElementById) return false;
  if (!document.getElementById("intro")) return false;
  var intro = document.getElementById("intro");
  var slideshow = document.createElement("div");
  slideshow.setAttribute("id","slideshow");
  var frame = document.createElement("img");
  frame.setAttribute("src","images/frame.gif");
  frame.setAttribute("alt","");
  frame.setAttribute("id","frame");
  slideshow.appendChild(frame);
  var preview = document.createElement("img");
  preview.setAttribute("src","images/slideshow.gif");
  preview.setAttribute("alt","a glimpse of what awaits you");
  preview.setAttribute("id","preview");
  slideshow.appendChild(preview);
  insertAfter(slideshow,intro);
  var links = document.getElementsByTagName("a");
  for (var i=0; i<links.length; i++) {
    links[i].onmouseover = function() {
      var destination = this.getAttribute("href");
      if (destination.indexOf("index.html") != -1) {
        moveElement("preview",0,0,5);
      }
      if (destination.indexOf("about.html") != -1) {
        moveElement("preview",-150,0,5);
      }
      if (destination.indexOf("photos.html") != -1) {
        moveElement("preview",-300,0,5);
      }
      if (destination.indexOf("live.html") != -1) {
        moveElement("preview",-450,0,5);
      }
      if (destination.indexOf("contact.html") != -1) {
        moveElement("preview",-600,0,5);
      }
    }
  }
}
addLoadEvent(prepareSlideshow);
```

Now if you hover over any of the links in the navigation list, the slideshow animation will be triggered:

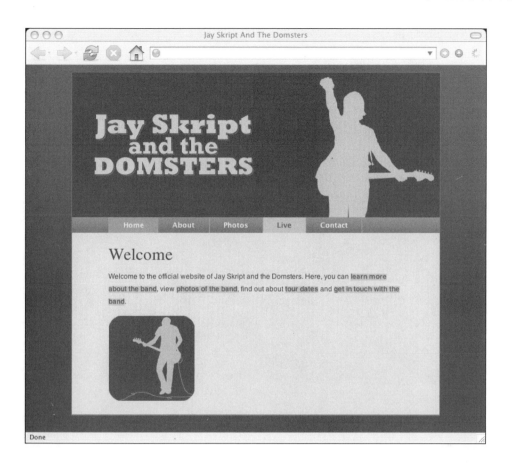

Internal navigation

The next page in the site is the "about" page. Add this markup in the "content" div of
`template.html`:

```
<h1>About the band</h1>
<ul id="internalnav">
  <li><a href="#jay">Jay Skript</a></li>
  <li><a href="#domsters">The Domsters</a></li>
</ul>
<div class="section" id="jay">
  <h2>Jay Skript</h2>
  <p>Jay Skript is going to rock your world!</p>
  <p>Together with his compatriots The Domsters,
Jay is set for world domination. Just you wait and see.</p>
  <p>Jay Skript has been on the scene since the mid nineties.
His talent hasn't always been recognized or fully appreciated.
In the early days, he was often unfavorably compared to bigger,
similarly-named artists. That's all in the past now.</p>
```

11

```
    </div>
    <div class="section" id="domsters">
      <h2>The Domsters</h2>
      <p>The Domsters have been around, in one form or another,
for almost as long. It's only in the past few years that The Domsters
have settled down to their current, stable line-up.
Now they're a rock-solid bunch: methodical and dependable.</p>
    </div>
```

Save the file as about.html. The "about" page looks like this:

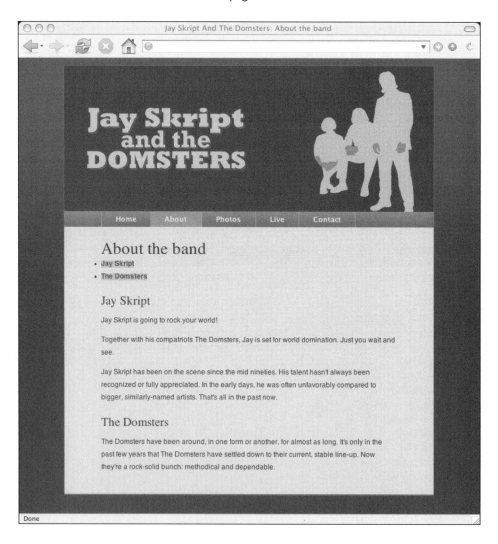

The page looks and works fine. It's a little bit long, though. That's why there are internal links at the top of the page, inside the list with the "internalnav" id. Each of these links leads to a div with a class attribute of "section".

Using JavaScript and the DOM, you can selectively show and hide these sections so that only one is visible at any one time.

Here's a function that will show a "section" div with a specified id, while hiding all the other "section" divs:

```
function showSection(id) {
  var divs = document.getElementsByTagName("div");
  for (var i=0; i<divs.length; i++ ) {
    if (divs[i].className.indexOf("section") == -1) continue;
    if (divs[i].getAttribute("id") != id) {
      divs[i].style.display = "none";
    } else {
      divs[i].style.display = "block";
    }
  }
}
```

The showSection function updates the display style property of each section. The display property is set to "none" on all the sections, except for the one with the specified id. The id is passed as an argument to the function. The display property for the div with this id is set to "block".

The showSection function needs to be executed whenever someone clicks on a link in the "internalnav" list.

Create a function called prepareInternalNav. Start looping through all the links in the "internalnav" list:

```
function prepareInternalnav() {
  if (!document.getElementsByTagName) return false;
  if (!document.getElementById) return false;
  if (!document.getElementById("internalnav")) return false;
  var nav = document.getElementById("internalnav");
  var links = nav.getElementsByTagName("a");
  for (var i=0; i<links.length; i++ ) {
```

The href value of each link is the id of a div, but with the "#" symbol at the start to indicate that the link is internal. You can extract the id of the div by using the split method. This is a handy way of splitting a string into two or more parts based on a dividing character:

```
array = string.split(character)
```

11

269

In this case, you want everything after the "#" character. Split the href value on this character. The resulting array will contain two values: the first is everything before the "#" character, the second is everything afterward. Remember that the first element in an array has an index of zero. You're interested in the second element of the array, which has an index of one:

```
var sectionId = links[i].getAttribute("href").split("#")[1];
```

This will extract everything after the first "#" character and assign the result to the variable sectionId.

Add a short test to make sure that an element with this id actually exists. If it doesn't, carry on to the next iteration of the loop:

```
if (!document.getElementById(sectionId)) continue;
```

When the page loads, you'll want to hide all the sections by default. Do that by adding this line:

```
document.getElementById(sectionId).style.display = "none";
```

Now you can add the onclick event handler for the link. When the link is clicked, you want to pass the variable sectionId to the showSection function.

There's a problem of scope, however. The variable sectionId is a local variable. It only exists while the prepareInternalnav function is being executed. It won't exist within the event handler function.

You can get around this problem by creating your own custom property for each link. Call the property destination and assign it the value of sectionId:

```
links[i].destination = sectionId;
```

That property has a persistent scope. You can query that property from the event handler function:

```
links[i].onclick = function() {
  showSection(this.destination);
  return false;
}
```

Close up the prepareInternalnav function with some closing curly braces. Call the function with onLoadEvent:

```
addLoadEvent(prepareInternalnav);
```

Save both functions to a file called about.js in the scripts folder:

```
function showSection(id) {
  var divs = document.getElementsByTagName("div");
  for (var i=0; i<divs.length; i++ ) {
    if (divs[i].className.indexOf("section") == -1) continue;
```

```
      if (divs[i].getAttribute("id") != id) {
        divs[i].style.display = "none";
      } else {
        divs[i].style.display = "block";
      }
    }
  }

  function prepareInternalnav() {
    if (!document.getElementsByTagName) return false;
    if (!document.getElementById) return false;
    if (!document.getElementById("internalnav")) return false;
    var nav = document.getElementById("internalnav");
    var links = nav.getElementsByTagName("a");
    for (var i=0; i<links.length; i++ ) {
      var sectionId = links[i].getAttribute("href").split("#")[1];
      if (!document.getElementById(sectionId)) continue;
      document.getElementById(sectionId).style.display = "none";
      links[i].destination = sectionId;
      links[i].onclick = function() {
        showSection(this.destination);
        return false;
      }
    }
  }

  addLoadEvent(prepareInternalnav);
```

Call this file from about.html using a <script> tag in the head element:

```
<script type="text/javascript" src="scripts/about.js"></script>
```

Load about.html in a web browser and test the functionality. Clicking on one of the internal links shows the relevant section only. Here's the "about" page with only part of the content displayed:

11

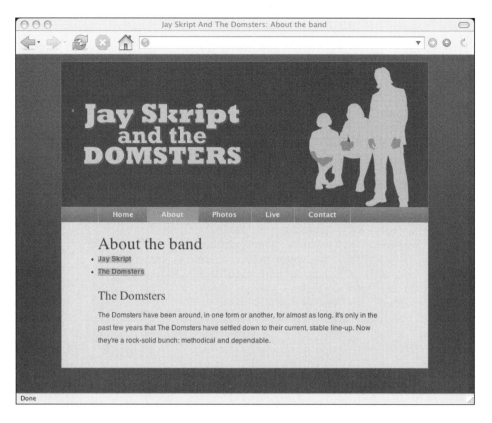

This function could be very useful on much longer pages. If you had a page of frequently asked questions, for example, each question could be an internal link. Clicking on a question would reveal the answer to that question while keeping all the other answers hidden.

JavaScript image gallery

The next page you're making is `photos.html`. This is the ideal place for the JavaScript image gallery that you've been perfecting.

The client has provided you with four 400 by 300 pixel photos of Jay Skript and the Domsters in action:

- `concert.jpg`
- `bassist.jpg`
- `guitarist.jpg`
- `crowd.jpg`

Create a new folder called photos in the images folder. Put these four images in the photos folder.

Make 100 by 100 pixel thumbnails of each image:

- thumbnail_concert.jpg
- thumbnail_bassist.jpg
- thumbnail_guitarist.jpg
- thumbnail_crowd.jpg

Place these in the photos folder, too.

Create a list of links pointing to the full-sized images. Give this list the id "imagegallery".
Put an <img> tag in each link. The src of each image is a thumbnail image:

```
<h1>Photos of the band</h1>
<ul id="imagegallery">
  <li>
    <a href="images/photos/concert.jpg" title="The crowd goes wild">
      <img src="images/photos/thumbnail_concert.jpg"
➥ alt="the band in concert" />
    </a>
  </li>
  <li>
    <a href="images/photos/bassist.jpg" title="An atmospheric moment">
      <img src="images/photos/thumbnail_bassist.jpg"
➥ alt="the bassist" />
    </a>
  </li>
  <li>
    <a href="images/photos/guitarist.jpg" title="Rocking out">
      <img src="images/photos/thumbnail_guitarist.jpg"
➥ alt="the guitarist" />
    </a>
  </li>
  <li>
    <a href="images/photos/crowd.jpg" title="Encore! Encore!">
      <img src="images/photos/thumbnail_crowd.jpg"
➥ alt="the audience" />
    </a>
  </li>
</ul>
```

Put this list in the "content" div of template.html and save the file as photos.html.

Update the layout.css file so that the thumbnails appear horizontally rather than
vertically:

```
#imagegallery li {
  display: inline;
}
```

11

You need one more image for the image gallery script to work. Make a placeholder image. Call it placeholder.gif and put it in the images folder.

Now you can take your image gallery scripts from Chapters 6 and 7 and put them in a file called photos.js in the scripts folder:

```
function showPic(whichpic) {
  if (!document.getElementById("placeholder")) return true;
  var source = whichpic.getAttribute("href");
  var placeholder = document.getElementById("placeholder");
  placeholder.setAttribute("src",source);
  if (!document.getElementById("description")) return false;
  if (whichpic.getAttribute("title")) {
    var text = whichpic.getAttribute("title");
  } else {
    var text = "";
  }
  var description = document.getElementById("description");
  if (description.firstChild.nodeType == 3) {
    description.firstChild.nodeValue = text;
  }
```

```
      return false;
    }

    function preparePlaceholder() {
      if (!document.createElement) return false;
      if (!document.createTextNode) return false;
      if (!document.getElementById) return false;
      if (!document.getElementById("imagegallery")) return false;
      var placeholder = document.createElement("img");
      placeholder.setAttribute("id","placeholder");
      placeholder.setAttribute("src","images/placeholder.gif");
      placeholder.setAttribute("alt","my image gallery");
      var description = document.createElement("p");
      description.setAttribute("id","description");
      var desctext = document.createTextNode("Choose an image");
      description.appendChild(desctext);
      var gallery = document.getElementById("imagegallery");
      insertAfter(description,gallery);
      insertAfter(placeholder,description);
    }

    function prepareGallery() {
      if (!document.getElementsByTagName) return false;
      if (!document.getElementById) return false;
      if (!document.getElementById("imagegallery")) return false;
      var gallery = document.getElementById("imagegallery");
      var links = gallery.getElementsByTagName("a");
      for ( var i=0; i < links.length; i++) {
        links[i].onclick = function() {
          return showPic(this);
        }
      }
    }

    addLoadEvent(preparePlaceholder);
    addLoadEvent(prepareGallery);
```

There's just one small change. The description text has been placed above the place-holder image.

Call the photos.js file from photos.html with a <script> tag:

```
<script type="text/javascript" src="scripts/photos.js"></script>
```

11

Load photos.html in a web browser to see the image gallery in action:

Table enhancements

You've been given a list of tour dates for Jay Skript and the Domsters. For each concert, there is a date, a city, and a venue. This is tabular data, so the "Live" page will consist of a <table> of concert dates:

```
<h1>Tour dates</h1>
<table summary="when and where you can see the band">
  <thead>
  <tr>
    <th>Date</th>
    <th>City</th>
```

```
      <th>Venue</th>
    </tr>
    </thead>
    <tbody>
    <tr>
      <td>June 9th</td>
      <td>Portland, <abbr title="Oregon">OR</abbr></td>
      <td>Crystal Ballroom</td>
    </tr>
    <tr>
      <td>June 10th</td>
      <td>Seattle, <abbr title="Washington">WA</abbr></td>
      <td>Crocodile Cafe</td>
    </tr>
    <tr>
      <td>June 12th</td>
      <td>Sacramento, <abbr title="California">CA</abbr></td>
      <td>Torch Club</td>
    </tr>
    <tr>
      <td>June 17th</td>
      <td>Austin, <abbr title="Texas">TX</abbr></td>
      <td>Speakeasy</td>
    </tr>
    </tbody>
  </table>
```

Put this `<table>` in the "content" div of `template.html` and save the resulting file as `live.html`.

You can add some table cell styling to `layout.css`:

```
td {
  padding: .5em 3em;
}
```

Update `color.css` with declarations for table headers and rows:

```
th {
  color: #edc;
  background-color: #455;
}
tr td {
  color: #223;
  background-color: #eb6;
}
```

If you load `live.html` in a web browser, you will see a perfectly normal, somewhat non-descript table:

11

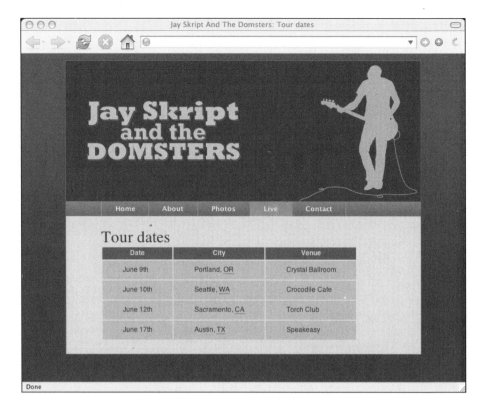

This is the perfect opportunity to use the table styling functions from Chapter 9: stripeTables and highlightRows. You can also add the displayAbbreviations function.

Put them all in a file called live.js and call them with addLoadEvent:

```
function stripeTables() {
  if (!document.getElementsByTagName) return false;
  var tables = document.getElementsByTagName("table");
  for (var i=0; i<tables.length; i++) {
    var odd = false;
    var rows = tables[i].getElementsByTagName("tr");
    for (var j=0; j<rows.length; j++) {
      if (odd == true) {
        addClass(rows[j],"odd");
        odd = false;
      } else {
        odd = true;
      }
    }
  }
}

function highlightRows() {
  if(!document.getElementsByTagName) return false;
```

```
    var rows = document.getElementsByTagName("tr");
    for (var i=0; i<rows.length; i++) {
      rows[i].oldClassName = rows[i].className
      rows[i].onmouseover = function() {
        addClass(this,"highlight");
      }
      rows[i].onmouseout = function() {
        this.className = this.oldClassName
      }
    }
}

function displayAbbreviations() {
  if (!document.getElementsByTagName || !document.createElement
➥ || !document.createTextNode) return false;

  var abbreviations = document.getElementsByTagName("abbr");
  if (abbreviations.length < 1) return false;
  var defs = new Array();
  for (var i=0; i<abbreviations.length; i++) {
    var current_abbr = abbreviations[i];
    if (current_abbr.childNodes.length < 1) continue;
    var definition = current_abbr.getAttribute("title");
    var key = current_abbr.lastChild.nodeValue;
    defs[key] = definition;
  }
  var dlist = document.createElement("dl");
  for (key in defs) {
    var definition = defs[key];
    var dtitle = document.createElement("dt");
    var dtitle_text = document.createTextNode(key);
    dtitle.appendChild(dtitle_text);
    var ddesc = document.createElement("dd");
    var ddesc_text = document.createTextNode(definition);
    ddesc.appendChild(ddesc_text);
    dlist.appendChild(dtitle);
    dlist.appendChild(ddesc);
  }
  if (dlist.childNodes.length < 1) return false;
  var header = document.createElement("h3");
  var header_text = document.createTextNode("Abbreviations");
  header.appendChild(header_text);
  var container = document.getElementById("content");
  container.appendChild(header);
  container.appendChild(dlist);
}

addLoadEvent(stripeTables);
addLoadEvent(highlightRows);
addLoadEvent(displayAbbreviations);
```

11

The highlightRows function has been updated slightly. Instead of applying a style property directly, it uses the addClass function from global.js to apply the highlight class. This class is applied when the user hovers over a row. Before that, the function takes a snapshot of the old className property and stores it as a custom property called oldClassName. When the user moves off the table row, the className property is reset to the value of oldClassName.

Add some styles for the definition list to layout.css:

```
dl {
  overflow: hidden;
}
dt {
  float: left;
}
dd {
  float: left;
}
```

Update typography.css as well:

```
dt {
  margin-right: 1em;
}
dd {
  margin-right: 3em;
}
```

Finally, add the color information for the odd and highlight classes to color.css:

```
tr.odd td {
  color: #223;
  background-color: #ec8;
}
tr.highlight td {
  color: #223;
  background-color: #cba;
}
```

Add the usual <script> tag in the head of live.html:

```
<script type="text/javascript" src="scripts/live.js"></script>
```

Load live.html in a web browser to see the enhanced <table>. Every second row has been given a class of odd:

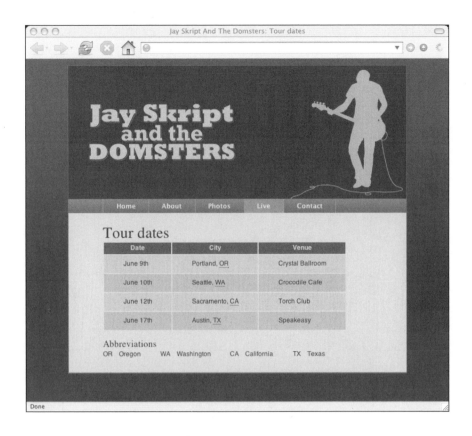

Form enhancements

There's just one more page of the site to build. It's an important page. There needs to be some kind of way for visitors to get in touch with the band.

Just about every website lists some kind of contact information, even if it's just an email address. For this website, you're going to build a contact form.

Contact forms require some kind of server-side technology to process the data entered in the form. This can be done with Perl, PHP, ASP, or just about any other server-side programming language. For this example, however, the data isn't going anywhere. It's a fictional band, remember.

Make a file called `contact.html`. It should have the same structure as `template.html`, but with this <form> inside the "content" div:

```
<h1>Contact the band</h1>
<form method="post" action="#">
  <fieldset>
    <p>
      <label for="name">Name:</label>
      <input type="text" id="name" name="name" value="Your name"
```

```
➥ class="required" />
    </p>
    <p>
      <label for="email">Email:</label>
      <input type="text" id="email" name="email"
➥ value="Your email address" class="email required" />
    </p>
    <p>
      <label for="message">Message:</label>
      <textarea cols="45" rows="7" id="message" name="message"
➥ class="required">Write your message here.</textarea>
    </p>
    <input type="submit" value="Send" />
  </fieldset>
</form>
```

Update the layout.css file:

```
label {
  display: block;
}
fieldset {
  border: 0;
}
```

The contact form looks like this:

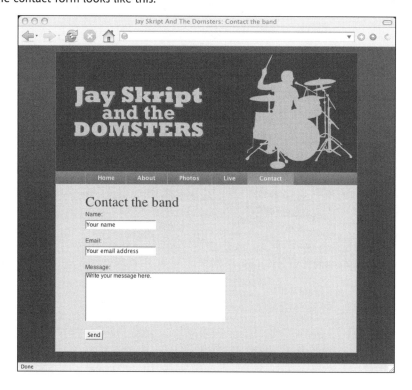

Labels

There are three form fields, name, email, and message. Each field has a corresponding <label> tag.

The label element is a very useful aid to accessibility. Using the for attribute, it specifically associates a piece of text with a form field. This can be of tremendous value to screen-reading software.

The label element can be equally valuable to visitors without any visual impairments. Many browsers create a default behavior for label elements: if the text within a label is clicked, the associated form field is brought into focus. This is a really nice little usability enhancement. Unfortunately, not all browsers implement this behavior.

The behavior might not be implemented by default, but there's no reason why you can't add it yourself. All you need is a few lines of JavaScript.

- Get all the label elements in the document.
- If the label has a for attribute, attach an event handler.
- When the label is clicked on, extract the value of the for attribute.
- This value is the id of a form element.
- Make sure the form element exists.
- Bring that form element into focus.

Call the function focusLabels. Execute the function when the page loads using addLoadEvent:

```
function focusLabels() {
  if (!document.getElementsByTagName) return false;
  var labels = document.getElementsByTagName("label");
  for (var i=0; i<labels.length; i++) {
    if (!labels[i].getAttribute("for")) continue;
    labels[i].onclick = function() {
      var id = this.getAttribute("for");
      if (!document.getElementById(id)) return false;
      var element = document.getElementById(id);
      element.focus();
    }
  }
}
addLoadEvent(focusLabels);
```

11

Save this in a file called contact.js in the scripts folder. Add a <script> tag to the head of contact.html:

```
<script type="text/javascript" src="scripts/contact.js"></script>
```

Load contact.html in a web browser. Clicking on the text in a label brings the associated form field into focus. Depending on the browser you're using, this may have always been the case. However, you've leveled the playing field. All browsers will execute this behavior now.

Default values

Each field in the contact form has some default placeholder text. The name field has a value of "your name", the email field has a value of "your email", and so on.

Again, this is useful from an accessibility viewpoint. Checkpoint 10.4 of the Web Accessibility Initiative guidelines states, "Until user agents handle empty controls correctly, include default, place-holding characters in edit boxes and text areas. [Priority 3]"

Historically, some browsers have had problems recognizing empty form fields. This made keyboard navigation particularly difficult. Visitors weren't able to tab to empty fields.

Much like using <label> tags, this accessibility enhancement turns out to be useful for everybody. Even if users aren't navigating by keyboard, it's still very handy for them to be able to see what they should be writing in each form field.

There's one drawback to having default values in form fields. When the user comes to write something in a field, they must first delete the placeholder text. This can become tedious. It would be useful if this deletion could happen automatically.

You can make this happen using JavaScript. This time, though, you won't be using methods and properties of the DOM Core. You'll be using one of the most useful objects in the HTML-DOM: the Form object.

The Form object

As you know, every element in a document is an object. Each element has DOM properties like nodeName, nodeType, etc.

Some elements have even more properties than those provided by the DOM Core. Every form element in a document is an object of the type Form. Each Form object has a property called elements.length. This value returns the number of form elements contained by a form:

> *form.elements.length*

This is a different value to childNodes.length, which returns the total number of nodes contained by an element. The elements.length property of a Form object returns only those elements that are form elements, e.g. input elements, textarea elements, etc.

Collectively, all of these form fields are the elements property of a Form object. This is an array that contains all the form elements:

> *form.elements*

Again, this differs from the childNodes property, which is also an array. The childNodes array will return every node. The elements array will only return input, select, textarea and other form fields.

Each form element in the elements array comes with its own set of properties. The value property, for instance, gives you the current value of a form element:

> *element.value*

This is equivalent to:

```
element.getAttribute("value")
```

Another property you can query is the defaultValue of a form element:

```
element.defaultValue
```

This will give you the initial value of any field in a form. That's exactly what you need for the function you're going to write.

Every form field in contact.html has a default initial value. These values are useful for indicating to the user what they should type in each field. However, it can be tedious for the user to delete these default values. It would be useful if the default values were automatically deleted whenever a form field is brought into focus. Likewise, if the user moves on without entering a value in the field, the default value should reappear.

Write a function called resetFields that takes a Form object as its single argument.

- Loop through all the elements in the form.
- If the element is a submit button, move on to the next iteration of the loop.
- If the element doesn't have a default value, move on to the next iteration.
- Otherwise, add an event handler for when the element is brought into focus:
  - Set the value of the element to empty.
- Add another event handler for when the element no longer has focus:
  - If the value of the element is empty, change it back to its default value.

Here's the function:

```
function resetFields(whichform) {
  for (var i=0; i<whichform.elements.length; i++) {
    var element = whichform.elements[i];
    if (element.type == "submit") continue;
    if (!element.defaultValue) continue;
    element.onfocus = function() {
      if (this.value == this.defaultValue) {
        this.value = "";
      }
    }
    element.onblur = function() {
      if (this.value == "") {
        this.value = this.defaultValue;
      }
    }
  }
}
```

11

The function is using two event handlers. The onfocus event is triggered when the user tabs to or clicks on an element. The onblur event is triggered when the user moves out of the form element.

Save the resetFields function in contact.js. You need to activate the function by passing it a Form object. Write another function called prepareForms that loops through each Form object in the document and passes each one to the resetFields function:

```
function prepareForms() {
  for (var i=0; i<document.forms.length; i++) {
    var thisform = document.forms[i];
    resetFields(thisform);
    }
  }
}
```

Call the prepareForms function using addLoadEvent:

```
addLoadEvent(prepareForms);
```

Reload contact.html to see the effects of the scripts.

Click on any form field, or any label for that matter. The default value will disappear. If you move on to another field without writing anything, the default value reappears. If you write something, the default value doesn't reappear.

Form validation

The last task that you're going to perform on the contact form involves one of the oldest uses of JavaScript.

Client-side form validation has been around almost as long as JavaScript. The theory is simple. When a user submits a form, run some tests on the values provided. If required fields haven't been provided, the user is told with an alert dialog which fields need fixing.

It sounds straightforward and it usually is. But if JavaScript form validation is implemented badly, it can cause more harm than good. If the code has been written sloppily, the user may end up never being able to submit the form.

There are two things to remember when you are writing JavaScript form validation functions:

- Bad form validation can be worse than no validation at all.
- Never rely solely on JavaScript. It's not a substitute for server-side validation. Just because you validate a form with JavaScript doesn't mean you shouldn't check the values again when they are sent to the server.

With those thoughts in mind, it's best to keep form validation as simple as possible. A very simple test would be to see if the user has provided a value at all.

Here's a function called isFilled. It takes an element from a form as its single argument. The function will return a value of true if the field has been filled in. It will return a value of false if the user hasn't filled in the field:

```
function isFilled(field) {
  if (field.value.length < 1 || field.value == field.defaultValue) {
    return false;
  } else {
    return true;
  }
}
```

By checking the length property of the value property, you can see if the value has less than a single character. If it does, the function returns a value of false. Otherwise, it continues on to the next line.

By comparing the value property to the defaultValue property, you can find out if the user has simply left the placeholder text in the field. If the two values are the same, the function returns a value of false.

If both tests are passed, the isFilled function returns a value of true.

Here's a similar function called isEmail. It tests whether the value of a form field looks like an email address:

```
function isEmail(field) {
  if (field.value.indexOf("@") == -1 || field.value.indexOf(".") == -1)
{
    return false;
  } else {
    return true;
  }
}
```

This function runs two tests using the indexOf method. This method finds the first occurrence of a string within another string. If the search string is found, it returns the position. If the search string isn't found, it returns a value of -1.

The first test looks for the "@" character in the value property of the form field. This character must be present in an email address. If the "@" isn't found, the isEmail function returns a value of false.

The second test works exactly the same way, except this time the test is looking for the "." character. If it can't be found in the value property of the field, the function returns false.

If both tests are passed, the isEmail function returns true.

11

The isEmail function isn't foolproof. It's still entirely possible to enter fake email addresses or even strings that could never be email addresses. Still, it's not worth getting too clever. The more complicated a test becomes, the greater the likelihood of false positives. In other words, as the validation gets more complex, there's more chance that valid values will be rejected.

You have two functions, isFilled and isEmail. You don't want to run those functions on every form field. You need some way of indicating which fields need to be filled and which fields should be email addresses.

In your markup, you're using a class called required:

```
<input type="text" id="name" name="name" value="Your name"
➥ class="required" />
```

You're also combining this with a class called email:

```
<input type="text" id="email" name="email" value="Your email address"
➥ class="email required" />
```

You can use these classes in your CSS files. If you want, you could style required fields with a thicker border or a different background color.

You can also use the classes in your JavaScript.

Write a function called validateForm. This function will take a Form object as its single argument.

- Loop through the elements array of the form.
- If the string "required" is found in the className property of the element, then pass the element to the isFilled function.
  - If the isFilled function returns a value of false, display an alert message and have the validateForm function return a value of false.
- If the string "email" is found in the className property of the element, then pass the element to the isEmail function.
  - If the isEmail function returns a value of false, display an alert message and have the validateForm function return a value of false.
- Otherwise, the validateForm function returns a value of true.

Here's the finished function:

```
function validateForm(whichform) {
  for (var i=0; i<whichform.elements.length; i++) {
    var element = whichform.elements[i];
    if (element.className.indexOf("required") != -1) {
      if (!isFilled(element)) {
        alert("Please fill in the "+element.name+" field.");
        return false;
      }
```

```
          }
          if (element.className.indexOf("email") != -1) {
            if (!isEmail(element)) {
              alert
➥("The "+element.name+" field must be a valid email address.");
              return false;
            }
          }
        }
      return true;
    }
```

Now you just need to run your forms through the validateForm function when they are submitted. You can add the behavior for the onsubmit event handler in the prepareForms function:

```
    function prepareForms() {
      for (var i=0; i<document.forms.length; i++) {
        var thisform = document.forms[i];
        resetFields(thisform);
        thisform.onsubmit = function() {
          return validateForm(this);
        }
      }
    }
```

Whenever a form is submitted, the submit event is triggered, which is intercepted by the onsubmit event handler. When this happens, the form is passed to the validateForm function. If validateForm returns true, the form is submitted to the server. If validateForm returns false, the submission is cancelled.

Save all of the form validation functions in contact.js.

Refresh contact.html in a web browser. Try submitting the contact form with empty or default values. You will be greeted with a terse alert message telling you the first thing that needs to be fixed:

11

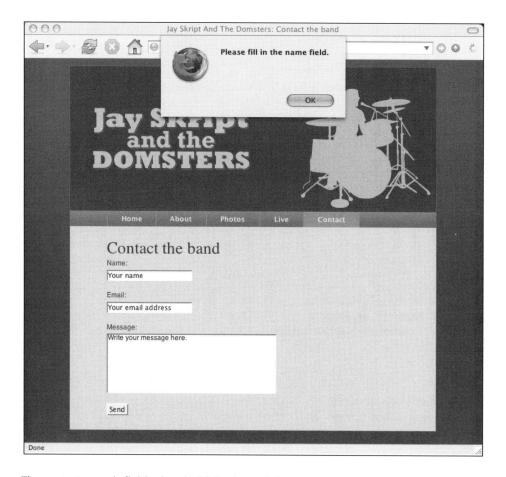

The contact page is finished and with it, the website.

Summary

The website for Jay Skript and the Domsters is ready to be unleashed on the Web. You've created a stylish online presence for the band. You wrapped the content in valid, semantically meaningful XHTML. You implemented the design with external style sheets. Finally, you added some extra behavioral pizzazz and usability enhancements using the power of JavaScript and the Document Object Model.

It almost seems a shame that the band is completely fictional. Still, there's no reason not to put the final result online. You can see the finished website at http://domscripting.com/domsters/index.html.

- The home page has a slideshow.
- Content is selectively hidden and displayed on the "about" page.

- Photos are presented in a JavaScript image gallery.
- The table of tour dates has been styled with JavaScript to make it more readable.
- The contact form can't be submitted without filling in the required fields.

If you removed any or all of those enhancements, the site would still look and work perfectly fine. The DOM scripts aren't essential, but together, they make visiting the site more pleasurable.

What's next?

In one sense, you're done!

Not only have you learned the theory behind DOM Scripting, you have applied it in building an entire website. You can build practical and powerful functions using the methods and properties that you've learned about.

In another sense, you're just beginning.

I've shown you just some of things that you can do with just a few DOM methods. There are many more uses for those methods. There are other methods I haven't even mentioned.

The number of methods and properties you know about isn't the most important part of good DOM Scripting. It's more important that your scripts are built in a robust way so that they degrade gracefully. Most importantly of all, ensure that structure, presentation, and behavior remain separate.

JavaScript and the DOM are being used more and more every day. DOM Scripting is taking web design to some exciting places. In the final chapter, I'm going to take a peek into the future.

11

12 THE FUTURE OF DOM SCRIPTING

What this chapter covers:

- The state of the Web
- Ajax and XMLHttpRequest
- Applications on the Web

I'm going to finish with a look at some of the ways that JavaScript and the Document Object Model are being used today. These uses point to an exciting future.

I began this book with an over-the-shoulder look at the history of JavaScript and the emergence of a standardized Document Object Model. Describing the past is relatively easy. Hindsight is 20/20 vision. Trying to predict the future is a much trickier proposition, but that's what I'm going to attempt now. I may turn out to be completely wrong in my predictions, and I might very well end up with egg on my face. With that caveat in mind, let's take a look at the Web as it exists today.

The state of the Web

The World Wide Web is a difficult entity to categorize. It can be a thousand different things to a thousand different people. For some people, the Web is all about e-commerce. For others, the Web is one giant art gallery. For many, the Web is a virtual community where friendships are formed and strengthened.

The Web is all these things and more. It's pointless to even try to pin down the nature of the Web by examining its content.

On a more fundamental level, the World Wide Web is pretty easy to describe. It's a collection of web pages. People, often web designers, build these pages. The pages are usually gathered together in groups called websites. In most cases, people using web browsers visit these websites.

That's a simplistic view, but it does help to view websites in terms of how they're made and how they are displayed.

Web browsers

Compared to the situation in the mid to late nineties, the web browser marketplace of today seems positively blissful.

In the past, web browsers differed in fundamental ways, each one offering proprietary Document Object Models and HTML extensions. These days, web browsers differ only in their level of support for standards like CSS and the W3C DOM.

Having won its war against Netscape, Microsoft's Internet Explorer dominated the marketplace for a long time. On the one hand, this was good news for web designers. A predictable, stable browser landscape meant that web designers could dismiss many of the uncertainties that were previously intrinsic to publishing on the Web. Internet Explorer also has pretty good standards support, so designers were in a position to move forward and work with web standards.

On the other hand, the lack of competition meant there was no incentive for Microsoft to improve its browser. The CSS support in Internet Explorer, for instance, could be improved tremendously, with just a few more additions, to bring it even more in line with the specifications.

Web designers have had to deal with this state of inertia for the past few years. It's a frustrating environment. Standards support in the dominant web browser is good, but it could be better. The browser marketplace has been stable, but imperfect, for quite a while.

Now something has happened to upset this equilibrium.

Crazy like a Firefox

The Firefox browser from the Mozilla organization (http://www.mozilla.org/products/firefox/) is built on the open source Gecko rendering engine. Gecko, and therefore Firefox, has excellent support for web standards. It is also constantly undergoing improvement.

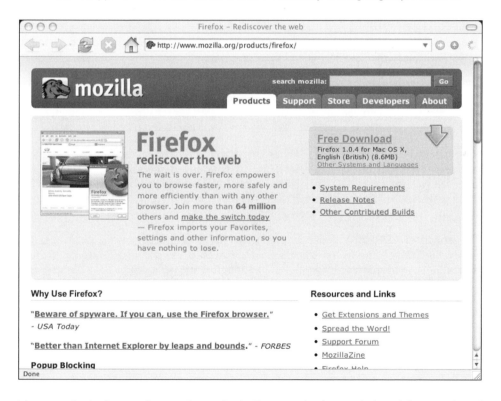

12

Most people don't care about web standards. Few people choose their web browser based on its support for W3C recommendations. They do, however, care about speed, ease of use, and security. For those reasons, a lot of people are switching from Internet Explorer to Firefox.

The balance of the browser market has shifted. Microsoft is paying attention. The development of Internet Explorer has been revived from its long slumber.

The stage is set for another browser war. This time, however, I think things are going to be different. The second browser war will be fought with conventional means, rather than with the dirty bombs of the first browser war that polluted the web development environment for years afterward.

Hopefully, the battle between Internet Explorer, Firefox, and other browsers that want to compete will be fought like any other fight for market share. Competing products are released, each one attempting to improve on its rivals by providing better features. For most people, this means tabbed browsing, pop-up blocking, and security patches. For web designers, it means better support for standards like CSS2 and the DOM.

Web designers

The term "web designer" has no formal definition. It can mean different things to different people. It can also mean different things at different times. Take this definition from Wikipedia, http://en.wikipedia.org/wiki/Web_designer:

"Web design is the design or designing of a Web page, Website or Web application. The term generally refers to the graphical side of Web development using images, CSS and XHTML."

Just a few years ago, there would have been no mention of web applications in any definition of web design. The emergence of CSS is also a relatively recent phenomenon. At the start of the twenty-first century, CSS was a fringe technology that most web designers had little knowledge of. These days, it's a vital weapon in every web designer's arsenal.

Some designers use CSS purely to change colors and fonts. Others use CSS for everything, including the layout of page elements. This latter group is still in the minority, but the ranks are growing every day. The question is no longer *if* CSS will be used for layout, but rather *when*. Individual designers will make the move from table-based layout at their own pace, but the move itself seems inevitable.

The growth of CSS-based design is gratifying, but it is also somewhat surprising. The biggest hurdle faced by web designers moving to CSS is the problem of varying browser support. Internet Explorer's incomplete CSS support is the bane of CSS development.

DOM Scripting, by contrast, seems like a walk in the park. There are some browser inconsistencies but nothing too major.

Yet many more web designers know CSS than know JavaScript and the Document Object Model. There are a number of reasons for this.

- The early days of JavaScript were a wild and lawless time. The technology was misused to create some very dubious "enhancements."
- Due to a lack of forethought, many early scripts were inaccessible. This has given rise to the myth that JavaScript is somehow an inherently inaccessible technology.

- There is a misconception that the Document Object Model is implemented differently on competing browsers. This was true during the dark days of DHTML and the browser wars, but it is no longer true today.

- JavaScript is a programming language. Many web designers are visually oriented and are wary of anything with a whiff of code.

In short, the biggest hurdle standing in the way of the widespread adoption of DOM scripting is simply a public relations issue. Slowly but surely, this PR problem is being solved. Web designers are beginning to realize that there is a gap in their knowledge.

The three-legged stool

Many web designers come from a background in print design. The most common initial approach to designing websites is to treat them just like printed pages, but on a screen instead of paper. This approach is doomed to fail. The Web is a different medium. Whereas content and presentation are intermingled in print design, web design works best when these aspects are separated.

The most accurate way to approach web design is to view web pages in terms of three layers:

1. Structure
2. Style
3. Behavior

Each one of these layers requires a different technology. The respective technologies are

1. (eXtensible) HyperText Markup Language
2. Cascading Style Sheets
3. JavaScript and the Document Object Model

These three technologies are like three legs of a stool. In order to have a balanced skill set, web designers should able to call upon each technology as and when they are needed. Right now, DOM Scripting is the shortest leg of the stool.

Many web designers are becoming aware of this gap in their skill set. They've mastered structure and style. Now they are starting to tackle behavior.

Learning a programming language like JavaScript will seem like a daunting task to these designers. Luckily, help is at hand.

The DOM Scripting Task Force

In July 2005, a task force was set up under the auspices of the Web Standards Project, http://domscripting.webstandards.org/. The DOM Scripting Task Force encourages the use of standards-compliant, unobtrusive JavaScript that degrades gracefully.

12

This book is just one part of a larger movement promoting best practices in DOM Scripting. Members of the task force regularly publish articles and tutorials aimed at helping web designers who want to expand their skill set.

I believe the DOM Scripting Task Force will find a receptive audience. Something has happened to change the image of JavaScript. That something is Ajax.

Ajax

On February 18th, 2005, Jesse James Garrett of Adaptive Path published an essay titled "Ajax: A New Approach to Web Applications" (http://www.adaptivepath.com/publications/essays/archives/000385.php). He coined the term "Ajax," but not to describe a legendary Trojan warrior, or a household cleaning product, or even Flash Gordon's spaceship. The term **Ajax** refers to a revolutionary way of using JavaScript.

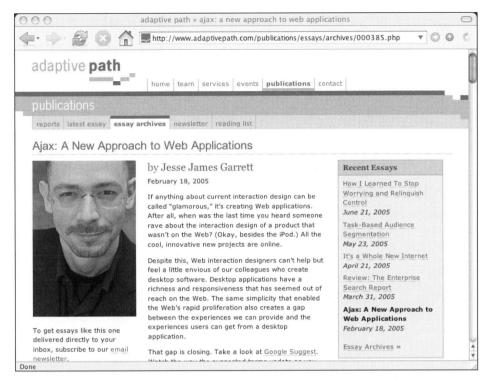

Ajax involves the use of JavaScript, CSS, the DOM, and (X)HTML. There's nothing new about that. In fact, that pretty accurately describes what DHTML was supposed to be. The difference is that Ajax uses **asynchronous** server-side processing.

Traditionally, web applications involve lots of page refreshes. The user makes a choice or enters data on one page. This information is sent back to the server. The server then sends back a new page based on the user's actions. Even if the user only needed to make a small query to the server, a whole new page would need to be served.

Take the example of a login page. This page would probably have branding, navigation, and footer elements as well as the obligatory login form. Every time a user tries to log in, a call must be made to the server to check the inputted data against a database. If the login is incorrect, the same page is served up again, complete with the same branding, the same navigation, and the same footer. The only difference between this page and the previous page is the error message informing the user that the attempted login was un- successful. Despite the fact that only a small portion of the page needed to be updated, the entire page was reloaded. Each page load is synchronous with a user request.

In the Ajax version, only the login portion of the page changes. Everything else—the branding, the navigation, and the footer—remains the same. The user fills in the login form and presses submit. This time, if the login is unsuccessful, an error message appears on the page that is already loaded in the browser.

12

The difference between the traditional login page and the Ajax version is that with Ajax, the server-side processing occurs asynchronously. Instead of serving up a whole new page every time the user sends a request, the server can process requests in the background.

Perhaps the best description of this difference comes from Derek Powazek, who said that the traditional Web is to Ajax as email is to instant messaging.

There has always been a very clear divide between client-side processing and server-side processing. On the client side, which is the browser, JavaScript can manipulate the contents of the currently loaded page. If any server-side processing is required, a request is sent to a program on the server, written in PHP, ASP, Perl, ColdFusion, or any other server-side programming language. Traditionally, the only way for the server to send back a response was to serve up a new web page.

Whenever the client (the web browser) needed something from the server, a request had to travel all the way to the server, and a corresponding response had to travel all the way from the server back to the client.

The magic of Ajax is achieved by placing a way station between the client and the server. Using JavaScript, a request is sent from the client to this way station, instead of going all the way back to the server. The request is then passed along to the server. The server sends a response back to the way station. This response is then passed on to the client where it can be processed using JavaScript.

The way station is the XMLHttpRequest object.

The XMLHttpRequest object

Don't bother looking for XMLHttpRequest in the W3C DOM specifications because you won't find it. It's not a standard, but it is very widely supported in modern web browsers.

Unfortunately, different browsers implement XMLHttpRequest in different ways. As is so often the case when dealing with non-standard JavaScript, you'll need to branch your code.

Microsoft first implemented something called XMLHTTP as one of their proprietary ActiveX objects. Here's how you would create a new instance of the object in Internet Explorer:

```
var waystation = new ActiveXObject("Microsoft.XMLHTTP");
```

Other browsers achieve the same result by using XMLHttpRequest:

```
var waystation = new XMLHttpRequest();
```

In order to satisfy both implementations, you would need to write something like this getHTTPObject function to create an instance of the right object:

```
function getHTTPObject() {
  if (window.ActiveXObject) {
    var waystation = new ActiveXObject("Microsoft.XMLHTTP");
  } else if (window.XMLHttpRequest) {
```

```
      var waystation = new XMLHttpRequest();
    } else {
      var waystation = false;
    }
    return waystation;
  }
```

That's a very simple example. In a real-world situation, you might have to write something even more convoluted!

The getHTTPObject function returns a reference to a new XMLHttpRequest object. You can assign this reference to a variable:

```
request = getHTTPObject();
```

This object has a number of methods, the most useful of which is open. The open method is used to point the object at a file on the server. You can also specify what sort of HTTP request you want to make: GET, POST, or SEND. A third parameter specifies whether the request should be processed asynchronously.

This will initiate a GET request to a file called example.txt in the same directory as the JavaScript file:

```
request.open( "GET", "example.txt", true );
```

You also need to specify what happens when the XMLHttpResponse object receives a response from the server. You can do this by utilizing the onreadystatechange property. This is an event handler that is triggered when the server sends a response back to the XMLHttpRequest object.

This will cause a function called doSomething to be executed when onreadystatechange is triggered:

```
request.onreadystatechange = doSomething;
```

Once you've specified where the object should send a request and what it should do once it receives a response, you can start the process using the send method:

```
request.send(null);
```

The whole process looks like this:

```
request = getHTTPObject();
request.open( "GET", "example.txt", true );
request.onreadystatechange = doSomething;
request.send(null);
```

You'll need to write a function called doSomething to handle the response from the server.

12

When the server sends a response back to the XMLHttpRequest object, a number of properties are made available. The readyState property is a numerical value that is updated while the server deals with the request. There are five possible values:

0 uninitialized

1 loading

2 loaded

3 interactive

4 complete

Once the readyState property has a value of 4, you have access to the data sent by the server.

You can access this data as a string of text provided by the responseText property. If the data is sent back with a Content-Type header of "text/xml", you can also access the responseXML property, which is effectively a DocumentFragment. You can use all the usual DOM methods to manipulate this DocumentFragment. This is where the XML part of XMLHttpRequest comes from.

In this example, the doSomething function waits for a readyState value of 4 and then dumps the entire responseText property into an alert dialog:

```
function doSomething() {
  if (request.readyState == 4) {
    alert(request.responseText);
  }
}
```

If the example.txt file contains a piece of text saying "Hello world," then that will appear in the alert box.

That's a very simple and unimpressive way of using the XMLHttpRequest object, but with a little imagination, it can be put to astounding use.

An explosion of Ajax

Given the recent interest in Ajax, you'd be forgiven for thinking it was a new technology. In fact, the XMLHttpRequest object has been around for years. In technical terms, asynchronous JavaScript interaction with the server is nothing new. All of the other elements of the Ajax model have also been around for quite some time: CSS, (X)HTML, and DOM Scripting.

Yet in 2005, interest in this methodology soared. Could it really be that simply giving this approach a snappy name like Ajax was responsible for the sudden interest?

In truth, interest in the new approach to building websites was on the rise even before Jesse James Garrett coined the term "Ajax." This increase in interest was fueled by the appearance of new web applications from Google.

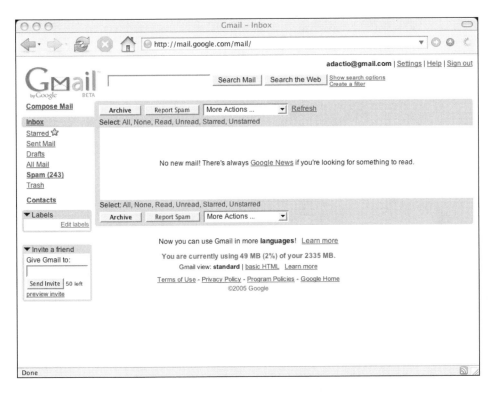

When Google launched Gmail, a web-based email service, the initial focus was on its large storage capacity (http://mail.google.com/). Once people began to interact with the service, other features came to the fore. Gmail employs spellchecking, auto-completion of addresses, and other processes that are carried out transparently in the background. The front end of the web application is asynchronously transferring data to, and receiving data from, the server.

Interest in the XMLHttpRequest object was piqued further when beta testing began on Google Suggest, http://www.google.com/webhp?complete=1. When the user begins typing a phrase into the search field, suggestions for completed phrases appear in a list below. Every time the user types a letter, a call is made to the server for a new list of suggestions. This kind of feature is effective because the client/server interaction is happening asynchronously. If the page were reloaded every time the user typed a letter, Google Suggest would be far less usable.

12

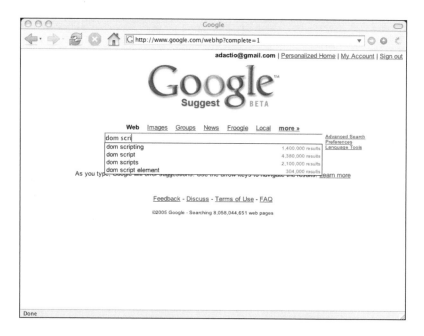

As innovative as Gmail and Google Suggest are, they pale in comparison to Google's mapping service, Google Maps, `http://maps.google.com/`. Searches are performed, maps are dragged and zoomed; all of this is done without any page refreshes. Although Google Maps doesn't make heavy use of the `XMLHttpRequest` object (it uses a hidden `iframe`), it exemplifies the Ajax methodology of asynchronous data transfer.

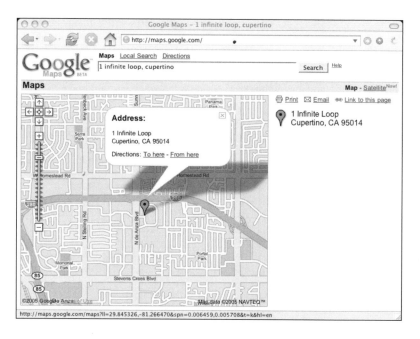

Google supplied the working examples, and Jesse James Garrett provided a snappy marketing term. Ajax is primed and ready for take-off.

Ajax challenges

Ajax is here to stay, of that I am certain. On the whole, I think that the Ajax methodology will bring a lot of benefits. It can improve the usability of websites by providing very fast responses to user actions without refreshing the whole page. At the same time, this new approach also presents a number of challenges.

One of the features of Ajax applications is a reduced number of individual page loads. The downside to this state-saving technology is that it interferes with browsing conventions such as using the back button or being able to bookmark individual pages.

The ability to update just part of a page also alters user expectations. Ideally, every action taken by the user should have a clear and obvious result. Web designers must rise to the challenge of providing meaningful feedback when the user initiates a request to the server and when the server provides a response.

There's no doubt that Ajax is a powerful tool but, as with any powerful tool, it could be misused. There is a danger that, right now, at the very moment that JavaScript is becoming an accepted technology, Ajax could return us right back to square one if it garners a reputation for being awkward and inaccessible. This is something that we as web designers need to avoid.

The key to building a successful Ajax application is to treat it like adding any other JavaScript enhancement. Apply progressive enhancement in order to provide graceful degradation.

Progressive enhancement with Ajax

Because Ajax applications can provide fast, transparent responses to user actions, they are often likened more to desktop applications than traditional websites. There is a certain amount of truth to this comparison, but it can be taken too far. There is a danger that the use of Ajax could be seen as carte blanche to ignore usability and accessibility considerations associated with traditional websites.

Already, sites are emerging that use Ajax and specify JavaScript as a requirement for accessing content. The argument offered as justification for this approach is that the features that are provided are so rich in nature that they couldn't possibly degrade gracefully.

I don't buy it. In fact, I believe that Ajax applications, by their very nature, can always offer a non-Ajax alternative. It all depends on how the Ajax functionality is applied.

If Ajax is included as part of the functionality from the start, then it will be very hard to decouple it at a later stage to provide a non-Ajax version. If, on the other hand, the application is first built using old-fashioned page refreshes, Ajax can be applied on top of the existing framework to intercept requests to the server and route them through XMLHttpRequest. The Ajax functionality then sits like a layer over the regular site.

12

Does this sound familiar? This is no different from the technique of progressive enhancement that you've seen employed throughout this book.

Building Ajax functionality into the core of an application from the start is equivalent to using the javascript: pseudo-protocol every time you want a link to trigger an action. It's far better to just use a normal link and intercept the default action. The best way to build an Ajax website is to simply build a normal website. Then Hijax it.

Hijax

If the success of Ajax has shown one thing, it's that having a short, snappy name for something helps sell an idea. Just as it's easier to say Ajax instead of "XMLHttpRequest with DOM Scripting, CSS, and (X)HTML," it's simpler for me to say Hijax instead of "progressive enhancement using Ajax."

Ajax relies on the server for its power. A server-side programming language carries out most of the real work. The XMLHttpRequest object acts as a gateway between the browser and the server, transferring requests and responses. If that gateway is removed, it should still be possible to send requests and receive responses. It will just take longer.

Think back to the example of a login form. The simplest way to build this is to use the time-honored approach of having a form submit the entire page to the server, which then transmits a new page containing feedback. All the processing is done on the server, where the values that have been entered in the form are compared to values stored in a database in an attempt to find a match.

In order to apply the Ajax methodology to the login process, the submission of the form needs to be intercepted (hijacked) and passed to the XMLHttpRequest object instead. The submission of a form triggers a submit event. If this event is captured using the onsubmit event handler, the default action—submitting the whole page—can be cancelled and replaced with a new action: sending the data to the server via XMLHttpRequest.

Once the login form has been Hijaxed, the login process becomes more convenient for the user. Response times are increased, and lengthy page refreshes are eliminated. Crucially, however, if JavaScript is unavailable to the user, the application will still work. It will take longer and the experience won't be as seamless, but because the login processing is done on the server, there is no reason to turn the user away.

The fact that Ajax applications rely so heavily on server-side, rather than client-side processing means that they can degrade gracefully.

Admittedly, some applications will seem painfully slow when they rely on page refreshes, rather than Ajax, every time the user initiates an action. But a slower degraded experience is still better than no experience at all.

I put together my own little Ajax application to demonstrate the idea of Hijaxing, http://elsewhere.adactio.com/:

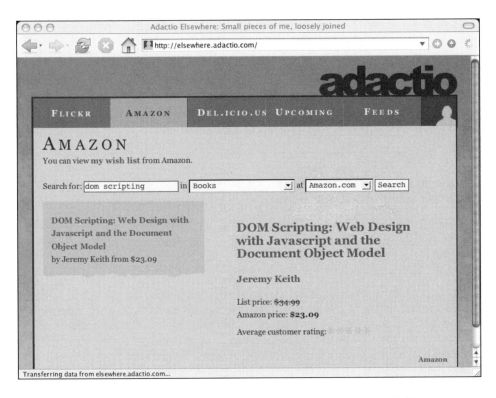

If you disable JavaScript, you will see that all the same content is still available.

The future of Ajax

I'm certain that we will see an increase in the use of Ajax. Personally, I would like to see Ajax used in the same way that any other kind of DOM Scripting should be used: as an enhancement to, rather than a requirement of, the user experience. I would like to see the idea of Hijaxing applied to page elements like feedback forms and shopping carts.

To me, the Hijax technique seems like the simplest way to apply Ajax. Unfortunately, the majority of high-profile Ajax applications haven't been built that way. Gmail and Google Maps were both built with Ajax tightly integrated from the start. This makes it a lot harder to provide a non-Ajax version.

If Google Maps had been built like any other mapping website, the Ajax enhancements could have been applied on top. As it is, it will involve a lot of work to provide a "separate but equal" non-Ajax version.

Google Suggest, on the other hand, is a good example of progressive enhancement in action. The core functionality is the ability to search the Web for a term. With JavaScript enabled, that process is enhanced by suggesting possible search terms using Ajax. If JavaScript is disabled, the core functionality remains.

12

There is no doubt that Ajax is a wonderful technology, but I hope it won't be abused in such a way as to shut out browsers that don't meet the minimum entry requirements. Instead, I hope that it will be used like CSS, as a way of enhancing the user experience without sacrificing access to content.

Applications on the Web

Gmail is an example of a web application. More and more tasks that have traditionally been performed by desktop software are migrating to the Web: reading and writing emails, managing projects, and storing photos, to name just a few. Web design is beginning to resemble software development.

As more and more applications move to the Web, the role of the operating system may become increasingly irrelevant. It could be that in the near future, all you'll need to accomplish your daily tasks is an Internet connection and a standards-compliant web browser. Your home computer could be a dumb terminal connected to a network of smart servers.

Building applications on the Web appears to be fraught with difficulties. Software developers bemoan the lack of control over forms and other interface elements. It's true that, compared with the richness of desktop user interfaces, the browser can seem primitive. But importantly, the browser is just good enough to warrant using it as an interface. There are benefits to having a centralized application on a web server rather than many copies of an application sitting on desktops. Changes and improvements can be carried out instantaneously with immediate effect. If using a browser, rather than a richer Graphical User Interface, is the price to pay, it seems worth it.

Alternatively, the browser may become just one of many possible tools for interacting with web applications. Apple's Tiger operating system includes an application called Dashboard. Dashboard contains a collection of widgets, many of which interact with web applications. These widgets use all the familiar web technologies: CSS, XHTML, and DOM Scripting, with a few desktop enhancements thrown in. Dashboard is effectively offering an alternative to using a browser.

Other alternatives may be forthcoming. Mozilla's XUL and Microsoft's XAML technologies both promise the means to build rich user interfaces that can interact with web applications. Nobody seems quite sure whether this means we will see lots of desktop applications on the Web or lots of web applications on the desktop.

Personally, I love the idea of the Web as an application platform. However, there is a danger in comparing web applications to desktop applications. Whereas the Web is open to any and all user agents, desktop applications are tied to a specific operating system. When creating web applications with technologies like DOM Scripting and Ajax, it's very tempting to demand a similar lock-in. The simplest solution often seems to be to demand a minimum technology requirement, such as a DOM-compliant browser, or worse yet, to limit applications to specific browsers.

While this may seem like the easiest way to build web applications, I believe that this approach should be resisted at all costs.

What's next?

DOM Scripting is a powerful technology. I hope that this book has given you a taste of what can be accomplished with JavaScript and the Document Object Model.

How you use DOM Scripting is up to you, but I am hopeful that you will employ it in a responsible, usable way. It's all too easy to get bogged down in the minutiae of using a particular tool to the detriment of the final product. I find it helpful to step back occasionally and take a look at the bigger picture. The grand vision of the World Wide Web is the same today as when it was invented by Tim Berners Lee:

"The power of the Web is in its universality. Access by everyone regardless of disability is an essential aspect."

Hypertext documents on the Web are inherently accessible. They only become restricted when we choose to make them that way. Using a combination of web standards and best practices, we can ensure that the Web remains an open, accessible place:

- Use meaningful markup to structure your content.
- Keep presentational information separate using CSS.
- Apply behavioral changes responsibly using unobtrusive JavaScript that degrades gracefully.

We are at a crossroads in the development of the Web. Some people have already started talking about the next stage of the Web, a Web 2.0, as something that is being created right now. The boundary between desktop software and Web applications is becoming blurred with the emergence of methodologies like Ajax. Together, we will face many challenges as we strive to move the Web forward while remaining true to its original purpose as a universal medium.

What happens next is up to you. This is an exciting time to be a web designer.

12

REFERENCE

What this section covers:

- Creating nodes
- Duplicating nodes
- Inserting nodes
- Removing nodes
- Replacing nodes
- Manipulating nodes
- Finding nodes
- Node properties
- Traversing the node tree

This section contains a list of some of the most useful methods and properties provided by the Document Object Model. They are arranged by task.

Methods

These methods are part of the DOM Core. This isn't a complete list of all the methods available. These are the most useful methods.

Creating nodes

Use these methods to create new nodes.

createElement

The createElement method creates a new element node with the specified tag name. This method returns a reference to the newly created element:

```
reference = document.createElement(element)
```

The method takes a single parameter: the name of the element to be created. This is a string:

```
reference = document.createElement("p")
reference = document.createElement("h1")
```

The reference returned by createElement is a node object. It is an element node, so its nodeType property will have a value of 1:

```
var para = document.createElement("p");
```

In this example, para.nodeType would return a value of 1. para.nodeName would return a value of "p" or "P".

An element created with createElement is not automatically added to the document. The new node has no parentNode property. Instead, it exists only in JavaScript as a

DocumentFragment. To add the DocumentFragment to your document, you will need to use the appendChild or insertBefore methods (see "Inserting nodes") or else replaceChild (see "Replacing nodes"):

```
var para = document.createElement("p");
document.body.appendChild(para);
```

This example will create a paragraph element and append the newly created element as the lastChild of the body element.

You can apply methods to the newly created element at any time. For instance, you can set an attribute on the element even before the element is inserted into the document (see "Manipulating nodes"):

```
var para = document.createElement("p");
para.setAttribute("title","My paragraph");
document.body.appendChild(para);
```

Alternatively, you can manipulate the newly created node after it has been inserted into the document:

```
var para = document.createElement("p");
document.body.appendChild(para);
para.setAttribute("title","My paragraph");
```

createTextNode

The createTextNode method creates a new text node containing the specified text. This method returns a reference to the newly created text node:

reference = document.createTextNode(text)

The method takes a single parameter: the string of text to be created:

reference = document.createTextNode("hello world")

The reference returned by createTextNode is a node object. It is a text node, so its nodeType property will have a value of 3:

```
var message = document.createTextNode("hello world");
```

In this example, message.nodeType would return a value of 1. message.nodeName would return a value of "#text".

A text node created with createTextNode is not automatically added to the document. The new node has no parentNode property. To add the newly created text to your document, you will need to use the appendChild or insertBefore methods (see "Inserting Nodes") or else replaceChild (see "Replacing Nodes"):

```
var message = document.createTextNode("hello world");
var container = document.getElementById("intro");
container.appendChild(message);
```

This example will create a text node with the value "hello world". This text node is then appended to the element with the id "intro".

The createTextNode method is often used in conjunction with createElement method to create chunks of markup that can then be inserted into the document:

```
var message = document.createTextNode("hello world");
var container = document.createElement("p");
container.appendChild(message);
document.body.appendChild(container);
```

In this example, a text node containing the string "hello world" is created. The createTextNode method returns the reference message. A paragraph element is created using the createElement method, which returns the reference container. The message text node is placed inside the container element node using the appendChild method. This updated container element is then appended to the body element of the document.

Duplicating nodes

The Document Object Model provides a method for copying a node.

cloneNode

The cloneNode method creates a copy of a specified node. This method returns a reference to the newly cloned node:

reference = *node*.cloneNode(*deep*)

The method takes a single parameter that can have a Boolean value of true or false. This parameter specifies whether or not the newly created node contains the same child nodes as the copied node. If the parameter's value is true, the newly created node will have all the same children as the node from which it was cloned. If it is false, the newly created node will have no child nodes. If the node is an element node, it means that any text within the original element will not be duplicated (the text is a child node), but attributes will be duplicated:

reference = *node*.cloneNode(**true**)
reference = *node*.cloneNode(**false**)

The reference returned by the cloneNode method is a node object. This node will have the same nodeType and nodeName properties as the original node from which it was cloned:

```
var para = document.createElement("p");
var newpara = para.cloneNode(false);
```

This example creates a new element node: para. Then, another new element node, newpara, is created, which is a clone of the para element node. The value of para.nodeType is 1 (an element node) so the value of newpara.nodeType is also 1.

Here's another example:

```
var message = document.createElement("hello world");
var newmessage = message.cloneNode(false);
```

In this case, a new text node is created: message. This text node is cloned to make newmessage. The value of newmessage.nodeType is 3 (a text node) because the value of message.nodeType is 3. newmessage.nodeName is "#text", the same value as message.nodeName.

In the following example, a node is cloned complete with child nodes:

```
var para = document.createElement("p");
var message = document.createTextNode("hello world");
para.appendChild(message);
var newpara = para.cloneNode(true);
```

Because the value true was passed to para.cloneNode, the newly created element node, newpara, has a child text node with the value "hello world".

Here, a node is cloned without cloning the node's children:

```
var para = document.createElement("p");
var message = document.createTextNode("hello world");
para.appendChild(message);
var newpara = para.cloneNode(false);
```

The new node, newpara, is an element node just like the original para. But whereas para had a child text node with the value "hello world", newpara has no child nodes.

When a node is duplicated using the cloneNode method, the newly created node is not automatically added to the document. The new node has no parentNode property. You will need to use the appendChild or insertBefore methods (see "Inserting Nodes") or else replaceChild (see "Replacing nodes"):

```
var para = document.createElement("p");
var message = document.createTextNode("hello world");
para.appendChild(message);
document.body.appendChild(para);
var newpara = para.cloneNode(true);
document.body.appendChild(newpara);
```

In this example, a new paragraph element called para is created. Also, a new text node called message is created. The message text node is inserted into the para element node and then para is inserted into the body of the document. Using the cloneNode method, para is duplicated (along with its child node) to create the element node: newpara. newpara is inserted into the body of the document. Two identical paragraphs of text have been added to the document.

If you clone an element that has a unique id, you should always change the value of the new element's id. An id attribute must be unique within a document.

Inserting nodes

There are two methods for inserting nodes into a document.

appendChild

The appendChild method adds a new child node to an element node:

```
reference = elment.appendChild(newChild)
```

The new child node becomes the last child node of the element to which it has been appended. This method returns a reference to the newly appended node.

This method is usually used in conjunction with createElement and createTextNode, which are used to generate new nodes.

In this example, a paragraph element, para, is created with createElement. A text node, message, is creating with createTextNode. The text node is then inserted into the paragraph using appendChild:

```
var para = document.createElement("p");
var message = document.createTextNode("hello world");
para.appendChild(message);
```

The para element (and its child, message) can then be inserted into the structure of the document, again using appendChild:

```
document.body.appendChild(para);
```

In this case, the para element is appended to the body of the document.

New nodes can be attached to any element in the document. In the following example, a new text node is appended to the element in the document with the id of "headline":

```
var message = document.createTextNode("hello world");
var container = document.getElementById("headline");
container.appendChild(message);
```

The lastChild property of container is the new text node with the value "hello world".

As well as working with newly created elements, appendChild can also be used to move existing elements in the document.

In this example, there is one element with the id "content" and another with the id "fineprint". The "fineprint" element is moved from wherever it was in the document and is appended at the end of the "content" element:

```
var message = document.getElementById("fineprint");
var container = document.getElementById("content");
container.appendChild(message);
```

The element with the id "fineprint" is first removed from the document tree and then reinserted in its new position as the last child node of the "content" element.

insertBefore

The insertBefore method is used to insert a new node into an element before a specified child node of the element:

```
reference = element.insertBefore(newNode,targetNode)
```

The node newNode is inserted into the node element before the node targetNode. The node targetNode must be a child node of element. If targetNode is not specified, newNode will be appended at the end of the child nodes of element. In that case, it behaves just like the appendChild method.

The insertBefore method is often used with createElement and createTextNode to insert newly created nodes into the document tree.

In this example, a document has an element with the id "content". This element contains an element with the id "fineprint". A new paragraph element is created using createElement. This newly created element is then inserted into the "content" element, right before the "fineprint" element:

```
var container = document.getElementById("content");
var message = document.getElementById("fineprint");
var para = document.createElement("p");
container.insertBefore(para,message);
```

If the node being inserted has any child nodes, these will also be inserted before the target node:

```
var container = document.getElementById("content");
var message = document.getElementById("fineprint");
var para = document.createElement("p");
var text = document.createTextNode("Here comes the fineprint");
para.appendChild(text);
container.insertBefore(para,message);
```

As well as working with newly created nodes, insertBefore can also be used to move existing nodes in the document.

In this example, a document has an element with the id "content". This element contains an element with the id "fineprint". Elsewhere in the document, there is an element with the id "headline". The "headline" element is moved into the "content" element and placed before the "fineprint" element:

```
var container = document.getElementById("content");
var message = document.getElementById("fineprint");
var announcement = document.getElementById("headline");
container.insertBefore(announcement,message);
```

The element with the id "headline" is first removed from the document tree and then reinserted into its new position before the "fineprint" element inside the "content" element.

Removing nodes

The DOM provides a method for removing nodes from a document.

removeChild

The removeChild method removes a child node from a specified parent element:

> *reference = element.removeChild(node)*

This method returns a reference to the node that has been removed.

When a node is removed with removeChild, any child nodes contained by that node are also removed.

In this example, the element with the id "content" contains an element with the id "fineprint". The "fineprint" element is removed from the "content" element using removeChild:

```
var container = document.getElementById("content");
var message = document.getElementById("fineprint");
container.removeChild(message);
```

If you want to remove a node but you don't have a reference to its parent node, you can use the parentNode property of the node you want to remove:

```
var message = document.getElementById("fineprint");
var container = message.parentNode;
container.removeChild(message);
```

If you want to move a node from one part of the document tree to another, there is no need to use removeChild. The appendChild and insertBefore methods will automatically remove nodes from the document tree before reinserting them in their new positions.

Replacing nodes

The DOM provides a method for replacing nodes in a document tree.

replaceChild

The replaceChild method replaces one child node of a specified parent element with another node:

> *reference = element.replaceChild(newChild,oldChild)*

The oldChild node must be a child node of element. This method returns a reference to the node that has been replaced.

In this example, an element with the id "content" contains an element with the id "fineprint". A new paragraph element is created using createElement. Using replaceChild, this newly created element replaces the "fineprint" element:

```
var container = document.getElementById("content");
var message = document.getElementById("fineprint");
var para = document.createElement("p");
container.replaceChild(para,message);
```

If the new node has any child nodes, they will also be inserted into the document tree.

The replaceChild method also works on nodes that are already part of the document tree. If the newChild node already exists in the document tree, it will first be removed before replacing the oldChild node.

In this example, the element node with the id "headline" replaces the element with the id "fineprint" within the element "content":

```
var container = document.getElementById("content");
var message = document.getElementById("fineprint");
var announcement = document.getElementById("headline");
container.replaceChild(announcement,message);
```

This example does the same as the previous one, but this time a reference to the replaced node is used to reinsert it into the document (as the last child node of "content"):

```
var container = document.getElementById("content");
var message = document.getElementById("fineprint");
var announcement = document.getElementById("headline");
var oldmessage = container.replaceChild(announcement,message);
container.appendChild(oldmessage);
```

Manipulating nodes

The DOM provides a mechanism for manipulating attribute nodes.

setAttribute

The setAttribute method adds a new attribute value or changes the value of an existing attribute of a specified element node:

```
element.setAttribute(attributeName,attributeValue)
```

The name and the value of the attribute are passed to the method as strings. If this attribute already exists, its value will be updated. If the named attribute doesn't exist, it will be created and given a value. The setAttribute method can only be used on element nodes.

In this example, a title attribute with the value "this is important" is added to an element with the id "fineprint":

```
var message = document.getElementById("fineprint");
message.setAttribute("title","this is important");
```

Regardless of whether or not the element had an existing title attribute, it now has a title attribute with the value "this is important".

Attribute nodes can be set on elements that have not yet been added to the document tree. If you create a new element using the createElement method, you can set attributes on that element before adding it to the document tree:

```
var para = document.createElement("p");
para.setAttribute("id","fineprint");
var container = document.getElementById("content");
content.appendChild(para);
```

The corollary to setAttribute is getAttribute, which allows you to retrieve the value of an attribute.

Finding nodes

The Document Object Model provides a number of methods for locating nodes in a document tree.

getAttribute

The getAttribute method returns the value of a named attribute node of a specified element:

```
attributeValue = element.getAttribute(attributeName)
```

The name of the attribute is passed to the method as a string. The value of the named attribute is returned as a string. If the named attribute doesn't exist, getAttribute returns an empty string.

This example retrieves the title attribute of an element with the id "fineprint" and stores it in a variable called titletext:

```
var message = document.getElementById("fineprint");
var titletext = message.getAttribute("title");
```

This next example takes the value of the title attribute and creates a new text node with that value. This text node is then appended to the end of the "fineprint" element:

```
var message = document.getElementById("fineprint");
var titletext = message.getAttribute("title");
var newtext = document.createTextNode(titletext);
message.appendChild(titletext);
```

The corollary to getAttribute is setAttribute, which allows you to specify the value of an attribute.

getElementById

The getElementById method finds an element with a specified id attribute:

    element = document.getElementById(ID)

This method returns an element node with the specified id. If there is no such element, getElementById returns null. The getElementById method can only be applied to the document object.

The element node returned by getElementById is an object, complete with properties such as nodeName, nodeType, parentNode, childNodes, etc.

This example retrieves the element with the id "fineprint" and stores it in the variable message. The parent node of message, also an element, is stored in the variable container:

    var message = document.getElementById("fineprint");
    var container = message.parentNode;

If an element has an id, using the getElementById method is the simplest and quickest way to reference that element. You can then apply methods like setAttribute, cloneNode, or appendChild.

The following example finds an element with the id "fineprint" and stores it in the variable message. The title attribute of this element is then updated with the value "this is important":

    var message = document.getElementById("fineprint");
    message.setAttribute("title","this is important");

The id of an element should be unique within a document. If more than one element share the same id, the getElementById method may behave unpredictably.

getElementsByTagName

The getElementsByTagName method finds all the elements with a specified tag name:

    elements = document.getElementsByTagName(tagName)

This method returns a list of elements. This list can be treated as an array. The length property of the list is equal to the number of elements in the document with the specified tag name. Each element in the array is an object, complete with properties such as nodeName, nodeType, parentNode, childNodes, etc.

This example retrieves all the paragraphs in a document. The length property of the returned list is stored as the variable howmany:

    var paras = document.getElementsByTagName("p");
    var howmany = paras.length;

The getElementsByTagName method is often used together with a for loop to go through each element in the returned list. In this way, each element can be queried or manipulated using methods like setAttribute, cloneNode, appendChild, etc.

The following example loops through all the paragraphs in a document and sets the title attribute of each one to a blank string:

```
var paras = document.getElementsByTagName("p");
for (var i=0; i < paras.length; i++) {
  paras[i].setAttribute("title","");
}
```

In that example, paras is a nodeList. The items in this list can be accessed like any other array: paras[0], paras[1], paras[2], and so on. Alternatively, you can use the item method: paras.item(0), paras.item(1), paras.item(2), and so on.

The getElementsByTagName method doesn't have to be used on the entire document. It can also be used to find elements with a specified tag name that are children of a specified element.

In the following example, a document contains an element with the id "content". The getElementsByTagName method is applied to this element to find all the paragraphs it contains:

```
var container = document.getElementById("content");
var paras = container.getElementsByTagName("p");
var howmany = paras.length;
```

The variable howmany now contains the number of paragraphs within the "content" element, not the number of paragraphs within the entire document.

hasChildNodes

The hasChildNodes method can be used to find out if a specified element has any child nodes:

```
booleanValue = element.hasChildNodes
```

This method returns a Boolean value of either true or false. If the specified element has any children, hasChildNodes returns true. If the element has no children, hasChildNodes returns false.

Text nodes and attributes cannot contain any children. The hasChildNodes method will therefore always return a value of false.

This method is often used in an if statement. The following example finds an element with the id "fineprint" and stores it in the variable message. If this element has any child nodes, they are stored as an array in the variable children:

```
var message = document.getElementById("fineprint");
if (message.hasChildNodes) {
  var children = message.childNodes;
}
```

The hasChildNodes method does not return the child nodes of an element. The child nodes can be retrieved from the childNodes property of the element. If hasChildNodes returns a value of false, the childNodes property is an empty array.

Likewise, if hasChildNodes returns false for a specified element, that element's firstChild and lastChild properties will be null.

Properties

Here are some properties of nodes in a DOM tree.

Node properties

Every node in a document has the following properties.

nodeName

The nodeName property returns a string containing the name of the specified node:

> *name = node.nodeName*

If the specified node is an element node, the nodeName property will return the name of the element. This is equivalent to the tagName property.

If the specified node is an attribute node, the nodeName property will return the name of the attribute.

If the specified node is a text node, the nodeName property will return the string "#text".

The nodeName property is read-only. It can be queried, but it can't be manipulated directly.

nodeType

The nodeType property returns an integer indicating what type of node the specified node is:

> *integer = node.nodeType*

There are twelve possible values for the nodeType property. The numerical value returned by nodeType corresponds to one of twelve types of nodes:

1. ELEMENT_NODE
2. ATTRIBUTE_NODE
3. TEXT_NODE
4. CDATA_SECTION_NODE
5. ENTITY_REFERENCE_NODE
6. ENTITY_NODE
7. PROCESSING_INSTRUCTION_NODE

8. COMMENT_NODE
9. DOCUMENT_NODE
10. DOCUMENT_TYPE_NODE
11. DOCUMENT_FRAGMENT_NODE
12. NOTATION_NODE

Of these twelve types, the first three are the most important. Most DOM Scripting on the Web involves the manipulation of elements, attributes, and text nodes.

The nodeType property is often used in an if statement to ensure that illegal actions aren't performed on the wrong kind of node. In this example, a function takes a single argument, mynode, which can be any element in the document. The function adds a title attribute and value to the element. Before doing that, the nodeType property is checked to make sure that mynode is in fact an element node:

```
function addTitle(mynode) {
  if (mynode.nodeType == 1) {
    mynode.setAttribute("title","this is important");
  }
}
```

The nodeType property is read-only.

nodeValue

The nodeValue property returns the value of a specified node:

value = node.nodeValue

This property returns a string.

If the specified node is an attribute node, nodeValue returns the value of the attribute.

If the specified node is a text node, nodeValue returns the content of the text node.

If the specified node is an element node, nodeValue returns null.

The nodeValue property is read/write. However, you can't set a value if it is defined as null. In other words, you can't set a nodeValue for an element node. You can set a value for a text node.

This example will not work. It attempts to set a value for an element node:

```
var message = document.getElementById("fineprint");
message.nodeValue = "this won't work";
```

This example will probably work. It attempts to set a value for the first child of an element node. As long as this first child is a text node, the new value is set:

```
var message = document.getElementById("fineprint");
message.firstChild.nodeValue = "this might work";
```

This example will certainly work. There is a test to make sure that the first child of the element is a text node:

```
var message = document.getElementById("fineprint");
if (message.firstChild.nodeType == 3) {
  message.firstChild.nodeValue = "this will work";
}
```

The nodeValue property provides the simplest mechanism for updating the value of text nodes. To update the value of attribute nodes, it is usually easier to use the setAttribute method on the attribute's parent element.

Traversing the node tree

These properties can be read to extract information about neighboring nodes.

childNodes

The childNodes property returns an array of child nodes for a specified element node:

```
nodeList = node.childNodes
```

The array returned by this method is a nodeList. Each node in the nodeList is a node object. These node objects have all the usual node properties such as nodeType, nodeName, nodeValue, etc.

Text nodes and attribute nodes cannot contain any children. Their childNodes property always returns an empty array.

To find out if a node has any child nodes at all, use the hasChildNodes method.

To find out how many child nodes an element has, use the length property of the childNodes array:

```
node.childNodes.length
```

If an element has only one child node, the childNodes property will still return an array of nodes, not a single node. The length of the array will be 1. For instance, in a web page, the document has just one child, the html element. The value of document. childNodes[0].nodeName is "HTML".

The childNodes property is read-only. To add child nodes to an element, use the appendChild or insertBefore methods. To remove child nodes from an element, use the removeChild method. Whenever you use those methods, the childNodes property of the altered element is updated automatically.

firstChild

The firstChild property returns the first child node of a specified element node:

```
reference = node.firstChild
```

This property returns a reference to a node object. This node object has all the usual node properties such as nodeType, nodeName, nodeValue, etc.

Text nodes and attributes cannot contain any children. Their firstChild property always returns a value of null.

The firstChild property of an element is equivalent to the first node in an element's childNodes nodeList:

```
reference = node.childNodes[0]
```

To find out if a node has any child nodes at all, use the hasChildNodes method. If a node has no child nodes, the firstChild property will return a value of null.

The firstChild property is read-only.

lastChild

The lastChild property returns the last child node of a specified element node:

```
reference = node.lastChild
```

This property returns a reference to a node object. This node object has all the usual node properties such as nodeType, nodeName, nodeValue, etc.

Text nodes and attributes cannot contain any children. Their lastChild property always returns a value of null.

The lastChild property of an element is equivalent to the last node in an element's childNodes nodeList:

```
reference = node.childNodes[elementNode.childNodes.length-1]
```

To find out if a node has any child nodes at all, use the hasChildNodes method. If a node has no child nodes, the lastChild property will return a value of null.

The lastChild property is read-only.

nextSibling

The nextSibling property returns the next node after a specified node:

```
reference = node.nextSibling
```

This property returns a reference to a node object. This node object has all the usual node properties such as nodeType, nodeName, nodeValue, etc.

If there are no nodes immediately following the specified node, the nextSibling property returns a value of null.

The nextSibling property is read-only.

parentNode

The parentNode property returns the parent of a specified node:

> reference = node.parentNode

This property returns a reference to a node object. This node object has all the usual node properties such as nodeType, nodeName, nodeValue, etc.

The node that is returned will always be an element node, as only element nodes can contain children. The only exception to this is the document node, which has no parent. In that case, parentNode returns a value of null.

The parentNode property is read-only.

previousSibling

The previousSibling property returns the previous node before a specified node:

> reference = node.previousSibling

This property returns a reference to a node object. This node object has all the usual node properties such as nodeType, nodeName, nodeValue, etc.

If there are no nodes immediately before the specified node, the previousSibling property returns a value of null.

The previousSibling property is read-only.

INDEX

INDEX

A

abbr tag
  Internet Explorer, 161
  marking up content, 148, 149
abbreviations, 148
  browsers applying styling to, 151
  CSS overriding browser default styling, 151
  default browser behavior for, 152
  definition list structuring, 155
  displayAbbreviations function, 153–161
  displaying for content enhancement, 152–164
about.html
  Jay Skript & Domsters website, 268, 271
absolute value, position property
  style property, DOM, 209
abstraction, 203
  functions running animation, 215–221
access keys
  convention for using, 171
  displayAccesskeys function, 173–174
  displaying for content enhancement, 171–174
  too many access keys, 171
accessibility statement, 172
accesskey attribute, 171
acronym tag, 148
acronyms, 148
addClass function, 202, 203
  Jay Skript & Domsters website, 257
addLoadEvent function
  calling displayAbbreviations, 160
  calling displayCitations, 169
  calling moveMessage, 210
  calling positionMessage, 209
  executing onload events when page loaded, 103
  JavaScript image gallery, 138
  Jay Skript & Domsters website, 256
  styling elements in node tree, 191
Ajax, 298–308
  challenges and concerns, 305
  examples of current use of, 302–305
  future of, 307
  Hijax, 306
  progressive enhancement with, 305
  XMLHttpRequest object, 300–302
alert function, JavaScript, 34
alt attribute
  displaying content of attributes, 147
and (&&) operator, JavaScript
  logical operators, 29
animation, 208–241
  abstraction of functions running, 215–221
  annoying visitors, 222
  changing elements position, 210
  clearTimeout function, 211

  CSS and JavaScript, 208
  displaying image associated to link at onmouseover
    event, 222–241
    CSS, 225–227
    existence of style properties, 236
    insertAfter function, 240
    JavaScript, 227–230
    layout.css, 240
    prepareSlideshow function, 238
    questioning assumptions, 236
    refining, 233–236
    scope, 231–233
    situation, 222–223
    solution, 223–225
    topics.gif, 224
  incremental movement, 212–214
  introduction, 208–221
  position and animation, 208–210
  position property of style property, 208
  reusable functionality, 215–221
  setTimeout function, 211–212
  time and animation, 211–214
  W3C recommendations, 222
anonymous function, 101
APIs (Application Programming Interfaces)
  real world examples of, 8
appendChild method, 127–128, 316
  uses of, 129, 130, 134
arguments, JavaScript
  functions, 33
arithmetic operations, JavaScript, 25
arrays, JavaScript, 22
  Array object, 38
  arrays of arrays, 24
  associative arrays, 24
  declaring, 22, 23
  index of element, 23
  objects, 38
  populating, 23
  using Array keyword, 22, 23
assignment, JavaScript
  comparison/assignment operators, 29
  JavaScript variables, 18, 19
associative arrays, JavaScript, 24
attribute nodes, 46
attributes
  accesskey attribute, 171
  getAttribute method, 52–53, 320
  getting value of, 69
  setAttribute method, 54, 319
  tags and semantic information, 147
  web browsers displaying content, 147
auto value, CSS overflow property, 225

B

behavior layer
  separating layers, 180
    className property, 200–203
  web content, 179
Berners Lee, Tim, 309
block level elements, CSS
  blockquote element containing, 166
  displaying, 147
block value, display property, 147
blockquote element
  cite attribute
    displaying citations, 165
    marking up content, 148, 149
  elements contained, 166
  finding element nodes, 167
body tag
  family tree model of web page, 45
  inheritance, 47
BOM (Browser Object Model), 42
  creating new browser windows, 82
Boolean data, JavaScript, 22
bottom property
  style property, DOM, 209
Browser Object Model
  see BOM
browser sniffing, 90
browsers
  backward compatibility, 88
  effect of variation of browsers, 7
  host objects, 42
  innerHTML property, 122–125
  support for DOM, 9
  W3C and DOM development, 7
  WaSP recommendations, 9
built-in functions, JavaScript, 34

C

camel casing
  JavaScript naming conventions, 35
  style properties, 183, 184
Cascading Style Sheets
  see CSS
case sensitivity
  HTML and XHTML, 149
  JavaScript variables, 19
checkpoints
  JavaScript image gallery, event handlers, 97
child nodes
  appendChild method, 127–128, 316
  childNodes property, 66–67, 325
  firstChild property, 70, 325
  hasChildNodes method, 322

insertBefore method, 135, 317
  lastChild property, 70, 326
  nextSibling property, 180, 326
  parentNode property, 180, 327
  previousSibling property, 327
  removeChild method, 318
  replaceChild method, 318
childNodes property, DOM, 66–67, 325
  form elements, 284
citations
  displayCitations function, 165–170
  displaying for content enhancement, 164–170
cite attribute, blockquote element
  displaying citations, 165
  marking up content, 148, 149
class attribute
  CSS, 48, 147
  striped effect on tabular data, 196
className property, 200–203
clearTimeout function, JavaScript, 211
  scope of variables in animation example, 231
cloneNode method, 314
closing tags
  HTML and XHTML, 149
color property of style property
  measurement units of properties returned, 184
color.css style sheet
  Jay Skript & Domsters website, 250–251
    odd and highlight classes, 280
    styles for here class, 258
    table headers and rows, 277
comments, JavaScript, 16
comparison operators, JavaScript, 29
compiled languages, 15
concatenation operators, JavaScript, 26
conditional statements, JavaScript, 27
  do...while loop, 31
  for loop, 32
  if statement, 28
  while loop, 31
contact.html
  Jay Skript & Domsters website, 281–290
    form validation, 286
content
  marking up in XHTML, 149
  tags and content, 147
content enhancement, 146–175
  displaying abbreviations, 152–164
  displaying access keys, 171–174
  displaying citations, 164–170
continue keyword, 165, 167
createElement method, 126–127, 312
createTextNode method, 128–130, 313

CSS (Cascading Style Sheets), 47–48
  animation, 208
  animation example, 225–227
  attributes influencing, 147
  declaring styles, 47
  displaying block level elements, 147
  inheritance, 47
  Jay Skript & Domsters website, 248–255
    color.css style sheet, 250–251
    importing CSS files, 248
    layout.css style sheet, 251–253
    typography.css style sheet, 254–255
  lessons for website programming, 84
  overflow property, 225
  overriding browsers default styling, 151
  separating presentation functionality, 85
  setting element position, 208
  sharing hooks with CSS, 112–114
  state of the web today, 296
CSS-DOM, 178–205
  className property, 200–203
  CSS properties, 183, 184
  presentation layer, 178, 180
  repetitive styling, 193–197
  responding to events, 198–200
  separating layers, pseudo classes, 180
  style property, 180–189
  styling elements in node tree, 189–193
  using tables with, 193
  when to use DOM styling, 189

D

Dashboard, 308
data types, JavaScript, 20
  boolean, 22
  numbers, 21
  objects, 36
  strings, 20
Date object, JavaScript, 38
dd tags
  structure of definition list, 155
default values
  Jay Skript & Domsters website, 284–286
defaultValue property, DOM
  form elements, 285
definition list
  displayAbbreviations function, 153
  DOM overriding default browser behavior, 152
  steps to create using DOM, 152
  structure of, 152
  structuring abbreviations, 155
degradation
  see graceful degradation

design
  Jay Skript & Domsters website, 247
DHTML (Dynamic HTML)
  description, 6
  DOM Scripting and, 10
  effect of variation of browsers, 7
display property values, 147
displayAbbreviations function, 153–161
  Internet Explorer, 161, 163
  Jay Skript & Domsters website, 279
displayAccesskeys function, 173–174
displayCitations function, 165–170
div tag
  Jay Skript & Domsters website, 246
dl tags
  structure of definition list, 155
do...while loop, JavaScript, 31
doctype declaration
  family tree model of web page, 44
  HTML or XHTML, 149
document object
  JavaScript host objects, 38, 42
  write method, 120–122
Document Object Model
  see DOM
document.write
  see write method, document object
DOM (Document Object Model), 42–55
  behavior layer, 179, 180
  browsers and DOM
    browser support for, 9
    checking browser understands, 158
    overriding default browser behavior, 152
  className property, 200–203
  description, 5
  documents, 42
    attaching information to, 175
    retrieving information from, 175
    updating text on web page, 66
  DOM Core methods, 115
  DOM level 0, 6
  DOM scripting
    Ajax, 298–308
    DHTML and, 10
    state of the web today, 294–298
    today and in the future, 294–309
    Web and, 309
  family tree model, 43
  graceful degradation, 81–84
  HTML-DOM, 115
  markup, extracting and recreating, 147
  markup, inserting using DOM methods, 130–132
  models compared, 43
  node properties, 323–325

nodes, 45
  attribute nodes, 46
  copying nodes, 314–315
  creating nodes, 312–314
  element nodes, 45
  finding nodes, 320–323
  inserting nodes, 316–318
  manipulating attribute nodes, 319–320
  removing nodes, 318
  replacing nodes, 318–319
  text nodes, 46
  text node or element node, 166
  traversing node tree, 325–327
objects, 42
real world examples of APIs, 8
style property, 180–189
  externally/internally declared styles, 186–187
  getting styles using, 182–186
  setting styles using, 188–189
  repetitive styling, 193–197
  responding to events, 198–200
  styling elements in node tree, 189–193
  when to use DOM styling, 189–200
web pages
  altering structure of, 180
  using DOM to insert content into, 146
W3C and DOM development, 7
W3C definition, 8
DOM methods, 125–132, 135–138, 312–323
  appendChild method, 127–128, 316
  cloneNode method, 314
  createElement method, 126–127, 312
  createTextNode method, 128–130, 313
  getAttribute method, 52–53, 320
  getElementById method, 49–50, 321
  getElementsByTagName method, 50–51, 321
  hasChildNodes method, 322
  insertBefore method, 135, 317
  removeChild method, 318
  replaceChild method, 318
  setAttribute method, 54, 319
DOM properties, 323–327
  childNodes property, 66–67, 325
  className property, 200–203
  firstChild property, 70, 325
  lastChild property, 70, 326
  nextSibling property, 180, 326
  nodeName property, 180, 323
  nodeType property, 67–68, 323
  nodeValue property, 69, 324
    updating description, 70–74
  parentNode property, 180, 327
  previousSibling property, 327
DOM Scripting Task Force, 297
dt tags
  structure of definition list, 155

E
ECMAScript
  origins of JavaScript, 4
element nodes
  nodes, DOM, 45
  style property and, 180
  text nodes or, DOM, 166
elements
  checking existence of element, 105
  counting number of children of, 67
  createElement method, 126–127, 312
  getElementById method, 49–50, 321
  getElementsByTagName method, 50–51, 321
  getting children of elements, 66
  insertBefore method, 135, 317
else clause
  if statement, JavaScript, 28
enhancing content
  see content enhancement
escaping characters
  JavaScript strings, 20
event handlers
  how event handling works, 64
  inline event handlers, 82
  JavaScript image gallery, 63–65, 97–102
    changing behavior of links array elements, 101
    checkpoints for DOM methods, 97
  onclick event, 63
  onload event, 102
  separating behavior functionality, 86
events
  displaying image associated to link at onmouseover
    event, 222–241
  setting styles in response to, 198–200
explanation.html, 160
external files, JavaScript, 86
externally declared styles
  retrieving styles of style property, 186–187

F
family tree model, 43–45
Firefox browser, 295–296
first-child (:first-child) pseudo class, CSS2, 193
firstChild property, DOM, 70, 325
Flash, 79
floating-point numbers, JavaScript, 21
focus (:focus) pseudo class, CSS, 180
focusLabels function
  Jay Skript & Domsters website, 283
fontFamily property of style property, 183, 184
fontSize property of style property, 185, 186
for loop, JavaScript, 32
  JavaScript image gallery, 100

for/in loop
   displayAbbreviations function, 155, 156
form enhancements
   Jay Skript & Domsters website, 281–290
Form object
   Jay Skript & Domsters website, 284
form validation
   Jay Skript & Domsters website, 286–290
functions, JavaScript, 33
   abstraction, 203
   alert function, 34
   anonymous function, 101
   arguments, 33
   built-in functions, 34
   naming conventions, 35
   return statement, 34
   variable scope, 35

G

gallery.html file, 140
   JavaScript image gallery, 59, 140
Garrett, Jesse James, 298
getAttribute method, 52–53, 320
   extracting path to image, 61
   Jay Skript & Domsters website, 259
   testing for existence of title attribute, 107
   updating text on web page, 66
getElementById method, 49–50, 120, 321
   getting placeholder image, 61
getElementsByTagName method, 50–51, 120, 321
   getting children of elements, 66
getNextElement function, 190
global variables, JavaScript, 35
Gmail
   current uses of Ajax, 303
   future of Ajax, 307
Google Maps
   current uses of Ajax, 304
   future of Ajax, 307
Google Suggest
   current uses of Ajax, 303
   future of Ajax, 307
graceful degradation
   CSS lessons for programming websites, 84
   from JavaScript, 81–84
   JavaScript image gallery, 95–96
   JavaScript inserting content into web pages, 146
   popUp function, 83
   progressive enhancement, 85
   searchbots ranking websites, 83
   using DOM appropriately, 146

H

h1 tag
   family tree model of web page, 45
hasChildNodes method, 322
head tag
   executing JavaScript, 14
   family tree model of web page, 45
   referring to JavaScript in XHTML, 63
here class
   Jay Skript & Domsters website, 258
hidden value, CSS overflow property, 225, 226
highlightPage function
   Jay Skript & Domsters website, 259, 261
highlightRows function
   changing styles based on events, 198
   Jay Skript & Domsters website, 278, 280
Hijax, 306
   future of Ajax, 307
home page
   Jay Skript & Domsters website, 255
hooks
   gallery.html file, 140
   Jay Skript & Domsters website, 261
   sharing hooks with CSS, 112–114
   unobtrusive JavaScript, 96
host objects, JavaScript
   document object, 38, 42
   window object, 42
hover (:hover) pseudo class, CSS, 180
   changing styles based on events, 198
HTML
   see also XHTML
   case sensitivity of tags/attributes, 149
   closing tags, 149
   deprecation, 149
   HTML or XHTML, 149
   result of ease of use, 78
html tag
   family tree model of web page, 44
HTML-DOM
   properties, 115
   web document specificity, 116
   XHTML using, 149

I

id attribute
   attributes influencing CSS, 147
   CSS, 48
   JavaScript image gallery, 60
if statement, JavaScript
   conditional statements, 28
   else clause, 28
      ternary operator, 108

image gallery, JavaScript
  see JavaScript image gallery
incremental movement
  animation, 212–214
index.html
  Jay Skript & Domsters website, 255
indexOf method
  Jay Skript & Domsters website, 259
inheritance, CSS, 47
inline declared styles
  retrieving styles of style property, 186–187
inline event handlers, 82
inline value, display property, 147
innerHTML property, 122–125
  XHTML using, 149
insertAfter function
  Jay Skript & Domsters website, 257
  refining animation example, 238, 240
insertAfter method, 136–138
  JavaScript image gallery, 139
insertBefore method, 135, 317
Internet Explorer
  abbr tag, 161
  displayAbbreviations function, 161
  DOM support, 9
  effect of variation of browsers, 7
interpreted languages, 15
isEmail function
  Jay Skript & Domsters website, 287
isFilled function
  Jay Skript & Domsters website, 287

J

JavaScript
  Ajax, 298–308
  animation, 208, 227–230
  arithmetic operations, 25
  arrays, 22
  asking "Are the bells and whistles necessary?", 80
  associative arrays, 24
  backward browser compatibility, 88
  behavior layer, 179
  Boolean data, 22
  browser sniffing, 90
  changing description with, 69
  choosing variable names, 99
  clearTimeout function, 211
  comments, 16
  comparison operators, 29
  conditional statements, 27
    do...while loop, 31
    for loop, 32
    while loop, 31
  data types, 20

description, 5, 78
do...while loop, 31
effect of support for DOM, 10
event handlers, 63–65
executing, 14
external files, 86
floating-point numbers, 21
for loop, 32
functions, 33
  variable scope, 35
graceful degradation, 81–84
host objects, 38
interpreted languages, 15
Java and, 4, 78
JavaScript image gallery
  applying, 63–65
  JavaScript for, 61–62
Jay Skript & Domsters website, 256–290
logical operators, 29
looping statements, 30, 31
native objects, 38
numbers, 21
objects, 36
onclick event handler, 63
onkeypress event handler, 109–111
operations, 25
origins of, 4–5
pop-up windows, 80
pseudo-protocol, 82
questioning assumptions, 104, 114
  element existence, 104, 105
  link has title attribute, 107
referring to in XHTML, 63, 219
requirements to write and view, 14
result of ease of use, 79
reusable scripts file, 256
separating behavior functionality, 85, 86–88
  JavaScript image gallery, 96–104
setTimeout function, 211–212
state of the web today, 296
statements, 16
strings, 20
syntax, 16
  incorrect syntax, 79
this keyword, 63
toLowerCase method, 261
typeof operator, 49
unobtrusive JavaScript, 86–88, 121
  JavaScript image gallery, 96–104
  sharing hooks with CSS, 112–114
updating text on web page, 66
using self contained functions, 79
using to insert content into documents, 146
variables, 18
while loop, 31

JavaScript image gallery, 58–75, 94–116, 132–142
    adding description in markup, 68
    addLoadEvent function, 138
    applying JavaScript, 63–65
    changing description with JavaScript, 69
    displaying image associated to link at onmouseover
        event, 222–241
    event handlers, 63–65
        adding, 97–102
        checkpoints for DOM methods, 97
    gallery.html file, 140
    graceful degradation, 95–96
    image gallery script, 72
    insertAfter method, 139
    JavaScript for, 61–62
    Jay Skript & Domsters website, 272–276
    looping with for loop, 100
    prepareGallery function, 111, 138, 139
    preparePlaceholder function, 134, 138, 139
    showPic function, 94, 111, 138, 140
        checks and tests, 104–111
    unobtrusive JavaScript, 96–104
        sharing hooks with CSS, 112–114
    XHTML markup for, 58–60
Jay Skript and the Domsters website, 244–291
    about.html, 268, 271
    addClass function, 257
    addLoadEvent function, 256
    color.css style sheet, 250–251
        odd and highlight classes, 280
        styles for here class, 258
        table headers and rows, 277
    contact.html, 281–290
        form validation, 286
    CSS, 248–255
        importing CSS files, 248
    default values, 284–286
    design, 247
    directory structure, 245
    displayAbbreviations function, 279
    div tag, 246
    files, 245
    focusLabels function, 283
    folders, 244
    form enhancements, 281–290
    Form object, 284
    form validation, 286–290
    getAttribute method, 259
    here class, 258
    highlightPage function, 259, 261
    highlightRows function, 278, 280
    home page, 255
    index.html, 255
    indexOf method, 259

insertAfter function, 257
internal navigation, 267–272
isEmail function, 287
isFilled function, 287
JavaScript, 256–290
JavaScript image gallery, 272–276
JavaScript slideshow, 262–266
label element, 283
layout.css style sheet, 251–253
    definition list styling, 280
    table cell styling, 277
    updating for contact.html, 282
    updating for frame, 265
    updating for photos.html, 262, 273
    updating for slideshow, 265
live.html, 276–280
markup, 255–256
material provided, 244
moveElement function, 262
page highlighting, 257–262
page structure, 246
page template, 246
pages, 245
    common page structure, 246
photos.html, 272
prepareForms function, 286
    adding onsubmit event handler, 289
prepareGallery function, 275
prepareInternalNav function, 269, 270
preparePlaceholder function, 275
prepareSlideshow function, 263, 266
project outline, 244
resetFields function, 285
reusable scripts file, 256
scope, JavaScript, 270
showPic function, 274
showSection function, 269, 270
site map, 245
site structure, 244–245
slideshow.gif, 262
stripeTables function, 278
table enhancements, 276–280
template.html, 246
typography.css style sheet, 254–255
    definition list styling, 280
validateForm function, 288
js (.js) file extension
    executing JavaScript, 14

K

keyboard access to web pages, 109–111

L

label element
   Jay Skript & Domsters website, 283
last-child (:last-child) pseudo class, CSS2, 193
lastChild property, DOM, 70, 326
lastChildElement property, 167
layers
   separating behavior/presentation, 85
layout.css style sheet
   Jay Skript & Domsters website, 251–253
      definition list styling, 280
      table cell styling, 277
      updating for contact.html, 282
      updating for frame, 265
      updating for photos.html, 262, 273
      updating for slideshow, 265
left property
   style property, DOM, 209
length property, 50
li tag, 45, 46
links
   clicking and remaining on same page, 59
   clicking and seeing image on same page, 59
   displaying image associated to link at onmouseover
      event, 222–241
   graceful degradation, 95
literals
   JavaScript variables, 20
live.html
   Jay Skript & Domsters website, 276–280
local variables, JavaScript, 35
logical operators, JavaScript, 29
   and (&&) operator, 29
   not (!) operator, 30
   or (||) operator, 30
looping statements, JavaScript, 30
   do...while loop, 31
   for loop, 32
   while loop, 31

M

Macromedia Flash, 79
markup
   adding description in markup, 68
   creating markup, 120–143
   for JavaScript image gallery, 58–60
   inserting markup using DOM methods, 130–132
   Jay Skript & Domsters website, 255–256
meta tag
   family tree model of web page, 45
methods, DOM, 125–132, 135–138, 312–323
mime-type, XHTML, 149
models, DOM, 43

N

moveElement function
   abstraction of moveMessage, 215–221
   animation example, 227, 229
      scope of variables, 231–233
   Jay Skript & Domsters website, 262
   refining animation example, 233, 235, 237
moveMessage function, 210
   abstraction of, 215
   code for function, 214
   incremental movement, 212
   positionMessage calling, 211

naming conventions, JavaScript
   camel case, 35
   functions, 35
   variables, 19, 35
native objects, JavaScript, 38
   JavaScript object types, 42
navigation
   Jay Skript & Domsters website, 267–272
Netscape Navigator browser
   DOM support, 9
   effect of variation of browsers, 7
   origins of JavaScript, 4
nextSibling property, DOM, 180, 326
nodeName property, DOM, 180, 323
   examples using typeof operator, 181, 182
nodes
   appendChild method, 127–128, 316
   changing behavior of links array elements, 101
   childNodes property, 66–67, 325
   cloneNode method, 314
   createElement method, 126–127, 312
   createTextNode method, 128–130, 313
   DOM (Document Object Model), 45
      attribute nodes, 46
      element nodes, 45
      text nodes, 46
   DOM methods for copying, 314–315
   DOM methods for creating, 312–314
   DOM methods for finding, 320–323
   DOM methods for inserting, 316–318
   DOM methods for manipulating attribute nodes, 319–320
   DOM methods for removing, 318
   DOM methods for replacing, 318–319
   DOM node properties, 323–325
   DOM properties for traversing node tree, 325–327
   firstChild property, 70, 325
   getAttribute method, 52–53, 320
   getElementById method, 49–50, 321
   getElementsByTagName method, 50–51, 321
   hasChildNodes method, 322

insertBefore method, 135, 317
lastChild property, 70, 326
nextSibling property, 180, 326
nodeName property, 180, 323
nodeType property, 67–68, 323
nodeValue property, 69, 70–74, 324
parentNode property, 180, 327
previousSibling property, 327
removeChild method, 318
replaceChild method, 318
setAttribute method, 54, 319
styling elements in node tree, 189–193
nodeType property, DOM, 67–68, 323
nodeValue property, DOM, 69, 70–74, 120, 324
none value, display property, 147
not (!) operator, JavaScript
logical operators, 30
numbers, JavaScript, 21

O

object detection
backward browser compatibility, 88
objects, DOM, 42
objects, JavaScript, 36
Array object, 38
Date object, 38
host objects, 38
native objects, 38
types of, 42
ol tag
JavaScript image gallery, 58
onblur event, 286
onclick event handler, JavaScript, 63
functioning of, 111
onfocus event, 286
onkeypress event handler, JavaScript, 109–111
avoiding use of, 110, 111
onload event
calling displayAbbreviations function, 159
executing when page has loaded, 102
separating behavior functionality, 87
onmouseover event
changing styles based on events, 198
displaying image associated to link at, 222–241
onsubmit event handler, prepareForms function
Jay Skript & Domsters website, 289
open method, window object
creating new browser windows, 81
operations, JavaScript, 25
arithmetic operations, 25
perform operations on variables, 26
using parentheses, 26
variables containing, 26

operators, JavaScript
arithmetic operations, 25
comparison operators, 29
concatenation operators, 26
increment/decrement operators, 26
logical operators, 29
shorthand operators, 26, 27
typeof operator, 49
or (||) operator, JavaScript
logical operators, 30
overflow property, CSS
animation example, 225
possible values, 225

P

p tag, 45, 46
page highlighting
Jay Skript & Domsters website, 257
page loading
executing addLoadEvent after, 102
parentNode property, DOM, 180, 327
parseFloat function, JavaScript, 212
parseInt function, JavaScript, 212, 213
photos.html
Jay Skript & Domsters website, 272
pop-up windows, JavaScript, 80
making "this is a new window" clear to user, 81
popUp function
calling using JavaScript pseudo-protocol, 82
graceful degradation, 83
separating behavior functionality, 88
position
position and animation, 208–210
refining animation example, 233–236
position property
style property, DOM, 208
positionMessage function, 209
calling moveElement function, 219
calling moveMessage, 211
Powazek, Derek, 300
prepareForms function
Jay Skript & Domsters website, 286
adding onsubmit event handler, 289
prepareGallery function, 102, 107
JavaScript image gallery, 111, 138, 139
assuming showPic function working, 105
Jay Skript & Domsters website, 275
return false statements, 99
prepareInternalNav function
Jay Skript & Domsters website, 269, 270
preparePlaceholder function
JavaScript image gallery, 134, 138, 139
Jay Skript & Domsters website, 275

prepareSlideshow function
  animation example, 227, 229
  Jay Skript & Domsters website, 263, 266
  refining animation example, 238
presentation layer
  separating layers, 180
    className property, 200–203
  web content, 178
previousSibling property, 327
programming languages
  interpreted or compiled, 15
  structured programming, 99
progressive enhancement
  graceful degradation, 85
  using DOM inappropriately, 146
properties
  DOM properties, 323–327
  HTML-DOM, 115
pseudo classes, CSS
  separating layers, 180
pseudo-protocol, JavaScript, 82

R

recursion, 214
relative value, position property
  style property, DOM, 208
removeChild method, 318
replaceChild method, 318
reserved words, JavaScript, 99
resetFields function
  Jay Skript & Domsters website, 285
return false statements
  prepareGallery function, 99
return statement
  JavaScript functions, 34
right property
  style property, DOM, 209
rounding values
  never ending loops/conditional statements, 234

S

scope, JavaScript
  animation example, 231–233
  Jay Skript & Domsters website, 270
  variable scope, 35
script tags
  animation example, 229
  executing JavaScript, 14
  referencing addLoadEvent function, 160
  referencing displayAbbreviations function, 160
  referring to JavaScript in XHTML, 63
  refining animation example, 239

write method, document object, 121
scripting language, 5
scroll value, CSS overflow property, 225
searchbots
  ranking websites, 83
semantic information
  tags and semantic information, 147
setAttribute method, DOM, 54, 120, 126, 319
  changing src attribute, 61, 62
setTimeout function, JavaScript, 211–212
showPic function
  JavaScript image gallery, 94, 106, 111, 120, 138, 140
    checks and tests, 104–111
  Jay Skript & Domsters website, 274
showPic.js file, 138
showSection function
  Jay Skript & Domsters website, 269, 270
slideshow.gif
  Jay Skript & Domsters website, 262
src attribute, JavaScript
  changing, 61
    without using setAttribute, 62
  executing JavaScript, 14
statements, JavaScript, 16
  conditional statements, 27
  looping statements, 30
static value, position property
  style property, DOM, 208
strings, JavaScript, 20
  concatenation operators, 26
  escaping characters, 20
striped effect on tabular data, 196
stripeTables function, 196, 202
  Jay Skript & Domsters website, 278
strongly typed languages, 20
structural layer
  separating layers, 180
  web content, 178
structured programming, 99
style property, DOM, 180–189
  bottom property, 209
  camel casing style properties, 183
  externally/internally declared styles, 186–187
  fontFamily property, 183, 184
  incremental movement, 212
  left property, 209
  measurement units of properties returned, 184, 185
  position property, 208
  refining animation example, 236
  retrieving styles, 182–187
  right property, 209
  setting styles, 188–189
    repetitive styling, 193–197
    responding to events, 198–200

styling elements in node tree, 189–193
when to set styles using DOM, 189–200
top property, 209
style tags
declaring styles, CSS, 47
styleElementSiblings function, 203
styleHeaderSiblings function, 191, 192, 200, 201, 203
syntax, JavaScript, 16
incorrect syntax, 79

T

tables
Jay Skript & Domsters website, 276–280
using with CSS, 193
tags, HTML and XHTML, 178
template.html
Jay Skript & Domsters website, 246
ternary operator, 108
text
updating text on web page, 66
text nodes, DOM, 46
createTextNode method, 313
element nodes or, 166
this keyword, 63
time
clearTimeout function, 211
setTimeout function, 211–212
time and animation, 211–214
title attribute
attribute nodes, 46
displaying content of attributes, 147, 152
getAttribute method, 52
setAttribute method, 54
testing for existence of, 107
updating text on web page, 66
title tag, 45
toLowerCase method
Jay Skript & Domsters website, 261
top property
style property, DOM, 209
topics.gif
animation example, 224, 228, 230
typeof operator, JavaScript, 49
example using, 181
types of data, JavaScript
see data types, JavaScript
typography.css style sheet
Jay Skript & Domsters website, 254–255
definition list styling, 280

U

ul tag, 45, 46
attribute nodes, 46
JavaScript image gallery, 58
unobtrusive JavaScript, 121
user defined objects, JavaScript, 42

V

validateForm function
Jay Skript & Domsters website, 288
var keyword, JavaScript, 35
variable names, JavaScript
choosing, 99
variables, JavaScript, 18
case sensitivity, 19
containing operations, 26
data types, 20
declaring, 19
global variables, 35
literals, 20
local variables, 35
naming conventions, 19, 35
performing operations on, 26
variable scope, 35
visible value, CSS overflow property, 225

W

W3C
DOM development, 7
WaSP (Web Standards Project), 9
weakly typed languages, 20
web (WWW)
state of the web today, 294–298
web applications, 308
wrapping content in layers, 178–180
web browsers
dealing with XMLHttpRequest object, 300
displaying content of attributes, 147
Firefox browser, 295–296
scripting languages and, 5
state of the web today, 294–296
web design
how to view web pages, 297
separating layers, 180
state of the web today, 296–298
web pages
element tree of basic web page, 44
family tree model illustrated, 43
how to view for web design, 297
result of ease of use of HTML, 78
striped effect on tabular data, 196
updating text on web page, 66

Web Standards Project (WaSP), 9
websites
    backward browser compatibility, 88
    CSS lessons for programming, 84
    Jay Skript & Domsters website, 244–291
    searchbot rankings, 83
while loop, JavaScript, 31
Willison, Simon, 103
window object
    host objects, JavaScript, 42
write method, document object, 120–122
    XHTML using, 149

X
XHTML
    case sensitivity of tags/attributes, 149
    closing tags, 149
    for JavaScript image gallery, 58–60
    HTML or XHTML, 149
    marking up content, 149
    mime-type, 149
    structural layer, 178, 180
    using document.write, 149
    using HTML-DOM methods, 149
    using innerHTML property, 149
XMLHTTP, 300
XMLHttpRequest object, 300–302
    see also Ajax
    Hijax, 306
    web browsers dealing with, 300

friendsofed.com/forums

Join the friends of ED forums to find out more about our books, discover useful technology tips and tricks, or get a helping hand on a challenging project. *Designer to Designer*™ is what it's all about—our community sharing ideas and inspiring each other. In the friends of ED forums, you'll find a wide range of topics to discuss, so look around, find a forum, and dive right in!

■ **Books and Information**

Chat about friends of ED books, gossip about the community, or even tell us some bad jokes!

■ **Flash**

Discuss design issues, ActionScript, dynamic content, and video and sound.

■ **Web Design**

From front-end frustrations to back-end blight, share your problems and your knowledge here.

■ **Site Check**

Show off your work or get new ideas.

■ **Digital Imagery**

Create eye candy with Photoshop, Fireworks, Illustrator, and FreeHand.

■ **ArchivED**

Browse through an archive of old questions and answers.

HOW TO PARTICIPATE

Go to the friends of ED forums at **www.friendsofed.com/forums**.